# The Silent Movies of W. C. Fields:

## How They Created The Basis for His Fame in Sound Films

## By Arthur Frank Wertheim

The Silent Movies of W. C. Fields:
How They Created The Basis for His Fame in Sound Films
By Arthur Frank Wertheim
Copyright © 2020 Arthur Frank Wertheim
No part of this book may be reproduced in any form or by any means, electronic, mechanical, digital, photocopying, or recording, except for inclusion of a review, without permission in writing from the publisher or Author.

No copyright is claimed for the photos within this book. They are used for the purposes of publicity only.

Published in the USA by:

BearManor Media
4700 Millenia Blvd.
Suite 175 PMB 90497
Orlando, FL 32839
www.bearmanormedia.com

Paperback ISBN: 978-1-62933-591-9
Case ISBN: 978-1-62933-592-6
BearManor Media, Orlando, Florida
Printed in the United States of America
Book design by Robbie Adkins, www.adkinsconsult.com
Cover: To attract customers, Gabby Gilfoil (Fields) displays his talent as a bally advertising his attractions inside his sideshow. *Two Flaming Youths*. Author's Collection.

*In honor of Jim Willis, my very close friend since high school, who, among other accomplishments, opened the first public gallery in the United States dedicated to tribal art where he staged exhibitions for over thirty years in San Francisco. R.I.P. my dear friend.*

"Fields, of course, was ... the real thing: bulbous nose, fastidious fingers forever twiddling in air, the stroll of a somnambulist, about him pleasing a woman or mauling a child. The very air parted about him as he walked. But he was a major comedian under wraps. Today it is virtually unthinkable that Fields should ever have been a *silent* comedian: we remember him first as something heard, then something seen. People who have grown up on his sound-film and radio appearances are much surprised, even now, to learn that he had a considerable screen career long before his oracular natalities could be put to their normal use."

Walter Kerr, *The Silent Clowns* (1980)

# ACKNOWLEDGMENTS

First and foremost, I owe a debt of gratitude to the grandchildren of W. C. Fields: Dr. Harriet A. Fields, Ronald J. Fields, William C. Fields, III, and Allen Fields. All graciously granted me full support and cooperation to write about their grandfather. They consented to interviews, which yielded significant information and insights. During a visit to the Library of Congress to research Fields's copyrighted stage sketches, I learned that Harriet Fields lived in Washington, D.C. Over lunch we had an informative conversation about her grandfather, during which she encouraged my project and offered to assist me. From that time to the present, her help has proved to be invaluable. I would also like to acknowledge grandson Everett Fields for his insights pertaining to the story of his grandfather. The family's goal is to ensure that current generations and generations to come know the joy of their grandfather's art through humor, and most important, to make his work accessible to the world community.

Many thanks are extended to the diligent archivists in the Department of Special Collections at the Margaret Herrick Library for their aid in helping me research the Fields Papers: Barbara Hall, Research Archivist, and Howard Prouty, Acquisitions Archivist. Faye Thompson, Photograph Department Coordinator, helped me select the many photographs in the Fields collection and order digital copies. The staff behind the desk was extremely efficient in paging the material, making items available every day, and photocopying what I needed. Together they made my innumerable visits to the library a very pleasant experience. The Fields family chose a superb place to work and a wonderful home for their grandfather's valuable collection.

I might still be wading through the Fields Papers if it were not for my research assistant, Dr. Emily Carmen. I cannot thank her enough for her diligent work. She shared in the research at the library, typed documents unavailable for photocopying, and did numerous transcriptions. A film scholar, her knowledge of cinema history aided me in understanding Fields's movie career.

Individuals at libraries also deserve my gratitude for their help. Uppermost is the help of Dr. Barbara Bair, Historian, Manuscript Division at the Library of Congress. She helped guide me through the collections that deal with W. C. Fields, especially the large number of typed stage sketches, film press books, radio scripts, and photographs deposited at the library. My thanks are also extended to the staff of numerous other libraries who were very helpful: Ned Comstock, Cinematic Art Library, University of Southern California, who helped guide me through their various collections and oversaw the photocopying of important material; Geraldine Duclow, archivist, Free Library of Philadelphia; staff, Harvard Theatre Collection; Margaret Stevens-Garmon, Theatre Collections Archivist, Museum of the City of New York; Rick Watson, Research Associate, Performing Arts Collection, Harry Ransom Research Center, University of Texas, Austin.

I would be remiss if I failed to acknowledge the authors of several books on Fields. Their findings and writings were extremely helpful to me as guideposts to Fields's story. Uppermost are the two books by his grandson, Ronald J. Fields: *W. C. Fields by Himself* (1973) and *W. C. Fields: A Life on Film* (1984). The former is an excellent groundbreaking book comprising considerable letters and documents about his grandfather, which proved indispensable for my study. The latter book on his grandfather's films contains a gold mine of information about Fields's movie career. I very much appreciate his kindness in granting me permission to quote from the two books.

Five other books were valuable to my research. *W. C. Fields, A Bio-Bibliography* and *Groucho and W. C. Fields: Huckster Comedians* by Wes D. Gehring provide gems of information and insights into his subject's life and comedy. Gehring has also written about Fields's valuable *Follies* scripts, which the comedian deposited at the Library of Congress. They proved crucial to understanding the evolution of Fields's comedy in the *Follies*. David T. Rock's *W. C. Fields—An Annotated Guide* is also valuable for its list of chronology, bibliography, filmography, cartoons, recordings, and miscellaneous subjects. Two other books, *W. C. Fields: A Biography* by James Curtis and *Man on the Flying Trapeze: The Life and Times of W. C. Fields* by Simon Louvish, have uncovered a wealth of new information about their subject. They especially deserve credit for disproving many legends about Fields. Both books were helpful to my study, especially for cutting through the fog of fabrications about the comedian.

I very much appreciate the strong support of Don B. Wilmeth, editor, Palgrave Studies in Theatre and Performance History, and Asa Messer, Emeritus Professor of Theatre and English, Brown University. I very much wish to thank him for recognizing the important need for a study about the life and career of W. C. Fields. Crucial to the publication was Ben Ohmart, head, BearManor Media. Also invaluable was Rachel Nishan of Twin Oaks Indexing, who deserves my thanks for creating a revised manuscript and a first-rate index.

# Contents

Part I: Launching a Silent Screen Career . . . . . . . . . . . . . . . . . . 1
Fort Lee: The Silent Film Capital on the Hudson . . . . . . . . . . . . 2
Gaumont: The French Connection . . . . . . . . . . . . . . . . . . . . 12
The Pool Trickster . . . . . . . . . . . . . . . . . . . . . . . . . . . . . . 27
The Remittance Man . . . . . . . . . . . . . . . . . . . . . . . . . . . . 40
"It Gave Me My Opportunity" . . . . . . . . . . . . . . . . . . . . . . . 48
Part II: A Rendezvous with D. W. Griffith . . . . . . . . . . . . . . . . 59
6. *Poppy* on Broadway . . . . . . . . . . . . . . . . . . . . . . . . . . . 60
7. The Big House . . . . . . . . . . . . . . . . . . . . . . . . . . . . . . 79
8. *Sally of the Sawdust* . . . . . . . . . . . . . . . . . . . . . . . . . . . 91
9. "A Very Lame Idea" . . . . . . . . . . . . . . . . . . . . . . . . . . . 106
Part III: From the Footlights to the Silent Screen . . . . . . . . . . . 123
10. *The Comic Supplement* . . . . . . . . . . . . . . . . . . . . . . . . 124
11. *It's the Old Army Game* . . . . . . . . . . . . . . . . . . . . . . . 139
Part IV: Milquetoasts . . . . . . . . . . . . . . . . . . . . . . . . . . . . 165
12. The Henpecked Husband . . . . . . . . . . . . . . . . . . . . . . 166
13. "God Bless Our Home" . . . . . . . . . . . . . . . . . . . . . . . 178
14. "I'm a Lion!" . . . . . . . . . . . . . . . . . . . . . . . . . . . . . . 186
Part V: The Hollywood Debacle . . . . . . . . . . . . . . . . . . . . . 199
15. Welcome to the Dream Factory . . . . . . . . . . . . . . . . . . 200
16. Not Once, but Three Times . . . . . . . . . . . . . . . . . . . . . 214
Afterword: Fields's Silent Movies: The Basis for His Fame . . . 232
    in Sound Films
Index . . . . . . . . . . . . . . . . . . . . . . . . . . . . . . . . . . . . . . 238

# SYMBOLS AND ABBREVIATIONS

## Frequently Cited Names and Sources

| | |
|---|---|
| WCF | William Claude Fields |
| *WCFALOF* | Ronald J. Fields, *W. C. Fields: A Life on Film* (New York: St. Martin's Press, 1984). |
| *WCFBH* | *W. C. Fields by Himself: His Intended Autobiography*, commentary by Ronald J. Fields (Englewood Cliffs, NJ: Prentice-Hall, 1973). |
| WCFP | W. C. Fields Papers, Academy of Motion Picture Arts and Sciences, Margaret Herrick Library, Department of Special Collections, Beverly Hills, CA. |

## Manuscript Collections and Archive Symbols

| | |
|---|---|
| AEFTL | Actors' Equity Files, Tamiment Library, Robert F. Wagner Labor Archives, New York University, New York, NY. |
| AMPAS | Academy of Motion Picture Arts and Sciences, Margaret Herrick Library, Department of Special Collections, Beverly Hills, CA. |
| CFOHCU | Center for Oral History, Butler Library, Columbia University, New York, NY. |
| HTC | Harvard Theatre Collection, Houghton Library, Harvard University, Cambridge, MA. |
| MCNY | Museum of the City of New York, New York, NY. |
| MMIOHP | Museum of the Moving Image Oral History Program, Astoria, Queens, New York, NY. |
| MOMAFSC | Museum of Modern Art, Film Study Center, New York, NY. |

| | |
|---|---|
| MPD-LOC | Motion Picture Division, Library of Congress, Washington, D.C. |
| MRR-LOC | Main Reading Room, Library of Congress, Washington, D.C. |
| MSD-LOC | Manuscript Division, Library of Congress, Washington, D.C. |
| NYPLPA | New York Public Library for the Performing Arts, Billy Rose Theatre Collection & Robinson-Locke Collection, Lincoln Center, New York, NY. |
| PFL-TC | Philadelphia Free Library Theater Collection, Philadelphia, PA. |
| USC | University of Southern California, Los Angeles, CA, Cinema and Television Library. |

## Newspapers and Magazines

*BE* Brooklyn Eagle
*CDT* Chicago Daily Tribune
*CEP* Chicago Evening Post
*CEE* Chicago Evening Examiner
*CHE* Chicago Herald Examiner
*HR* Hollywood Reporter
*LADM* Los Angeles Daily Mirror
*LADN* Los Angeles Daily News
*LAE* Los Angeles Examiner
*LAEHE* Los Angeles Evening Herald Express
*LAHE* Los Angeles Herald Examiner
*LAT* Los Angeles Times
*LST* London Sunday Times
*MPC* Motion Picture Classic
*MPD* Motion Picture Daily
*MPH* Motion Picture Herald
*MPM* Motion Picture Magazine
*MPN* Motion Picture News
*MPW* Motion Picture World
*NYA* New York American

*NYDM* New York Dramatic Mirror
*NYDN* New York Daily News
*NYEJ* New York Evening Journal
*NYEP* New York Evening Post
*NYG* New York Graphic
*NYH* New York Herald
*NYHT* New York Herald Tribune
*NYMT* New York Morning Telegraph
*NYSN* New York Sunday News
*NYST* New York Sunday Telegraph
*NYT* New York Times
*NYTEL* New York Telegram
*NYW* New York World
*NYWT* New York World Telegram
*PPB* Paramount Press Book
*SEP* Saturday Evening Post
*SLGD* St. Louis Globe Democrat
*SLPD* St. Louis Post Dispatch
*SLT* St. Louis Times
*ZTN* Zit's Theatrical Newspaper

# List of Figures

Figure 1.1 . . . . . . . . . 7
Figure 2.1. . . . . . . . . 15
Figure 2.2 . . . . . . . . 19
Figure 3.1 . . . . . . . . 31
Figure 3.2 . . . . . . . . 33
Figure 4.1 . . . . . . . . 45
Figure 5.1 . . . . . . . . 57
Figure 7.1 . . . . . . . . 83
Figure 7.2. . . . . . . . . 88
Figure 8.1. . . . . . . . . 96
Figure 8.2. . . . . . . . . 82
Figure 9.1. . . . . . . . .110
Figure 9.2 . . . . . . . .112
Figure 9.3 . . . . . . . .119
Figure 10.1. . . . . . . .131
Figure 11.1 . . . . . . .149
Figure 11.2 . . . . . . .151
Figure 11.3. . . . . . . .153
Figure 11.4 . . . . . . .158
Figure 12.1. . . . . . . .169
Figure 12.2. . . . . . . .171
Figure 13.1. . . . . . . .181
Figure 14.1 . . . . . . .188
Figure 14.2. . . . . . . .189
Figure 14.3 . . . . . . .191
Figure 15.1. . . . . . . .201
Figure 15.2 . . . . . . .205
Figure 16.1. . . . . . . .218
Figure 16.2. . . . . . . .219
Figure 16.3 . . . . . . .225
Figure 16.4 . . . . . . .226
Figure Afterword.1. .236

Fields and cast in Ballyhoo(1930). Courtesy, Al Hirschfeld Foundation.

# INTRODUCTION

My life with W. C. Fields started on a spring day in May 2007. An article in *The Los Angeles Times* announced that the Academy of Motion Pictures Arts and Sciences was staging an exhibition on its fourth floor gallery titled, "The Amazing Peregrinations and Pettifoggery of One William Claude Dukenfield, late of Philadelphia, Pa., familiarly known to Crowned Heads and Hoi Polloi alike as W. C. Fields."

Entering the door to the show, I was bowled over by the sight. The walls were covered with colorful posters; original playbills; handwritten and typed personal letters; contracts; cartoons; photographs; stage scripts; movie scenarios; souvenirs from his performances abroad; and much more material. At one end of the room gales of laughter stemmed from visitors watching his films. The show embodied a treasure trove of memorabilia donated by the Fields family so that the public might encounter the astonishing career of an eminent comedian.

His complete papers remained unavailable for researchers until the family gifted them to the Academy. After perusing the multi-page inventory and the material for a few months, I became convinced that the seventy-one boxes in the Fields Papers are possibly the most voluminous and valuable collection of an American performer's career. The collection is a gold mine. It begins with his date book listing his first stage appearances in 1898 and ends with papers about his lengthy confrontational probate trial lasting until the mid-1950s.

A journey through Fields's career from 1898 to 1946 is an incredible ride that yields significant information about his appearances in practically every performance art during the first half of the twentieth century: club shows; burlesque; medicine, museum, and minstrel shows; American vaudeville; British music halls; leading European variety theaters; three Broadway revues, including performances in six annual *Ziegfeld Follies*; Broadway plays, including a starring role in the long-running show *Poppy*; twelve silent movies; thirty-two sound shorts and features; guest spots on radio comedy programs; and, six months before his death, studio recording.

While in Ziegfeld's spectacular revue, he created two comic characterizations, the good-natured charlatan and besieged husband, two impersonations which reappear in his silent and sound films. When he went to Hollywood permanently in 1930 to make films, he took with him not only his stage scenarios but the techniques he used in the theater: pantomime and masterful timing as a jokester. He repeats his vaudeville acts, juggling balls, manipulating cigar boxes, and pool tricks for the screen. His 1918 *Follies* sketch as a frustrated, bungling golfer is reused in *The Golf Specialist* (1930). Three of his four shorts for Mack Sennett stem from his stage scenes in the *Vanities*. Fields's hilarious "Sleeping Porch" scene from the 1925 *Ziegfeld Follies* is repeated in the silent picture *It's the Old Army Game* (1926) and sound film *It's a Gift* (1934). Three of his last movies can even be traced back to his stage career.

The Fields Papers unleashed the need for a three-part sequential series that reevaluates the evolution of his comedic art and its relationship to his personal life. The first book, *W. C. Fields from Burlesque and Vaudeville to Broadway: Becoming a Comedian*, discusses his early life and stage career until 1915. The second volume, *W. C. Fields at the* Ziegfeld Follies: *Becoming a Character Comedian*, dramatizes a momentous turning point in Fields's career. During his appearances in six *Follies* between 1915 and 1925, he moves from being typecast as a vaudeville comic juggler to a character comedian performing a variety of roles, which are repeated in silent and sound films. By the end of his Broadway performances, Fields has created his two most durable characters, an endearing con artist and harassed husband, an achievement that will bring him fame as a top film comedian.

Volume three highlights his astonishing career in sound films and radio that lead to his Phoenix-like rise to an American cultural icon during the 1960s and 1970s. His work and life in Hollywood resembles a roller coast ride of failures and successes. He nonetheless creates a remarkable oeuvre that includes two masterpieces, *It's a Gift* and *The Bank Dick*. Alcohol addiction, accidents, and other afflictions undermine his health and eventually cause studios to fire him. His last films are mainly cameo roles causing his fame to plummet. During the 1960s his biting iconoclasm is rediscovered by devotees of the counterculture, as well as respected film critics who hail his sound films, thereby creating a Fields resurgence. Volume three enlivens the saga of a virtuoso comedian, often called a comic genius, legendary iconoclast, and "Great Man," who brought so much laughter to millions while enduring so much anguish.

This current volume is devoted to Fields's significant career in silent pictures, material that was not included in the first three books. Although often forgotten in his oeuvre, his twelve silent movies reveal that they were exceptional stepping stones to his career in sound films. Fields's silent pictures should consequently be re-evaluated in order to illuminate their magnitude in his career.

# PART I:
# Launching a Silent Screen Career

# CHAPTER 1

## The Silent Film Capital on the Hudson

A carpet of fresh grass, the color of light green jade, lay over Central Park on the bright spring morning of May 19, 1915. Further downtown on Broadway near Times Square, the boulevard, known as The Great White Way, was relatively quiet compared to its evening explosion of theatergoers arriving at showplaces with brightly lit marquees. After completing his last and lengthy vaudeville world tour in 1913-14, Fields was stunned by the expansion of Times Square, hailed as the "crossroads of the world." The number of magnificent legitimate theaters, movie palaces, lavish restaurants, and elegant hotels had multiplied. The sparking illumination of countless electric lights cast a glittering glow, a radiance acclaimed as The Great White Way. The area pulsated with energy, excitement, and artistic power unleashing distinct stage productions, a cornucopia of drama, comedy, musicals, cabaret, variety, revues, and numerous other attractions.

At ten o'clock Fields entered through the stage door of the 1800-seat New Amsterdam Theatre to start a new adventure at the home of the *Ziegfeld Follies*, considered the most spectacular revue on the Great White Way. After arriving, he went up a few steps to a long and narrow low-ceilinged corridor that led to the stage. The auspicious day inaugurated Fields's lengthy association with Florenz Ziegfeld, Jr., impresario extraordinaire of his famous *Follies*. Fields performed in six annual productions between 1915 and 1925, and also made numerous appearances in shows at the Midnight Frolic, the swanky late-night supper club on the theater's roof.

At age thirty-five Bill looked fit and trim, his hair still whitish blond, despite his fifteen-year exhausting grind on the vaudeville circuits across the U.S. and around the world from 1900 to 1915. During these years Fields evolved from a tramp juggler to a silent humorist who used his pantomime skills in sketches he wrote to generate laughter. Instead of the weekly grind of traveling from one city after another, the *Follies* offered Bill an opportunity to stay in New York for several months before the show went on the road.

Before the revue opened, Fields made his inaugural appearance in a moving picture, a silent short that became an act in the show. Cast members boarded the 125th Street ferry boat to Fort Lee, New Jersey, a major early film locale overlooking the Hudson River. During the American Revolution, George Washington and his army used Fort Lee's environs as an encampment in defense of New York City. The site was later named in honor of Charles Lee, a general in the Continental Army. Needing to retreat, Washington's troops departed along a road that is now Fort Lee's Main Street. During the withdrawal, Thomas Paine supposedly wrote his pamphlet "The American Crisis" that began with the line, "These are the times that try men's souls."

With a population totaling 4,472 in 1910, Fort Lee reflected the ambience of a picturesque small town perfect for filmmaking. Fort Lee's population burgeoned when the modern-day double-decked suspension George Washington Bridge (1931) opened, connecting the Jersey town to the Washington Heights area of Manhattan. Before that time, Fort Lee offered a multitude of outdoor backdrops for moviemaking: the majestic Palisades, bucolic farmland, marshland, rolling hills, forests, waterfalls, and other ready-made surroundings. The town's ambience was used for outdoor scenes and Wild West shorts. The exterior of Rambo's Hotel was converted to look like the front of a Western saloon. Crews used the hotel as a place to eat, sleep, and change into costumes. Important for its growth was the fact that land was cheaper here compared to New York City and its environs. By September 1912, up to eight film production companies were operating in Fort Lee, including Coytesville, another picturesque small town one mile away.

At the time, Thomas A. Edison was the most powerful figure in the moving picture business. With his talented inventor, technician, and photographer, William K. L. Dickson, he had already invented the Kinetoscope, which presented to the public twenty-second shorts. They featured a wide range of subjects: dancers, acrobats, novelties (a sneeze), sports figures, boxing matches, actualities, and popular stars, among them strongman Eugen Sandow, sharpshooter

Annie Oakley, and Buffalo Bill and his Wild West Show. Edison's earliest shorts were shot in his Black Maria studio, a shed covered with tar paper and a retractable roof, constructed in 1893 on the grounds of his laboratory in West Orange, New Jersey. A year later Kinetoscope peep-show parlors began flourishing in amusement arcades and in storefronts. On April 14, 1894, Andrew Holland opened the first one in New York City in a converted shoe store at 1155 Broadway. Customers paid twenty-five cents to view shorts emanating from five Edison Kinetoscope machines accompanied by synchronized sound.

During 1898, W. C. Fields at age 18 was wandering around New York, lacking warm clothes, shivering from the freezing cold during a harsh winter, and desperately looking for work as a juggler. That year he entertained at a museum and joined the *Monte Carlo Girls*, a burlesque show that played a few dates in the city before going on tour. A curious, adventurous young man interested in entertainment, Fields might have entered a Manhattan Kinetoscope parlor. If he did, he never mentioned the experience in his letters home nor to friends. Compared to the more established popular stage, the fledgling moving pictures in these parlors must have looked amateurish to him.

On December 19, 1909, the *New York Times* reported that the population of Fort Lee "has become accustomed to bands of Indians yelling and dashing about the roads and by-paths, to troops landing on the river bank, to dancing villagers, and every variety of battle, murder, and sudden death at their very doors. Although the hamlet had indeed been invaded, it was not by hundreds of marauders, but by scores of film production crews armed with nothing more than picture cameras."[1]

Numerous film companies escaped to Fort Lee hoping to evade Thomas Edison's Motion Picture Patents Company (MPPC), a cartel in which leading film companies pooled their resources into a Trust that controlled its major three branches: production, distribution, and exhibition. Behind its formation in 1908 was the need of Edison and Trust members to protect their patents on cameras, projecting machines, and 35mm film. Fort Lee was mostly established by studios, called "independents," desiring to escape the Edison Trust. The Trust hired detectives to spy on competitive filmmakers who were evading the MPPC's dictates. Carl Laemmle, later founder of Universal Pictures, recalled that while filming *Hiawatha* (1909) at Fort Lee, the Trust sent "paid spies and plug-uglies to dog our footsteps."[2]

David Wark Griffith was a frequent visitor to Fort Lee and the New Jersey environs. In 1907, he appeared in the Edison short *Rescued from the Eagle's Nest*, which reflected his hope to become a screen actor, an ambition that ended when he became a director at Biograph. While directing, Griffith shot approximately 100 silent shorts on location in the area, including *The New York Hat* (1912) with Mary Pickford, Lionel Barrymore, and the Gish sisters. James Agee felt this film exposed Griffith's talent for "realism that has never been beaten."[3]

Linda Arvidson, Griffith's first wife and a leading actress at Biograph, recalled the trip from New York City to Fort Lee. She boarded the subway at 125th Street in order to take the 8:45 a.m. ferry boat to the Jersey shore. From the foot of the Palisades, she needed to walk a long path to the top, often carrying film equipment. At the summit was Fort Lee, a bustling town with numerous studios scattered haphazardly across the landscape.

Arvidson felt New Jersey "was a fruitful land for movie landscape; it didn't take long to get there, and transportation was cheap. Small wonder Fort Lee shortly grew to be the popular studio town it did." She performed in Griffith's shorts in the Palisades, and took advantage of the sparsely populated vistas, recalling, "I do believe that first summer I was made love to on every rock and boulder for twenty miles up and down the Hudson."[4]

In 1908, Griffith directed *The Curtain Pole* (1909), using the dusty streets in Fort Lee to produce a slapstick comedy featuring Mack Sennett. (This was a version of Pathé's *Le Cheval emballé*, a popular hit in 1907-1908.) Desiring to be an actor, Mack first worked as an extra and did bit parts for Griffith at Biograph. Eager to learn more about moving pictures, he took long walks after work with Griffith while asking him questions about the art of film. Hoping to end Sennett's pestering, Griffith gave Mack a longer part in *The Curtain Pole* playing M. Dupont, who breaks a curtain pole and buys an extra long one as a replacement. "He had to maneuver [the pole] through the streets of Fort Lee, New Jersey, by various modes of transportation and at considerable peril to himself and to innocent passersby," wrote Richard Schickel. A marketplace was constructed, recalled Mrs. Griffith, "in a clearing in the wooded part of Fort Lee, stalls for fruits, vegetables, and other foodstuffs." The plot called for Dupont to take a horse-drawn cab with the pole "sticking out four or five feet on either side." He enters the marketplace a bit inebriated from drinking absinthe frappes. Playing a market woman, Mrs. Griffith remembered Sennett destroying the booths while she was buying a cabbage. The pole banged her head, knocking her "generally unconscious in the centre of the stage."[5]

After the incident Linda Griffith lost her enthusiasm "about Sennett's starring ventures." Nevertheless, the slapstick comedian-to-be soon appeared in *The Politician's Love Story* (1909). Griffith was excited about making this film after a large snowstorm made the tree limbs in Central Park "look like fantastic crystal branches." According to Griffith's wife, these two pictures "started the grumbling young Mack Sennett on the road to fame and fortune." Sennett was appointed director of Biograph's comedy films in 1911; however, a year later he departed for Los Angeles, where he made film history making slapstick shorts for Keystone. He was now truly "on the road to fame."[6]

Fort Lee flourished as a major center for early moving pictures, especially between 1909 and 1918. In 1910, the Champion Film Company constructed the first permanent movie studio in nearby Coytesville, a secluded rural area picked to evade the Trust. Still standing, it is considered the oldest studio building in the country. Within months, great greenhouse studios began sprouting up all over the Fort Lee area.[7] The following year Éclair, a French film company, opened an American branch in the town. By 1918 about eleven facilities were operating. Fort Lee became so crowded that companies had to compete for the best photogenic locales. For example, in December 1916, *Moving Picture World* announced that Lewis Selznick's Picture Productions had four companies using three Fort Lee studios ready to release four quality films.

Several major film companies in Hollywood trace their roots back to Fort Lee: Universal, 20th Century-Fox, Goldwyn Pictures, and Selznick Enterprises. Before moving to California, William Fox rented a studio in 1914 where he filmed *A Fool There Was* starring the "vamp" Theda Bara (née Theodosia Goodman), an overnight sensation. The Fox studio produced the epics *A Tale of Two Cities* (1917) and *Les Miserables* (1918) in Fort Lee. In 1914, Universal built its massive studio on Main Street in the West Fort Lee section. Considered one of the largest and most modern studios in the country before 1918, it was dubbed "Universal City East" by Carl Laemmle. In 1916, Samuel Goldwyn's Picture Corporation initially began renting space in the Solax Studios, and a year later moved to Universal's facility. After signing with Goldwyn, Will Rogers, Fields's friend and *Follies* colleague, completed his first film, *Laughing Bill Hyde*, here in 1918.

The most popular stars of the silent era were spotted in Fort Lee: Mary Pickford, the Gish sisters, Lionel Barrymore, Roscoe "Fatty" Arbuckle, Rudolph Valentino, and Pearl White, among others. White created a sensation in the silent serial *The Perils of Pauline*, while dangling from a *cliff* high above the Hudson River, a scene that reportedly triggered the term "cliff hanger."

*Figure 1.1 The path on the Palisades leading to Fort Lee before the George Washington Bridge (1931) was built. Author's Collection.*

Small wonder, then, that the *Follies* management picked Fort Lee for their film. On the day of shooting, thirty cast members from the *Ziegfeld Follies* assembled in front of the New Amsterdam a little after nine o'clock. After disembarking from their ferry boat, the *Follies* group hiked up a trail to the town perched atop the steep Palisades cliffs overlooking the Hudson River. When the Ziegfeld party arrived, they saw actors wearing makeup and costumes, numerous crews filming in the area, and aspiring bit players waiting in front of casting room doors. The Ziegfeld writers had written a sketch called "Commotion Picture," a parody of Griffith's *The Birth of a Nation*, which had recently opened at New York's Liberty Theatre with a sold-out performance. The short was to be shown at the 1915 *Follies* with another film intended to lampoon the nascent film industry. "A comedian in the [New Amsterdam] auditorium was to direct figures on the screen that followed his every instruction," recalled playwright and critic Channing Pollock. "The movie had to be carefully made, of course, and accurately timed."[8] The short featured such Ziegfeld principals as comedian Leon Errol, the legendary Bert Williams, and Mae Murray, the vivacious beauty known as "the girl with the bee stung lips," destined to became a silent screen diva. The film's director was the comic Ed Wynn, who later gained fame as radio's Fire Chief. By around four o'clock in the afternoon, as light dwindled and a ferry boat was scheduled to leave, the crew headed to Manhattan backtracking along the same route they had taken in the morning.

After the *Follies* opened, a rivalry soon erupted between Fields and Wynn during Bill's pool table routine. While hiding under the pool table, Wynn made funny faces, clowned, and did antics to amuse the audience. Known as a joker whose tomfoolery often stole scenes, Wynn began to disrupt Fields's timing. After it happened again, Bill threatened to seek revenge. The *Follies* was on the road in Boston when the tension between the two exploded. Fields suddenly took his pool cue and beamed Wynn over the head. Depending on different versions of the incident, Wynn was either dazed or leveled unconscious.

Wishing to become the highlight of the silent short shot at Fort Lee, Wynn stood in the left aisle near the orchestra pit commanding the actors in the film. Fields suddenly appeared on screen balancing a few cigar boxes. "Hey, Fields! You're not on yet!" yelled Wynn. "Get off the screen!" Startled, Bill dropped the boxes, picked them up, and walked away. Although rather forgotten, the short technically remains Fields's first appearance on screen.⁹

Sime Silverman wrote in *Variety* that Fields was "prominent in the screen pantomime." *The New York Times* reviewer felt that the short film was a highlight and encouraged people to see it. "You should see the motion-picture rehearsal with the movie actors— Bernard Granville, Mae Murray, Leon Errol, and all—bobbing about the screen while Ed Wynn hoarsely directs them out front. . . . There is a good deal of . . . more fun in the antics of W. C. Fields, an expert juggler with a sense of humor, who comes from the halls of the two-a-day."¹⁰

Fields, however, never mentioned his experience going to Fort Lee. Nor did he make any remarks that he had visited a significant site for early filmmaking and that here was an opportunity to join a new medium. But having just debuted in the *Follies*, he was avidly committed to his goal to become a star in Ziegfeld's revues.

In 1918, an extremely cold winter, a flu epidemic, and a shortage of coal needed for the nation's World War I effort caused many Fort Lee studios to shut down, and its personnel to flee to the warm sunshine of Southern California. Although its heyday was over, the area still continued to be the site of a few studios. The Eastman Kodak Company, for instance, used the Paragon Studios to test their Two-Color Kodachrome process. Fires and explosions constantly destroyed studios, leaving Fort Lee a "ghost town."

An article in the *New York Times Magazine* on May 31, 1931 was its "kiss of death": "The cradle of the motion picture in America is now a ghastly cemetery, with monuments of scaling concrete, crumpling brick, warped steel, and shattered glass . . . . Here at Fort Lee . . . declining careers gained rebirth and fortunes were created—and lost and stolen. Now even the ivy on the walls that housed these phenomena is dead."¹¹

The Palisades in New Jersey represented the locale where Fields began his involvement in silent moving pictures. Coincidently, the area became the setting where he launched his career in sound films, when he appeared in the short *The Golf Specialist* (1930), an offshoot of a sketch he first did on stage at the *Ziegfeld Follies of 1918* and off and on for the next twelve years. Bill had sparked an interest in the skit when he performed a version at the famous Palace Theatre in March 1930 and in the revue *Earl Carroll Vanities*. Fields had recently been in Hollywood where he did three silent Paramount films with Chester Conklin during 1927-28, a time when studios were transferring their facilities to sound. While there, not one studio recognized that Fields, with his unique voice, was a natural to do a sound film. After searching in vain for an opportunity to do a Talkie, he returned to the Broadway stage annoyed with Hollywood's fickleness.

Excited by the chance to finally do a sound film, Fields crossed the Hudson to the Palisades area where fifteen years earlier he had made his inaugural silent moving picture. He headed for the Ideal Studios, a two-building state-of-the art plant opened in June 1916 in Hudson Heights, near Fort Lee, by producer-director Herbert Brenon. "I have been so fortunate as to secure this studio, which was built regardless of cost by men who were determined to incorporate in it all the latest ideas and equipment," said Brenon. "I am satisfied that nowhere in the world is there a studio with better facilities. . . . I consider it a perfect tool." When Brenon left for England, a series of filmmakers used the studio for short silent comedies, and later it was equipped for sound. After the mid-1930s, the facility was equipped for storage space and as a warehouse for scenery and props. On September 9, 1953, the *Newark News* reported that "decades of movie-making slipped into oblivion yesterday when a general alarm fire swept the Ideal Sound Studios."[12] The Fort Lee area therefore formed the book ends of Fields's screen career in both silent and sound film comedy.

**Notes**

1. Christopher Klein, "When New Jersey Was the Film Capital of the World," *History*, February 25, 2016.
2. Richard Koszarski, *Fort Lee: The Film Town* (Rome, Italy, John Libbey Publishing, 2004), 30.
3. Richard Schickel, *D. W. Griffith: An American Life* (1984; New York, Limelight Paperback, 2004), 182.
4. Mrs. S. D. W. Griffith [Linda Arvidson], *When the Movies Were Young* (1925; New York: Dover Publications, 1969), 82, 87; see also Paul C. Spehr, *The Movies Begin: Making Movies in New Jersey 1887-1920* (The Newark Museum, 1977), 52.
5. Schickel, 117-18, *When the Movies Were Young*, 79-80.
6. *When the Movies Were Young*, 79-81.
7. *Fort Lee, Birthplace of the Motion Picture Industry* (Arcadia Publishing, 2006), 7.
8. Channing Pollock, *Harvest of My Years: An Autobiography* (New York: Bobbs-Merrill, 1943), 219.
9. Ibid.
10. *Variety*, June 26, 1915, scrapbook #29, WCFP; *NYT*, June 22, 1915, 15.
11. Koszarski, *Fort Lee*, 337.
12. Ibid, 229.

# CHAPTER 2

## Gaumont: The French Connection

While Fields was in the 1915 *Ziegfeld Follies*, he was offered an exceptional opportunity to appear in his first commercial film. Motion picture companies were signing numerous stage stars to do their specialties for the silent screen. The vogue dated back to Edison's Kinetoscope, which had filmed the strongman Eugen Sandow and the dancer Carmencita, among others, in 1894. The Gaumont Film Company, a leading French production corporation, wanted Fields to perform his pool table sketch and do a second one-reel short for its comedy series at its American studio, located on Congress Street in Flushing, Queens, a borough of New York City. The area was settled in 1644 by English non-conformists who probably named the township after their residence in Flushing in Holland. By the early twentieth century, Flushing remained a rural community noted for its nurseries, the study of horticulture, beautiful suburban houses, and prosperous farms.

Sites in New York's boroughs and on Long Island had burgeoned into a major center for East Coast filmmaking due to the locale's rural scenery, inexpensive vacant land, and proximity to midtown Manhattan via the Queensboro Bridge (1909), assets which enabled it to lure Broadway stars to perform before the camera. Starting the invasion in 1905 was the Vitagraph studio in the Flatbush area of Brooklyn, which churned out hundreds of silent movies during the 1910s and 1920s. To take advantage of scenery on eastern Long Island in 1915, Edison opened a studio in Bay Shore. In his book *Hollywood on the Hudson*, Richard Koszarski links early silent studios "within commuting distance of Times Square," as a single "viable local film industry." Nicknamed "Hollywood East," the area of cinema "[stretched] from the Edison laboratory and Fort Lee studios in northern New Jersey to the Thanhouser and D. W. Griffith studios in Westchester, and out beyond the Paramount

Astoria studio and Brooklyn Vitaphone stages to the rental facilities in eastern Queens and Long Island."[1]

Gaumont was one of the two leading film companies in France, along with Pathé-Frères. Founded by the engineer and inventor Léon Gaumont in 1898, the studio was initially devoted to the technological aspects of filmmaking, since Gaumont himself was particularly interested in photography, projectors, cameras, developing machines, and systems for washing and drying film prints. As early as 1902, Gaumont had invented Phonoscène, a primitive talking picture system based on a singer projected on a screen who would lip-synch to a sound recording. The showings, called "singing pictures," were extremely popular in Europe.

In an effort to enter the growing American market, and hoping to avoid import taxes, Gaumont opened its facility in Flushing around 1908. Two other French companies had studios on the East Coast: Éclair in Fort Lee (1911), and Pathé-Frères (1910) in Jersey City. French studios were also the leading importer of foreign films into the U.S., controlling sixty to seventy percent of the market in 1910 and sustaining its commanding position until the outbreak of World War I in Europe.

Comedy was especially popular in France, where vaudeville originated. The etymology of the word vaudeville stems from French sources. The name derives from the lively drinking and satirical songs found in the Valley of the Vire, *Vau-de-Vire*, in Normandy, France, in the fifteenth century. By the eighteenth century, the satirical songs sung on Parisian stages came to be known as melodies that stemmed from *Vau-de-ville* (valley of the town). Humorous farces with music, dancing, and other specialties at the French opéra-comique were called *pièces en vaudeville* and *comédies avec vaudeville*. The nation was also considered a leader in the evolution of film, both in technology and first-rate moving pictures, from the late nineteenth century until the outbreak of World War I in 1914.

Both Gaumont and Pathé had numerous film comedians under contract. At Pathé Max Linder was their star comic who delighted audiences with his portrayal of Max, a wealthy and dapper man-about-town frequently in trouble due to his affairs with gorgeous women and the pursuit of a luxurious lifestyle. He appeared in more than 100 silent shorts, and by 1910 he was recognized as the most popular film actor in the world.

In 1916, Linder went to the U.S. under contract to appear in comedy shorts at Essanay as a replacement for Chaplin, who had moved to Mutual. While filming *Max and his Taxi* in Hollywood, he befriended Chaplin, regularly visited his home, and discussed cinema. Some film critics believe that Linder had a major influence on Chaplin's style and persona. During his many tours in Europe (1901-1913) as a vaudeville juggler, Fields appeared in music halls and popular variety theaters, including the famous Folies Bergére (1904) in Paris. Fields might have seen Linder and other French comics in France during his overseas trips.

In 1905, the Gaumont company constructed a new monumental studio, called the Cité Elgé, which by 1913 had more than two dozen buildings, ranging from studios for filmmaking, to factories producing technical and industrial products for the cinema. The firm also owned the spectacular, 3,400-seat Gaumont-Palace (1911) movie theater in Paris, considered at the time the largest cinema in the world.

Under the leadership of Louis Feuillade, the studio's output included making longer well-regarded moving pictures that helped the studio to dominate French cinema from 1913 to 1920. Considered one of France's great versatile auteurs, he produced melodramas, thrillers, historical movies, and comedies. In 1913, Gaumont's facility in Flushing distributed Feuillade's masterpiece, *Fantomas*, a crime series featuring a phantom crook played by Renée Navarre. The film was one of many imports from French studios that sent negatives to the U.S. in order to avoid expensive tariffs. Upon arrival, positive prints were made by European facilities on the East Coast. Until 1919, Feuillade continued to make longer detective serials, ranging from ten to twelve episodes, pictures that accented poetic imagery and pure fantasy and captured the imagination of French surrealists.

In France Gaumont was also known for its comedic films. The exhibition catalogue "French Comedy, Gaumont Style," at the Museum of Modern Art in 2010, emphasized the studio's importance in the area: "One genre that has been a constant over the

*Figure 2.1 The Gaumont Studio in Flushing, NY, with its famous filmmaker Alice Guy Blaché. Author's Collection.*

company's 110-year history is comedy—hardly surprising for a nation that has given the world both Molière and Voltaire." Early works by pioneers Émile Cohl, Jean Durand, Louis Feuillade and others were shown.

Starting in 1906, slapstick appeared in many Gaumont shorts during the early twentieth century. Among them were the studio's "Calino" films, which accented discontinuous scenes that mainly focused on a single gag. Gaumont's popular *"Onésime"* (1912-13) comedy series, produced by Jean Durand, quickly rose to popularity with its frenetic action, acrobatic tumbling, destruction of sets, and absurd situations. They are considered the highpoint of prewar slapstick comedy in France. Mack Sennett's Keystone comedies were influenced by Durand's work as well as Pathé's early slapstick films. "I have been posing for many years as the inventor of slapstick motion-picture comedy," said Sennett. "It is about time I confessed the truth. It was those Frenchmen who invented slapstick and I imitated them."[2]

The studio relied on talented filmmakers to direct and produce its numerous silent films. Employed initially as Gaumont's secretary, Alice Guy Blaché, who was passionate about cinema, directed, produced, and supervised nearly 600 silent pictures ranging in length up to thirty minutes. Her range of subjects was broad during her twenty-three-year career: comedies, adventures, romances, religious epics, thrillers, melodrama, and westerns. She experimented also with Gaumont's Phonoscène, considered a forerunner of sound film. She was once described as a woman "with crisp diction, faultless grammar, and a mild way of talking about even painful and contentious matters." In her memoir she wrote about her inspiration: "In the silent cinema we had discovered a fresh, limpid spring, joyously reflecting the grasses, watercress and willows that bordered it; we had only to wet our lips in it to staunch our thirst."[3]

Alice Guy is also recognized as cinema's first female director and owner of a movie studio. As a voice encouraging women to become filmmakers, she stated in 1914, "There is nothing connected with the staging of a motion picture that a woman cannot do as easily as a man, and there is no reason why she cannot completely master every technicality of the art."[4]

In early 1907, Gaumont sent Alice Guy and her husband, Herbert Blaché, a British cameraman, to Cleveland to create a Chronophone franchise, an early attempt to develop a synchronized sound system for talking pictures. "Synchronization was obtained by adjusting the speed of unwinding of the motion picture film to the speed of the disc," wrote Léon Gaumont. After nine months the project failed, but Gaumont hired inventor Arthur Kingston to experiment with the development of electric recordings "by placing a contact on the phonograph disc. A rheostat in the motor circuit controlled the speed of both and kept the projector in accurate step with the phonograph." By 1909 they were using their successful system making talking pictures, which were shown in French venues. Gaumont appointed Herbert Blaché to manage the studio's facility in Flushing Meadows Park. The French company spent $20,000 equipping the former printing plant to produce English-language Chronophone film. Alice Guy called the Flushing studio a laboratory for "the development and printing of film in the United States." She believed that the studio could be used for production, despite how much smaller it was than the facilities in France. "The Gaumont studio was not being used —every day," she wrote. "The temptation was too strong. I resolved to rent it and try making a few films."[5] For that purpose, Alice Guy founded the Solax Company in Flushing in 1910. Soon the plant was producing two one-reelers a week, many directed by Guy.

On November 4, 1911, *Moving Picture World*, a leading weekly trade magazine in the industry, published a five-paragraph article, headlined "SOLAX ENLARGING STUDIOS." The author described the Flushing's Gaumont Studio, rented by Solax, as having a park and lake on one side and on the other side structures "representing a small Western hotel, county store, and saloon used to make Western pictures." Plans were made to create a larger studio addition to the Flushing plant, one "better suited to the varied product of the Solax Company. It will ... contain conveniences not provided by the present studio facilites."[6]

Alice Guy was described as a "most competent director" who has "been connected with picture production almost from the inception of the business." At Solax she was involved with writing and editing of scenarios and directing or overseeing the studio's pictures: fantasies, comedies, melodramas and historical films. "She practically has a hand in the entire output of the company."[7] The Gaumont facility advertised that it was churning out three shorts a week during 1912.

The Flushing facility, however, did not meet Guy's needs. Two years later she moved Solax to Fort Lee where, as mentioned earlier, production occurred in a larger modern facility with stages under a glass roof. Here she wrote screenplays, oversaw the production of 325 one-reel and multi-reel movies, and directed between thirty-five and fifty silent pictures, ranging from fantasy period pieces with gorgeous costumes and decorative sets based on literary sources, to the surreal slapstick of *The Drunken Mattress* and the social satire of the *Consequences of Feminism*. In 1912, she directed *A Fool and His Money*, considered the first film with solely African-American actors, although it failed to present an honest portrayal of Blacks.

The studio advertised it as a "satiric comedy dealing with the pretensions of colored folks. The way they try to ape and imitate their white brothers forms the basis of the story."[8] Several emerging stars appeared in Guy's movies, including Lionel and Ethel Barrymore, and the diva Olga Petrova. Sadly, her ouevre went unrecognized both in France and the U.S. due to the pervasive sexism in the film industry. Only now has her importance been discovered by film historians, preservationists who rescued her moving pictures for DVD release, and documentarians who explore her work in the recent film *Be Natural*, named after the advice she told her performers.

Another prominent pioneer female director, actor, and writer initially associated with Gaumont in Flushing was Lois Weber. Born in Allegheny, Pennsylvania, in 1879, Weber (née Florence Pietz) had been a Church Army street-corner evangelist and a repertory actress before her employment at Gaumont in 1908, where she made sound tracks for moving pictures. That same year Weber acted in her first short, *Hypocrities,* a four-reel allegory featuring a reappearing naked woman named "Miss Truth." By 1911, she and her husband and co-actor-director, Phillips Smalley, were working for the Rex Motion Picture Company, where she directed *The Merchant of Venice* (1914). By that year Weber had directed twenty-seven pictures, and in addition, she wrote scenarios and subtitles, designed sets and costumes, and edited movies and other films. A year later they left for Hollywood, where the couple worked for Universal Studios making pictures dealing with social issues such as abortion, alcoholism, birth control, drug addiction, prostitution, and the exploitation of the poor. In total, she is credited with directing 135 films, writing 114, and acting in 100. In 1939, she died impoverished; friends paid for her funeral expenses. Weber's artistic oeuvre ranks her as the first American woman to direct a feature film and among the most significant female filmmakers during the silent era.

Gaumont's Flushing studio therefore had a rich history before Fields filmed his two commercial comedy shorts in 1915. By that date the facility's heyday was over. The seven-year-old plant in Flushing was primitive compared not only to the modern Solax facility in Fort Lee, but to all of New York's recent state-of-the-

*Figure 2.2 Alice Guy Blaché recognized as the foremost woman film pioneer—director, producer, and screenwriter—1896-1927.*

art studios featuring glass roofs, improved lighting, increased set space, back lots, expansive exterior acreage, and other superior features. By 1914, sprawling Los Angeles included more than seventy refurbished or newly constructed studios. They were topped by Carl Laemmle's massive Universal City in the San Fernando Valley, which opened to great fanfare in March 1915.

During 1912-13, the French invasion of its films into the U.S. market started to slow, especially when excellent American multi-reel features began to usurp the transatlantic trade. More U.S. moving pictures were exported to Europe, while fewer foreign films were imported. Another reason was that the international studios in the U.S., including Gaumont, faced an uncertain future when war broke out in Europe during August 1914.

On December 18, 1915, shortly after Fields completed his shorts, *Moving Picture World* announced Gaumont's plans to build a brand new studio on adjacent land in Flushing with all the latest facilities, costing as much as $200,000. This ambitious project was never carried out, probably due to the U.S. entering the war in 1917. Apparently, Gaumont soon abandoned its studio around this time. Fields's two shorts in 1915 were shot near the end of Gaumont's productions in Flushing.

Fields's Gaumont films were distributed through the Mutual Film Corporation, an independent exchange system formed in 1912 through financing provided by Kuhn, Loeb, and Company. Mutual soon became a leader in the distribution field, challenging the monopolistic control of Edison's Motion Picture Patents Company. Mutual eventually succeeded in signing half of the latter's members when it became a production company in 1917. Interested in comedy as a money maker, Mutual was also Keystone's distributor. But when its president, Harry E. Aitkin, left the company in May 1915 to form the Triangle Film Corporation, this organization assumed the distribution of Keystone's productions.

Needing to replace its loss, Mutual's new management contracted with the Gaumont Company to provide three types of comic films starring Broadway performers. In August 1915, Mutual announced "All-Star Comedies, featuring Broadway comedians in a new variety of comic films." Silent films featuring headliners from The Great White Way had become a hot item: Vitagraph's "Broadway Star Features," Universal's "Broadway Features," and Kalem's "Broadway Favorites." Paramount, too, planned to release shorts starring popular Broadway headliners. Looking for comedians to appear in its new one-reel "All-Star Comedies," Gaumont's general manager in its Flushing studio, F. G. Bradford, thought the *Follies* had the best comics. Noticing that all the principal stars except Fields were tied up with other studios, he selected him to commence the series with his hilarious pool routine.[9] With his pantomime skills, trickery, visual comedy, his repertoire seemed perfect entertainment for an early silent comedy short.

Although Fields's contract with Ziegfeld called for his exclusive services, the impresario agreed to the filming provided that Mutual Corporation, the distributor, acknowledged his consent in the film, with the following message: "It is only through the courtesy of Florenz Ziegfeld that the Mutual Corporation is enabled to present this star feature in its regular program." Fearing he would lose customers if Fields recorded his act on film, Ziegfeld later ordered him not to appear before the camera while the *Follies* was playing on Broadway. Given the long road trip after its Broadway run, Fields had little time to do a film. As Broadway's leading producer of revues and musicals, Ziegfeld showed little interest in the film business. His stubborn attitude prohibited Fields from performing in additional films while he was in the *Follies* until 1925.

Fields signed a stringent contract with the Gaumont Company to report to the studio no later than the first day of September 1915. The wording gave the studio complete control over production and bound Fields ("the artist") to strict compliance. If not, he could be sued, forced to repay any sums paid, and was liable for any damages the company sustained due to the "Artist's default." Fields needed to render his services to the company in a correct and painstaking manner. He was asked to make two films within one week at a salary of $450, and if the filming time exceeded the one week period, he would be paid one sixth of $450 for each day of extra work. The contract gave Gaumont the right to hire another actor if Fields failed to finish the two pictures, which would make the agreement null and void. Fields would soon learn that Hollywood studios made actors wage laborers subject to supervision, budgets, and legal enforcements. Multi-year contacts exposed them to being fired under option clauses, which granted employers the right to dismiss players at any time.

Ziegfeld was not the only problem that prevented Fields from becoming a standout star in silent moving pictures. After seventeen years on stage, Bill found that theater performance was deeply ingrained in his psyche. Fields was wedded to the idea that he needed a live audience for his timing and to measure the success of his routines. "The hardest thing for a former stage player to get used to in movie work is to do your stuff minus applause or encouragement before a handful of cameramen and technical directors," Fields stated. "You wonder if you are getting across, and there's no way of finding out." As long as his theatrical career was advancing, he had little incentive to try a novel entertainment form that was still evolving.

Bill must have been aware of the growing popularity of the movies. Philadelphia, where he grew up, was noted for its early film exhibition. Keith's Bijou premiered Edison films there in May 1896. Based in the city was pioneer filmmaker Siegmund Lubin, who during the late 1890s manufactured early projectors and produced silent moving pictures. While performing in the 1915 *Follies*, Fields could see movie palaces springing up on Broadway. In 1914, the huge million-dollar Strand, seating nearly 3,500 patrons and known for having the city's largest stage, opened in Times Square, near the New Amsterdam Theatre where the *Follies* was playing. Vaudeville theaters such as Proctor's 23rd Street Theater in Manhattan began showing silent films exclusively starting in December 1907 at its newly named Bijou Dream. According to the *New York Times*, weekly attendance at movie theaters jumped from 45 million in 1909 to 105 million by 1917. Space for film news and reviews grew exponentially in *Variety* and the *New York Dramatic Mirror*.

As a vaudevillian Bill noted the beginning of silent movies. Vaudeville theaters were major showplaces for early film exhibition since its format of rotating acts was conducive to early motion picture exhibition. Shorts, running ten to twenty minutes, were easily integrated into a playbill. Once they grew in popularity, they were not always placed at the program's end as "chasers" in order to prod the audience to go home. Practically every time Fields participated in a big-time vaudeville program, a silent movie short (Biograph, Lumières Cinématographe, Vitagraph productions, etc.), was shown during the program. While performing in Melbourne, Fields shared the program with the showing of George Méliès's famous picture, *A Trip to the Moon*. The first major commercial presentation of moving pictures in the U.S., Thomas Edison's Vitascope, occurred on April 23, 1896, at Koster and Bial's New Music Hall. On June 29, the U.S. premier of Lumière's Cinématographe occurred at Keith's Union Square. The Keith and Orpheum circuits showed Biograph releases from 1897 to 1903. Their showplaces played a leading role in introducing the American public to early cinema. The British music halls and variety theaters in Europe performed a similar function. Fields must have been aware of these early silent films as he played the Keith and Orpheum circuits, the English music halls, and European variety theaters numerous times from 1901 to 1914.

Once studios turned to making features, the competition between motion pictures and vaudeville became more intense. During 1915, Fields's first year in the *Follies*, D. W. Griffith's *The Birth of a Nation* was released. Despite its harsh racial overtones, the feature is considered a major advancement in the art of film due to Griffith's masterful direction, employing techniques ranging from close-ups to cross-cutting. When the multi-reel feature film became popular, with its long narrative story performed by a growing list of silent screen stars, more fans flocked to movie palace venues rather than vaudeville houses.

By the mid-1910s, the narrative feature, exhibited in the most prestigious theaters, also routed short films. French imports played a role in this development, especially *Film d'Arte* productions, which aimed to produce features that would attract a more upscale audience by making cinematic versions of popular stage plays and literature. Influenced by these happenings in 1912, Adolph Zukor, head of Famous Players Motion Picture Company, imported *Queen Elizabeth* and *Camille*, French productions starring the famous stage actress Sarah Bernhardt. A year later Zukor's firm merged with Jesse Lasky's Feature Play Company, an amalgamation that later became Paramount, where Fields excelled as a sound film comedian.

Fields's two 1915 shorts therefore had become passé in the evolution of American cinema. Instead of being the main attraction, one-reel pictures often were shown as part of a double bill featuring a multi-reel production. Reviews of shorts consequently received less notoriety in the press.

Another problem Fields faced in 1915 was that most popular comedy shorts largely depended on slapstick, a formula accenting knockabout clowning, buffoonery, pratfalls, pie-in-the-face, and other rowdy antics for laughs. Generating laughter through physical aggression can be traced back to *commedia dell'arte* and English pantomime. The form later surfaced as slapstick comedy on the burlesque and vaudeville stages. An extreme form, knockabout comedy or roughhouse humor, saw the comic thrashing his straight man or foil through violent actions.

The genre was best exemplified by Mack Sennett's side-splitting Keystone shorts from 1912 to 1917, which accented frenzied sight gags and madcap anarchism. In 1914, Sennett signed Charlie Chaplin, a British music-hall graduate from Fred Karno's comedy sketch company. Chaplin's early films for Keystone reflected the studio's roughhouse formula. Disliking Sennett's *modus operandi*, Chaplin soon developed a new persona, his iconic little tramp, a sympathetic underdog whose poverty underscores society's injustices. In 1915, he moved to the Essanay Company's studio and became so popular that a sensational craze, called Chaplinitis, swept the country, highlighted by a proliferation of books, cartoons, poems, dolls, and toys, among others. Fields was therefore making his first silent picture at the time Chaplin was making headlines.

Although Fields admired Chaplin's gift for pantomime, he viewed the comedian as a competitor, and at one envious moment called him "a ballet dancer." Chaplin's tramp character, or "Little Fellow," was not particularly new, although the way he depicted the figure as a self-suffering compassionate underdog was. A wave of tramps had appeared earlier on stage, including Fields, who started in vaudeville as an unsightly tramp juggler wearing thick facial makeup and tattered clothes that in comparison made Chaplin's impersonation look nearly suave.

The demands of Gaumont and its distributor Mutual to produce a slapstick picture ensnared Fields in a quandary. In contrast to the Keystone cutups, Fields had developed on the vaudeville stage a subtle comedic style based on his pantomime skills. Although he had done some slapstick antics, pies in the face, slipping on a banana peel, and knockabout comedy were not his forte. "It is much easier to be funny without saying anything," he once stated. Another time he explained, "I love to make people laugh, but not the short guffaws. They really don't count, to my mind. When you can make your audience take the long down laughs, then you know you're pleasing them. As I figure it, only such a laugh is the 'laugh' worthwhile—the laugh really to work for."[10]

Despite his reputation as a successful lead performer in the 1915 *Follies*, he was a newcomer to the screen and lacked the clout to challenge the executives at Gaumont and Mutual distribution. Later, as a more popular veteran film comedian during the 1930s, Fields constantly fought with studio moguls. When ordered to perform a scene he did not like, Fields argued vehemently and a few times threatened to walk out, sometimes causing the studio to form an exclusive unit for him under a new director. "The director in sixty cases out of a hundred is an actor who can't make the grade," he once declared.[11]

However, in 1915, he saw no other way to enter the film industry. Fields caved in to the pressure to do a slapstick short, a performance style that was completely at odds with his comedic *modus operandi*. Backing down proved to be an ominous decision.

**Notes**

1. Richard Koszarski, *Hollywood on the Hudson: Film and Television in New York From Griffith to Sarnoff* (New Brunswick, NJ: Rutgers University Press, 2008), 6.
2. Edward Wagenknecht, *The Movies in the Age of Innocence* (1962; New York: Limelight Edition, 1997), 40-41.
3. *The Memoirs of Alice Guy Blaché*, ed. Anthony Slide (Lanham, MD: Scarecrow Press, 1986), 30, 67; *NYT*, April 26, 2019, c 10.
4. *Alice Guy Blaché, Cinema Pioneer*, ed. Joan Simon (New Haven: Yale University Press, 2009), frontispiece, 82.
5. www.filmcolors.org/timeline-entry; Guy, *Memoirs*, 67.
6. *MPW*, November 4, 1911, 386.
7. Ibid.
8. Koszarski, *Hollywood on the Hudson*, 70.
9. James Curtis, *W. C. Fields* (New York: Knopf, 2003), 102.
10. Sally Benson, "It Is Much Easier to be Funny Without Saying Anything," *Sunday Telegraph*, scrapbook #10, WCFP; David T. Rocks, *W. C. Fields—An Annotated Guide* (Jefferson, NC: McFarland, 1993), 17; Arthur M. Longworthy, "W. C. Fields—and Why?" *Park Avenue Social Bulletin*, August 1925.
11. *Silver Screen*, February, 1921, scrapbook #3, WCFP.

# CHAPTER 3
## The Pool Trickster

The Gaumont company in Flushing wanted Fields to perform his pool table sketch and do a second one-reel short for its comedy series. *Pool Sharks* was the first short that Fields completed in 1915, followed by a second, entitled *His Lordship's Dilemma*, a lost picture in which he plays a remittance man. Fields was paid $450 a week for the two films and one-sixth of his salary per day if the shooting was not completed within one week.

Fields's passion for pool began as a youngster when he worked as an assistant racking the balls for players at one of Philadelphia's numerous halls. Here he watched skilled pool sharks sucker naïve newcomers to play for money by first pretending to lose. Next the hustler waged a higher amount against his overconfident opponent, ran the table, and pocketed his earnings. Bill studied the expert finesse and shot-making of the sharks by watching their mannerisms and maneuvers. "While hanging around pool halls as a kid, I noticed that every player went through the same gyrations," stated Fields. "So, I enlarged upon this routine and it became one of my bright spots of pantomime, for everyone who ever played pool recognizes himself and laughs heartily."[1]

While touring music halls in England, where billiards was a very popular game, Fields introduced his pool table routine in January, 1902 at a music hall in Leeds. When he returned to the U.S., he had a custom table built by a friend in Atlantic City, slightly shorter than standard size and collapsible for easier handling. The design allowed him to take the table on all his vaudeville tours, including to Europe, Australia, and South Africa. It also had rounded cushions that allowed the balls to fly into the air at various angles. The pool game sketch was a work in progress, and evolved over time to become the highlight of his vaudeville performance. His initial routine consisted of trick shots ricocheting the ball from the back cushion into a spacious hip pocket in the rear of his pants. As he became more proficient, he made the ball bounce from the cushion to his knee on his upright leg and from there to the top of his foot, which kicked it into the table's rear pocket.

The sketch's highlight became the trick of pocketing all the balls with one stroke, which generated gales of laughter every time he did the stunt. The balls were connected by an invisible string attached to screw eyes installed on each ball. A mirror placed above the table enabled the spectators in the gallery to see how one shot made the balls disappear. An assistant hidden under the table would cut or pull the string so that all the balls would go into various pockets. Fields also developed a socko ending by jamming his cue through a disguised hole in the pool table. He then departed the stage to thunderous applause followed by curtain calls.

His pool table stunt was actually an extension of his talent as a trickster, which he first displayed as a juggler who manipulated cigar boxes. The boxes, with holes at their end, were connected together with an elastic cord. As he tossed them into the air, the boxes would return and balance on his hand in a tall vertical column, and then by the flip of his wrist would quickly form a horizontal column. Before loudly applauding, theatergoers, wondering how he accomplished the trick, would stare in disbelief. What the spectators saw were the deceptive moves of a sly conjurer.

Given the Keystone vogue, the producers of *Pool Sharks* worried that Fields's less demonstrative style might not amuse the movie-going public. Seeking box-office profits, Gaumont and its Mutual distributors apparently wanted their films to reflect the popular slapstick formula. *Pool Sharks*, a ten-minute one-reel short, consequently emphasizes anarchy, vulgarity, and tomfoolery in a fast-paced setting.

To direct *Pool Sharks*, the producers hired Edwin Middleton, an ex-comedy trouper with Philadelphia's Girard Avenue Theatre stock company. At the time of his employment, he had already directed several shorts, but these were not slapstick pictures. Indeed, his last two shorts before *Pool Sharks* were dramas starring Lionel Barrymore and Lillian Russell. His lack of experience in the genre might explain the slipshod manner in which the film is directed. In one frame, for example, a hand can be seen near the pool table.

The plot sticks to a typical Keystone story line about two rivals fighting for the affection of the same girl, a theme that can be seen in Chaplin's first Keystone, *Making a Living* (1914). The opening scene shows Fields entering a garden. He wears an unappealing jacket, rumpled hat, and incongruous white socks. With his face covered with thick makeup and a clip-on bushy mustache, which he wore on stage for numerous years, Fields resembles a disreputable bully and lothario. In his hand is his trusty cane, a vaudeville juggling prop that he will often use during his career. Spotting a pretty young woman sitting on a hammock, he twirls his cane in greeting, accidentally walloping himself in the head.

Fields's numerous confrontations with menacing objects date back to his vaudeville years when he feigned fearing juggling props that might hit him. Fields regularly used this comedy ruse while portraying the besieged Everyman assaulted by life's annoyances. "The comedian gets his biggest laughs when he is in trouble of some sort, when he is undergoing some manner of discomfort," Fields stated. Laughter, Bill believed, surfaces when the audience can easily identify with the situation. Everybody at one time or another has felt threatened by outside forces. "I don't make people laugh," he said. "They make themselves laugh consciously or unconsciously. They're laughing at themselves all the time I am on the stage. I don't point a finger at them and say, 'That's you.' I just give them a cartoon of themselves." The basis of his humor stemmed from everyday life. "As long as the public can laugh at themselves, I'll never run out of material. I get quite twenty-five per cent of my lines spontaneously just watching people on the other side of the footlights."[2]

The physical comedy in *Pool Sharks* continues as he tries to impress the girl on the hammock. A young worker tosses a pail that strikes him in the head. A rival suitor appears, played by the character actor Bud Ross. The two join the woman on the hammock, where more accidents occur. As they sit down, a sharp pin pierces Ross's rump while the rear of Fields's pants is splattered with large sticky white spots that resemble marshmallows. When the hammock suddenly collapses, the suitors fall off, looking like fools.

Fields's accident-prone character faces more trouble when he and his rival join the woman at a picnic. Spotting a young boy seated next to her, Fields places his cane around the boy's neck and yanks him to the ground. The action represents the first time Bill displays an on-screen hostility to young brats, a precursor to his portrayal as a child-hater in later films. As he begins to eat, a piece of asparagus pokes him in the eye. A pellet from the boy's pea shooter knocks him in the head, causing him to spill coffee on the woman's lap. When Ross twists Fields's proboscis, he retaliates by poking the attacker in the eye with his finger. During the fight Ross bites and severs one of Fields's fingers. The fighting has drawn a crowd, who now encourage the two to settle their differences in a game of pool; the victor will win the girl.

For filming the pool sequence, the studio used a different table from the one in the *Follies*, which was needed for the evening performance. Since Fields's cue shots are filmed with stop-motion photography, the film is unfortunately not an authentic reproduction of his classic pool table act. Instead of showing Fields's trick shot that clears the table with one stroke, for example, the moviegoer sees the balls fly up into a rack on the wall.

Slapstick and trick photography dominate as the rivals fight, wielding their cues and pool balls as weapons. When Fields hurls a ball at Ross, it sticks to the side of his eye. For a few seconds, Fields juggles several balls, but the scene is so brief it fails to show the full range of his talent. The two antagonists use their cues to bash one another over the head. Ross sees the woman looking at their roughhousing through an open window. Fields throws a ball, intending to hit Ross, but it flies through the window instead, knocking over a fish bowl and dumping the fish onto the woman's hair. She is so angry that she rushes to the pool room to seek revenge. Fields hurls a ball at Ross's head that causes his toupee to fall off, and after another assault Ross falls out of the window into a barrel full of water.

Bystanders, riled on behalf of the woman's safety, begin to chase Fields. To escape the crowd, Fields flees to the basement, where he grabs a bottle of liquor, takes a swig, and rushes outside carrying the contents. (Liquor props and gags later become a staple of Fields's films.) Spotting Ross, Fields lifts him out of the barrel. As Ross emerges, he spits water on Fields, who pushes him back into the

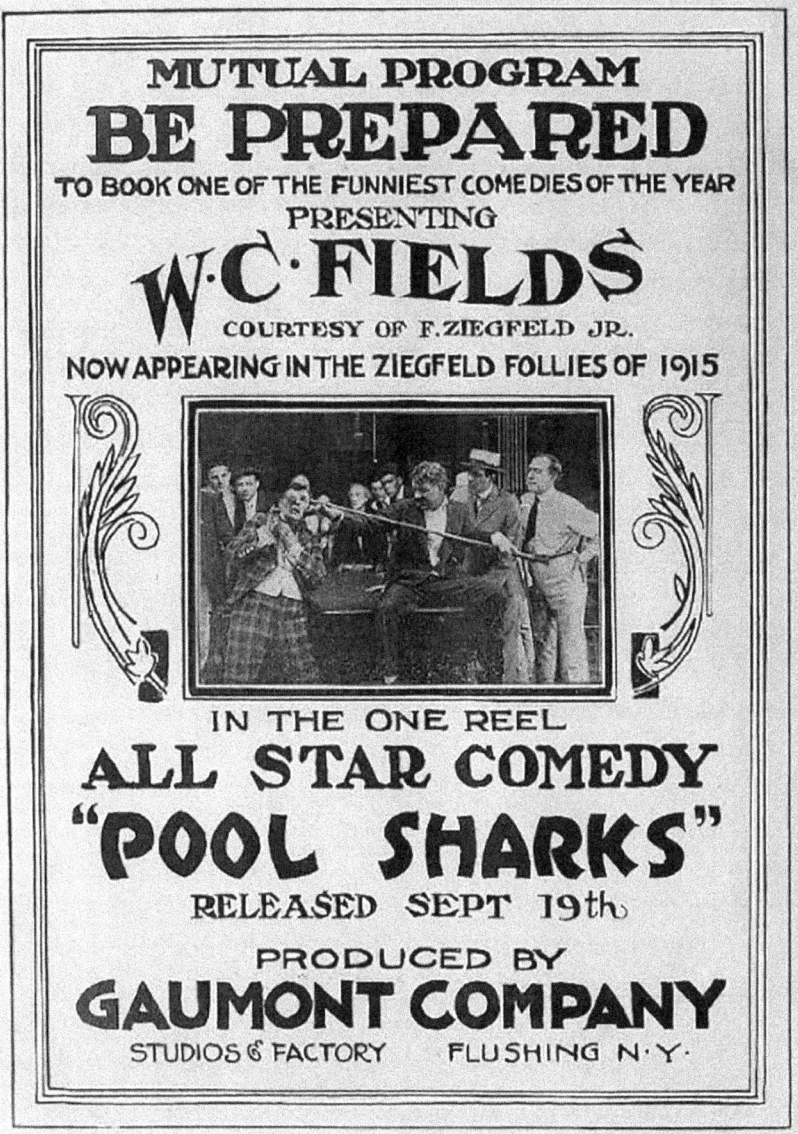

*Figure 3.1 Advertisement for* Pool Sharks. *Author's Collection.*

barrel. Finally, Fields escapes the hostile crowd, but fails to win the woman's affection.

At close inspection the short contains some redeeming features, especially when it captures Fields's trademark mannerisms. The way he flinches and ducks to avoid being hit by the pool balls exemplifies his reaction to perilous objects during his stage and screen career. To prepare his cue, he is unable to grasp the chalk which hangs from the ceiling, a sight gag that he repeats in other movies. While trying to put his loose hat back on his head, it gets entangled in his cane. Fields will often repeat his cane-hat gag, which originated in vaudeville. In *Pool Sharks* he plays the frustrated Everyman, a victim assaulted by inanimate objects, his rival Ross, and the crowd chasing after him at the end.

Some critics have recognized the significance of Fields's performance in *Pool Sharks*. *Moving Picture World* called the short, which opened on September 19, "an eccentric comedy number with amusing spots in it. . . . A comedy pool game is part of the picture. This contains some good nonsense." Two film historians also praised Fields. Nicholas Yanni commented, "What we can see in Fields' first experience with the new medium of motion pictures is his remarkable sense of timing and his skilled powers of understatement." William Everson found the film "well controlled," "mathematically precise" in its "timing," and "selective" in its "use of slapstick." "*Pool Sharks* is a minor masterpiece when viewed in the context of its period, and certainly a major milestone in the early evolution of screen comedy." Although the film fails to present an accurate portrait of Fields's pool act, the short remains a priceless preservation that documents Fields's first attempt to transfer a stage act to the screen. *Pool Sharks* exemplifies a significant factor in Fields's oeuvre: adaptations of his stage routines will play a substantial role in his film career.[3]

The pool-playing sketch evolved into Fields's signature act during his long career. Pool playing forms the bookends to his Broadway stage career in performances fifteen years apart. As discussed earlier, Fields performed the pool routine in his first *Ziegfeld Follies* (1915). He reprised the sketch in the play *Ballyhoo* (1930), his last appearance on the Great White Way. Reenactment of a favorite stage sketch became a habitual pattern as a showman. Fields fortunately possessed the talent to make each revival appear novel through slight unexpected variations, whether by altering the plot, gags, characters, or other aspects of the routine.

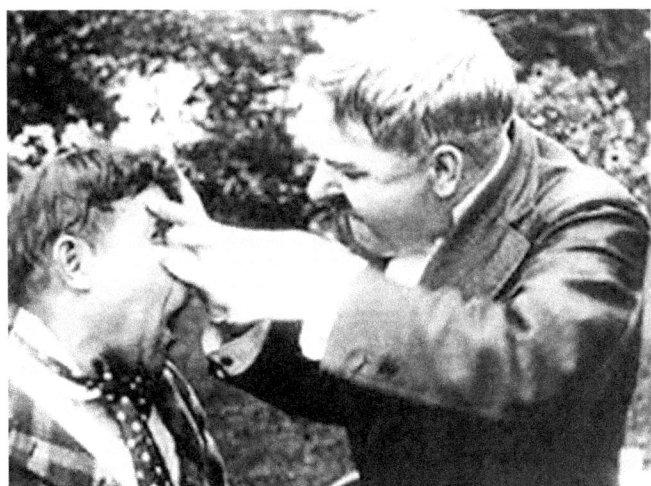

*Figure 3.2
Anarchy in
Pool Sharks.
Author's
Collection*

Because Fields believed that the act was a sure-fire hit, he regularly pestered film directors to include the routine. Sometimes he won; most times he lost when studio bosses insisted that it did not fit the plot. On other occasions they left the sequence on the cutting room floor, causing Bill to mope, cuss, and fume.

"My pool table and I have been pals for a long time, and we've made a lot of dough with our partnership." he said. Fields usually installed a pool table in a room in his large houses where he enjoyed fleecing challengers in a game. According to lore, when Fields opposed a newcomer, he sometimes pretended to have palsy; once the game started, his hands stopped shaking. Some nights Bill dreamed he was back in a Philadelphia pool parlor where he first learned the game. He could hear the hustlers ordering him to "Rack 'em up, boy!" Fields loved the look and feel of the green felt, which reminded him of a patch of grass. To ease a painful back, he sometimes slept on the table's top. In her memoir of living with Fields, Carlotta Monti recalled the time she screamed when first seeing him asleep on the table in his pajamas. Awakened, he looked up and declared, "A pool table was one of my early beds, and all of us unconsciously revert to our childhood."[4]

When Fields went to Hollywood in 1927 to continue his film career with Paramount, he insisted that his pool table accompany him. "I felt sort of lonesome without it," he confessed. "It's such an old friend that I like to have it around."[5] The studio agreed to pay for the transportation of his bulky table and props. He performed his pool routine in *Tillie's Punctured Romance* (1928), but it was cut from the final version.

The studio instead decided to include the scene in his last silent film, *Fools for Luck* (1928). A visual record of Fields's skill is unfortunately lacking, since the movie is lost. The action, however, is described in reviews. Fields plays Richard Whitehead (Whitey's white hair), a con man who pitches dry oil wells and is called "the most successful villain that the screen has exploited for many a day." A pool hustler, Whitehead challenges the town's champion, Samuel Hunter, played by the veteran walrus-mustached comedian Chester Conklin, a former Keystone Kop. Whitehead pretends he is an inept "mark" by handling the cue as a baseball bat and golf club. "The players get down to the last ball, with an easy shot for Mr. Hunter," wrote the *New York Times* reviewer. "As Mr. Whitehead has nothing that could be termed a conscience or sporting instinct he discovers a way to trick Mr. Hunter and win the game."[6]

Among the sound films that best illustrate Fields's pool playing skill is *Six of a Kind* (1934), directed by Leo McCarey, an illustrious comedy specialist. Fields initially balked at playing the part of a sheriff, called "Honest" John. He felt the script, which he read the night before the shooting, contained an anemic pool routine. He told McCarey that he had drunk a "quart of whiskey before he finally got to his part! I came to the conclusion that you were trying to kill me in pictures. I thought we were good friends but Caesar thought Brutus was too."[7] Fields threatened to walk out, but after arguing with McCarey, the director yielded and gave the comedian the freedom to improvise. Although the role was small, Fields stole the film with his pool playing sketch.

In the scene, Fields enters the pool room accompanied by his sidekick Doctor Busby, played by the character actor Tammany Young. With his expressionless face and reserved demeanor, Young was perfect for the part. The sheriff picks out a crooked cue and examines it. "It's crooked isn't it?" Young asks. "I'd like to see something in this joint that isn't crooked," the sheriff replies. Fields believed that he got more laughs by bending objects rather than breaking them. "It is never funny," he said, "to break anything. It is only funny to bend things."[8]

While standing next to the table, Young asks the sheriff how he got "the name of Honest John." The question gives Fields the opportunity to relate a tall tale during his pool routine. "At the time of which I speak, I'm tendin' bar up at Medicine Hat. Well, a guy used to come in there with a glass eye. I used to wait on him. Wasn't a bad guy. He used to take his glass eye out and put it in a tumbler of water. He comes in one day and he forgets the glass eye. I found it. The next morning when he comes in, I said 'Young man, here's your glass eye,' and I gave it back to him. Ever since that time—ever since that day, I've been known as Honest John."[9] The sheriff, of course, is not really "honest," but a petty crook who steals coins from a hotel pay phone in the film. A noted raconteur, Fields spun many other witty tall tales during his career.

The pool scene displays Fields's wonderful pantomime skills while depicting his determined but fruitless fight against the traps of everyday existence. Every object the sheriff touches rebuffs his efforts. He can't put chalk on the cue's tip because he is unable to grasp it as it moves back and forth on a string. A southpaw, Fields lines up his shot by gripping the stick's end with his left hand and placing the top part between the index fingers of his right hand. He starts to shoot, but extends his left hand too far, causing the cue to leave his right hand and bang against the bottom of the table. Frustrated, he places his hat on the table and takes off his coat. He places his cigar between two pieces of chalk on the side rail. When he picks up his cigar it is stuck to the chalk. Attempting to put the stogie in his mouth, the sheriff instead eats the chalk and spits its remnants out in disgust. When he tries again to break the balls, he hits the cue ball but misses the target, causing it to rebound off the cushion and bang him in the head. Recovering from the blow, the sheriff places his stick above the cue ball and tries a massé shot. When he misses the ball, his cue pierces the green cloth and rams through the table. Bill yanks the cue out of the table, places the ball basket over the hole to hide it, and he and the doctor exit the room.

Fields's performance was hailed by the critics. Richard Watts in the *New York Herald Tribune* felt Fields was "at the top of his form" and "walks off with the photoplay." The critic from the British journal *Film Weekly*, agreed. "It is [Fields] who, alone and unaided, performs the almost legendary feat of 'bringing down the house,' in his now-famous billiards match by himself."[10]

Fields was also "at the top of his form" in *The Big Broadcast of 1938*. The plot concerns a transatlantic boat race. Hoping to slow down the rival ship, the SS *Colossal*, Bellows (Fields) mistakenly arrives on his own boat, the SS *Gigantic*. On the boat Bellows challenges Lord Droopy (Lionel Page), a naïve English passenger, to a game of pool. The four and one-half minute sequence ranks among Bill's most humorous pool scenes. Not only does the scene portray his trick shots but also reveals his deceitful character as a hustler. Dressed smartly in shipboard attire, Bellows is an expert pool shark who knows that the nobleman has never played pool. Eager to make a quick buck, he coaxes Droopy to bet on the game. "Shall we say a pound?" the Englishman asks. "Make it ten?" replies Bellows. He hoodwinks his opponent whenever he is not looking. Bellows uses his hand and crooked cue to push his balls into the pockets and to prevent Droopy's shots from going in.

To distract his opponent, Bellows puts his straw boater over his opponent's fedora, asks him to carry his coat, and sticks his cigar in the Lord's mouth. Bellows tells him to stand behind him so that he cannot watch his shots too closely. "I don't want you to say I cheated afterwards." When Fields clears the table with one shot, his opponent thinks that the rolling ship caused the feat. Fields inadvertently shoots a ball through an open porthole and into a woman's ice cream dish. "Silly old monkey!" she blurts. A missed shot causes Bellows to rip the table top with the end of his cue. "How do you expect anyone to play pool on a moth-eaten torn table like that," he asks the steward. As Fields exits with the English Lord, he yells "is there a lawyer on the ship?" Once again Fields has used his beloved pool table act to create a laugh-getting sequence. A visitor to the set who witnessed Fields "trimming a harassed English gent at pool" wrote that the scene was "so funny that it reminded [him] of Milton's line about 'Laughter holding both sides.'"[11]

The pool scenes in *Six of a Kind* and *The Big Broadcast of 1938* are not verbatim renditions of Fields's pool sketch in vaudeville but an adaptation. To escape the charge that he is repeating himself, Fields takes the best parts of his stage routine, uses his pantomime skills to great effect, and adds humorous dialogue. The resulting sequences flourish on the screen.

As in his stage career, Fields's pool playing act became the bookends of his screen oeuvre. Nearly thirty years after *Pool Sharks*, the routine appeared in *Follow the Boys* (1944), among his last screen performances at age sixty-four. *Follow the Boys* was one of the many flag-waving war-time movies produced by studios to entertain the troops. Bill's five-minute cameo appearance for a reported $25,000 took only one and one-half days to shoot. For Fields, the film provided a means to show his support for the war effort, keep his name before the public, and hopefully halt his plummeting fame.

As the scene opens, a soldier rises from the front row of a camp's packed recreation hall to introduce "a man of spirit, a man who claims to be a bottle baby. . . . Mr. W. C. Fields." The comedian enters wearing a crumpled suit, white gloves to protect his hands, and his proverbial straw hat, singing "give me my books and my bottle."

As in his vaudeville years, he plays a blundering pool player who makes unintended gaffes. Fields twirls his cane around until it bangs his head, causing his straw hat to fall off (an old sight gag). The soldiers snicker at his foolishness. He saunters nonchalantly over to the cue rack and selects a warped cue. "Must have been near the fireplace," he quips as he picks out a better stick. Before taking a shot, he mistakenly eats a piece of chalk, spits it out in disgust, and puts a cigar in his mouth. Next he whacks the cue ball so hard that it ricochets off the rear cushion, bounces off the top of his cue, and goes into his coat pocket. Another shot causes the ball to rebound and crash into his head. "Who threw that?" Fields asks the soldiers.[12] Dazed, he removes his hat, causing the audience to hoot and howl when they saw the ball perched on his head.

"Here's what you call a massé shot, taken from an old French word," he announces. Positioning the cue's tip vertically over the ball's end, Fields misses his target and the stick rips through the table, a sure-fire venerable stage stunt that drew copious cheers. "They don't build billiard tables like they used to do in grandfather's day," he remarks. A soldier throws a ball made of paper that crumples when Bill puts a piece in his mouth. "Must be one of those secret weapons," he quips.

As his customary finale, he makes a shot that clears all the balls but one that stops in front of a pocket. "Come on, make up your mind," he shouts at the ball, which slowly goes into the pocket. As the soldiers clap wildly and whistle, Fields throws his cue on the table and strolls off the stage. "THE GREAT MAN IS BACK" was the headline in the *New York Times* about his performance.[13]

The well-respected film critic and author James Agee lauded the comedian for his strong performance. "W. C. Fields, looking worn-and-torn but noble as Stone Mountain, macerates a boozy song around his cigar butt and puts on his achingly funny pool exhibition with warped cues."[14] Agee's words, "looking worn-and-torn but noble as Stone Mountain," caught the essence of Fields's performance at age 64: an entertainer, tired and ill, yet appearing gallant and majestic while doing his last pool playing sketch.

## Notes

1. Arthur Frank Wertheim, *W. C. Fields from Burlesque and Vaudeville to Broadway: Becoming a Character Comedian* (New York: Palgrave Macmillan, 2014), 121.
2. *Hartford Courant*, September 26, 1924, scrapbook #10, WCFP; "Interview by Katherine Zimmerman," *NYT*, August 4, 1925, scrapbook #10, WCFP.
3. *MPW*, October 30, 1915, 792; Yanni, *W. C. Fields* (New York: Pyramid Publications, 1974), 23; William K. Everson, *The Art of W. C. Fields* (Indianapolis: Bobbs-Merrill, 1967), 22.
4. Wertheim, 121.
5. *Six of a Kind*, Paramount Press Book, LOC-MPD.
6. *NYT*, June 12, 1928, 33.
7. "Magnificent Rogue: The Adventures of W. C. Fields," *Biography and Sound,* narrated by Fred Allen, NBC, February 28, 1956.
8. Alva Johnston, "Who Knows What Is Funny?" *SEP*, August 6, 1938, 10.
9. Paramount Pictures Script Collection, *Six of a Kind*, Release Dialogue Script, January 27, 1934, AMPAS.
10. *NYHT*, March 10, 1934, clipping, scrapbook #30, WCFP; "Tribute to a Grand Film Clown," *Film Weekly* (London), July 6, 1934, scrapbook #OS-49, WCFP.
11. *LAT*, October 17, 1937, C4.
12. *NYHT*, January 24, 1944.
13. *NYT,* April 2, 1944.
14. *Time*, April 24, 1944, in James Agee, *Film Writing and Selected Journalism* (New York: Library of America, 2005), 395.

## CHAPTER 4

### The Remittance Man

Fields's second short, *His Lordship's Dilemma*, depicts the comedian impersonating a British remittance man trying to make a living after arriving in America. Ziegfeld was unhappy with Fields making another movie, believing that the extra job exhausted him and hurt his timing on stage. Bill, however, was obligated by his contract to make another short. The impresario regretted that he had granted Fields permission to do the Gaumont shorts; consequently, his attitude continued to damage their relations.

To direct the short, Gaumont hired an experienced director, William F. "Silent Bill" Haddock, who completed eighty-eight silent pictures between 1909 and 1918. Among them was *The Immortal Alamo* (1911), considered the first film about the 1836 Battle of the Alamo, a dramatic encounter between Mexican troops and Texans fighting for independence. An innovator, Haddock once directed a Talkie using synchronized records and also experimented making a color film. In an interview, "Silent Bill" recalled that he was walking on Broadway one day when he ran into a friend who told him that F. G. Bradford, who managed the Gaumont facility in Flushing, needed a director. He met Bradford at the Knickerbocker Hotel, where he won the job. "How could I lose?" Haddock recalled. "I found myself at Gaumont, a French outfit."[1]

Credits for the one-reel twelve-minute short do not list the source for the plot nor the name of the screenwriter. "Silent Bill" remembered that the omission was not unusual: "The pioneering days were probably the most satisfying and happiest. A director had no assistant, had to write his own continuity, or shoot off the cuff, look up locations, make up his own prop list, and sometimes act in the pictures."[2] This might have given Fields an opportunity to improvise, since there are several scenes in the picture that reflect his own experiences.

Fields impersonates a ne'er-do-well, pompous remittance man, "a young lord down on his luck [who] decides to try once anything he can get to do."[3] Although the film is considered lost, stills, advertisements, and reviews, like pieces of a jigsaw puzzle, help to reveal the picture.

Fields plays an unwanted younger son of an English aristocratic family, who is shipped to the U.S. Interestingly, autobiographical influences could be at play here. Fields's grandfather, John Dukinfield, traced his lineage to English ancestry. John's grandfather was Lord Dukinfield of Cheshire, a wealthy aristocratic landowner in northwest England. John's father was George Dukinfield, the Lord's third son, who failed to inherit the Lord's estate due to the laws of primogeniture that passed wealth to the firstborn son. Fields's grandfather and his extended family resided in industrial Sheffield, Yorkshire, where they earned a living in their cottage industry producing beautiful handmade hair combs and other products made from cow horns. Once synthetic hair combs began to be mass produced during the Industrial Revolution, such mechanization forced master craftsmen like John out of work. In search of a new life, Fields's grandfather, wife, and their six children immigrated to Philadelphia between 1854 and 1857.

Once settled, they faced hard times, much like the remittance man, who survives with money sent monthly until he receives a letter stating that his funds will be terminated. Among the numerous stills that exist, one shows a despondent Fields reading a letter. Forced to fire his servant (Bud Ross) and find a job, he works as a sandwich-board man carrying a heavy advertising sign on his back. On the street he runs into his servant, who is also carrying a sandwich board, and the two collide, causing their boards to interlock. Although the two have little money, they decide to enter a saloon, hoping to get free drinks and food. (Fields will return to the barroom locale in many subsequent films.) A photograph depicts Fields and his servant smoking cigars in the barroom, sandwich boards under their arms. Fields looks smugly at the bartender, played by his brother Walter. In 1903, Walter accompanied Bill to Australia, taking care of his pool table. On stage, he hid under the table and manipulated the strings to pocket all the balls. A still depicts Walter holding a cigar in his hand, which suggests that the remittance man has not paid for his stogie. According to a reviewer, Fields places a dollar on the bar to distract the bartender while his servant filches food from the lunch counter. Bill manages to obtain three drinks for the price of one, retrieves his dollar, and the two flee the barroom. (As a youngster in Philadelphia, Fields would often steal food from barrooms. Quite possibly he improvised part of this scene.)

Another still shows Fields as a restaurant worker, wearing a large apron. He stares at a crook who has stolen a lady's purse and is seemingly unconcerned about capturing him. The barroom and restaurant scenes reveal Fields playing a sly rogue for the first time in a film. The next sequence shows Fields and his servant eating their lunch in a park. (Exterior scenes were shot in Flushing Meadows Park and other nearby locations.) The latter reads a story from a newspaper that the remittance man has stolen. The article concerns Lord Swan, a skillful golfer, who is engaged to a Manhattan heiress. As the servant reads, Fields falls asleep, dreaming that he is the Lord whose golf playing impresses an attractive lady. (A still shows Fields dozing on a park bench as his servant reads from a newspaper. Other photos depict Fields on a golf course, including one that pictures him flirting with a pretty woman.) The sequence on the links reprises Fields's famous golf act, which debuted on vaudeville, premiered in the 1918 *Follies*, and became the sole subject of *The Golf Specialist* (1930), his first Talkie. Fields's golf sketch appears many times in his films, including in the silent *So's Your Old Man*. Fields also juggles golf balls and flips a golf club, which lands on his toe, reprising an earlier vaudeville trick. When anarchists suddenly throw a bowling-ball bomb on the golf course, Fields takes his driver, swings, and hits the explosive far away. Feeling that Fields has saved her life, the woman embraces him. (A photograph depicting a happy ending shows Fields with his arm around an attractive woman, and her father giving his blessing.)[4]

When the dream sequence ends, Fields discovers that he is hugging his valet. Disgusted, Bill throws his servant into a lake in the park. The scene reveals for the first time the temperamental and surly side of Fields's persona. Later, in *The Dentist* (1932), Fields flings his caddy into a pond on a golf course.

On October 3, *His Lordship's Dilemma* opened as a Gaumont Casino Star Comedy distributed by the Mutual Film Corporation. *Moving Picture World* described the picture as a "novel sort of comedy" with "a good many laughs."[5]

One reviewer, who went by the name of F. Gwynplaine MacIntyre, wrote in the International Movie Data Base (IMDB) that he had seen the movie in a Belgium archive. MacIntyre was an eccentric fabricator given to spinning fantastic tales. He was also a prolific author known for coining new words, writing an anthology of verse, a science fiction novel, mystery stories, and other works under aliases. "F. Gwynplaine MacIntyre lived in two dimensions," reported Corey Killigan in the *New York Times* after MacIntyre committed suicide on June 25, 2010, by setting his Brooklyn apartment ablaze. Neighbors knew him as Fergus, "a bearish pariah holed up in a fetid apartment stuffed with a lifetime of . . . trash" who once tortured a woman across the hall by stripping her, tying her to a chair, and spray painting her black. Others called him Froggy, and described him as "a witty bon vivant with an acerbic wit . . . with red hair, beard, and bushy sideburns."[6]

Most people believe that MacIntyre was a dishonest crackpot who invented the story. Since the reviewer never revealed the mysterious print's location in Belgium, the short has never been found. He was nonetheless an avid film buff who published other reviews in the IMBD. As a frequent traveler, his presence in Belgium would not be unusual. To his credit, the stills perfectly match the plot that he describes, and he also adds other plausible details. The coincidence leads to the conclusion that MacIntyre might have seen the short in an undisclosed Belgium location. If correct, *His Lordship's Dilemma* is a major loss, considering that it presents enticing clues to Fields's evolvement as a character comedian. Since the short contains much less slapstick than *Pool Sharks*, it reveals considerably more of Fields's vintage comedic style.

*Pool Sharks* and *His Lordship's Dilemma*, however, failed to convince Fields to leave the *Follies* and begin a film career. He lacked fond memories of the event and was not pleased with the process of filmmaking. As a stage comedian, he missed the presence of a live theater audience, which he needed for his timing and to gauge the success of a routine. After acting in front of a single stationary camera for four hours, he completed 1,500 feet of film. Unhappy about his performance in the Gaumont shorts, Fields called his debut a debacle. "If I missed my trick, I spoiled the picture so after a couple of trials at this, I lost interest in the movies." Nor did he like his performance before the camera. Slapstick, the primary genre in early screen comedy, was not his forte. The mistake of becoming a slapstick comic in *Pool Sharks* irked him.[7]

During 1915, numerous legitimate stage actors, attracted by the salaries paid to leading performers, were choosing a film career. That year drama critic Walter Prichard Eaton wrote about the cinema stampede in "Actor-Snatching and the Movies." "Money for every day you work, no free rehearsals, all your railroad and traveling expenses paid. Do you think twice about accepting it? No, you do not. You don't even think once. You pack your trunk and head for the coast."[8] In addition, actors were enticed by the prospect of increased celebrity. Compared to the theater's limited audience, a movie might draw millions during its run. Actors also imagined that a film appearance represented an opportunity to immortalize their work. Seemingly unaware of the fragility of nitrate film base and the need for preservation, early silent movie stars dreamed that their performance would remain forever on the screen. Florenz Ziegfeld contractually prevented his lead performers from joining the stage exodus, but that did not stop his wife, Billie Burke, from accepting a whopping $40,000 salary in 1915 from the New York Motion Picture Company.

Fields, by contrast, decided to become a holdout. Why give up the theater, he thought, and take a chance in a medium that he felt was in its formative stage? Compared to the limelight of Broadway, the experience of being cooped up in ramshackle studio in a dull suburb of Manhattan lacked ambience and excitement. Instead of the independence he craved, he was put under the supervision of a film director. Unimpressed with the entire occurrence, he walked away from the movies and back to the footlights of the *Follies*. He would not return to the screen for nine years.

Tracing the events following his decision reveals its calamitous consequences for his career trajectory. A renaissance in silent film

*Figure 4.1 Fields playing golf in* His Lordship's Dilemma. *On the ground is his valet, played by Bud Ross. Author's Collection.*

comedy occurred during Fields's absence, led by Charlie Chaplin, Buster Keaton, and Harold Lloyd. Compared to Fields, the trio chose to be in motion pictures because their stage careers were floundering during the second decade of the twentieth century. Chaplin was an itinerant comedian with Fred Karno's British music-hall troupe when he joined Keystone in 1914. Keaton teamed with his mother and father in a grotesque knockabout family act in vaudeville, and when it broke up in 1917, he decided on a film career. Lloyd was a struggling bit actor with touring and stock companies before his screen debut in 1912.

As a result of his nonappearance and late start, Fields unfortunately lost the opportunity to be rated among the first rank of silent film comedians. Despite generating some gems among the twelve silent pictures he completed up to 1928, he was unable to make up for the lost time. Moreover, half of Fields's silent films are unfortunately lost, making it impossible to judge his entire silent screen oeuvre.

Who knows what would have happened to Fields if he had decided to forgo the *Follies* for a film career? His theater career on Broadway between 1915 and 1925 gave birth to unforgettable hilarious characters in stage sketches that he later further evolved on the screen—precipitating his fame in sound films. Although he regretted his late start in the movies, had he left the stage earlier, he might never have developed the comic characterizations so crucial to his prominence.

**Notes**

1. Bernard Rosenberg and Harry Silverstein, *The Real Tinsel* (London: Macmillan, 1970), 331.
2. *WCFALOF*, 16.
3. *MPW*, October 9, 1915, 253.
4. The stills are in *WCFALOF*, 14-17.
5. *MPW*, October 9, 1915, 253.
6. Corey Killigan, "The Last Story of F. Gwynplaine MacIntyre," *NYT*, September 10, 2010.
7. Sara Redway, "W. C. Fields Pleads for Rough Humor," *Motion Picture Classic* (September 1925), 33.
8. Benjamin McArthur, *Actors and American Culture, 1880-1920* (Iowa City: University of Iowa Press paperback, 2000). 194; first published in the *American Magazine* (December 1915), 34.

## CHAPTER 5
### "It Gave Me My Opportunity"

One evening during March 1924, William LeBaron, a tall and handsome film executive, took his seat at the Apollo Theatre to watch the Broadway hit *Poppy* (1923-24), starring W. C. Fields. LeBaron watched intently while Fields played the kindhearted rogue, McGargle, a portrayal that earned Bill rave kudos. Midway during the play's run Fields became the show's sole star, delighting audiences.

His performance fascinated critics. George Jean Nathan, the dean of theater reviewers, wrote in *Smart Set* that Fields "is the most gorgeous Scaramouche of the season, a fellow out of the pages of Mark Twain . . . an actor of genuine parts." Joining him was the *Dial*'s critic, Edmund Wilson, who called Fields's characterization one of the season's "high spots." In *The World* Heywood Broun penned that Fields "gives us a real and complete portrait of as merry a rascal as the stage as seen in years."[1] McGargle would become the template for every mountebank and con-man that Fields impersonated on the screen.

LeBaron became Fields's most important mentor and champion during his film career. A talented and prolific composer and playwright, he had already authored numerous lyrics and books for Broadway shows, including the musical comedy *Moonlight*, then playing at the Longacre Theatre on 48th Street. Erudite, mild-mannered, and dignified, LeBaron differed from the rough and ruthless film executives who fought their way to the top in the cutthroat world of Hollywood. Louise Brooks, the flapper with the iconic jet-black bob hairstyle, believed LeBaron was "the most extraordinary man who was ever in pictures."[2]

LeBaron recommended roles to Fields, especially when the two were together at Paramount. As Bill's close friend and guardian angel, he produced more than twenty of the comedian's films between 1925 and 1938. In 1956, ten years after Fields's death,

LeBaron recalled that "his charm, his personality, and level of comedy made the audience actually love his skullduggery." Fields wooed audiences, he said, "because of the sort of elfin charm the man had, along with a tremendous mastery of pantomime and an air of timing."[3]

After a stint as managing editor at *Collier's Weekly* (1918-19), LeBaron joined William Randolph Hearst's Cosmopolitan Productions in 1920 as a scenario editor. In this position he promoted the development of screen writing specialists to improve the quality of motion pictures. Finding that LeBaron shared his idealism, Hearst quickly named him Director General in charge of such hits as *Humoresque* (1920) and *When Knighthood Was in Flower* (1922).

The newspaper tycoon inherited control of the family fortune when his mother, Phoebe Hearst, died in 1919. The windfall allowed him to spend more lavishly on his moving pictures. In 1920, Hearst acquired Cosmopolitan Productions' studio on land where Sulzer's Harlem River Park and Casino, an amusement center and beer garden, stood. The plant covered an entire city block bordered by First and Second Avenues and 126$^{th}$ and 127$^{th}$ Streets. Named after Hearst's *Cosmopolitan* magazine, the studio held film rights to every story published in his magazine and newspaper empire. New York, he felt, was the center of filmmaking due to the availability of Broadway stage luminaries. "It is folly," he said, "to minimize the screen's real need of the best artists on the stage in the casts of its worthwhile productions." He preferred making pictures with artificial lighting rather than depending on the vagaries of sunlight. At his new studio Hearst made thirty-five features before moving his company to California in 1924.

The newspaper tycoon believed that "making pictures is fundamentally like making publications.... I think I have learned various things in the publishing business that will be of value in the motion picture business." Hearst had already invested in moving pictures with his newsreel and animation enterprises, which featured his most popular newspaper comic strip characters. Among them were George Herrimann's *Krazy Kat*, Frederick Opper's *Happy Hooligan*, and Rudolph Dirks's *The Katzenjammer Kids*. His state-of-the-art animation studio in Manhattan was headed by Gregory La

Cava, whose innovations revolutionized "the content and style of American animation" through storyboarding and a novel method of depicting human motion called "rubber hose," developed by his colleague William Nolan.[4] La Cava later became a successful director, and in this capacity worked with Fields in *So's Your Old Man* (1926), considered one of Fields's best silent films, and *Running Wild* (1927).

The newspaper magnate aimed to produce twenty-four stylish "super-special" pictures per year, "an endeavor to entertain, enlighten, and uplift the public." Toward that end, he employed talented screenwriters, namely the brilliant Frances Marion, directors such as Allan Dwan, art designer and choreographer Joseph Urban from the *Ziegfeld Follies*, and made several scouting trips to Hollywood to sign stars. "The Chief," as Hearst was called, made a deal with Adolph Zukor's Paramount to distribute his moving pictures. When Zukor tried to take over production of his films, the ambitious Hearst told him that he intended to run his own studio: "If I am right then I ought to be able to develop something good and something distinctive, something that expresses my own purposes and personality."[5]

Hearst's main ambition was primarily to showcase motion pictures featuring Marion Davies, his lovely strawberry blond, curly-haired mistress, who starred in numerous features at the facility. Renowned screenwriter Frances Marion, who wrote three of her pictures for Hearst, felt he "concentrated his attention on Miss Davies certain that there was no limit to her future."[6] The daughter of a Brooklyn lawyer, she followed her two elder sisters into show biz and changed her last name to Davies, following her sister Reine, a successful stage actress.

Accounts differ regarding Hearst's initial encounter with Davies. According to biographer David Nasaw, Hearst first spotted the chorus girl in Irving Berlin's musical, *Stop! Look! Listen!* (1915), her fourth ensemble appearance on Broadway. Another story claims Hearst became captivated when he saw nineteen-year-old Davies in her next show, the 1916 *Ziegfeld Follies*, a blockbuster extravaganza that also featured Fields. She was given multiple roles, appearing as a member of the chorus; as the character Miss Believe, one of the

Avenue Girls, in the humorous sketch "Fifth Avenue." She performed in "Shakespeare's Juliet," a satire on the bard's plays; and in a burlesque of Henry VIII's wives, in which she sang the final line in Gene Buck's song, "He sure was a helluva king."

Davies and Fields shared the stage in the sketch "Puck's Pictorial Palace," with Marion impersonating a beauty contestant and Bill playing Theodore Roosevelt. An unsubstantiated story suggests that Davies, who desired to assume comedic roles, watched Fields from the wings. "He was doing something stupid with a golf ball," she recalled. Spotting her, Fields lambasted her backstage. "Where's that dirty jerk blond that was in the wings? Tell her I'm going to have her fired, whoever she is!" Petrified, she hid in a putrid prop trunk. Learning of the incident, Ziegfeld told Fields to "leave the kid alone."[7]

The *Follies* became sensationalized for the millionaire playboys who had affairs with the show's most heralded beauties. Hearst's ardor was the most publicized. "He was always a stage-door Johnny, just always," said his son Bill Jr. "He always used to take us backstage at the *Ziegfeld Follies*." The fifty-eight-year-old newspaper tycoon regularly sat in the second row ogling Davies as she danced and sang in the 1916 edition. Sometimes he purchased an extra seat for a friend or for his large hat. Davies's dressing room backstage was crammed with flower bouquets and expensive gifts from Hearst. Years later she recalled that he also sent her "silver boxes or gloves or candy ... all the girls thought he was particularly looking at me." The older performers warned her, "Look out for him. ... He's a wolf in sheep's clothing."[8]

After falling for Hearst, Marion felt different. She recalled, "He was the kindest, most innocent, naïve person you'd ever want to meet. He wouldn't have harmed anybody, ever." Thus began an infamous thirty-five-year courtship until Hearst's death in 1951. Orson Welles's *Citizen Kane* (1941), about a newspaper tycoon and his talentless mistress Susan Alexander, overshadowed Davies's reputation. Welles admitted in 1975 that Susan Alexander "bears no resemblance at all" to Marion Davies.[9]

Both Hearst and Fields were trapped in unhappy marriages to Catholic wives who refused to grant their husbands divorces. Coincidentally, Bill was wooing Bessie Poole, a chorus girl in the same *Follies*, and beginning an affair that lasted seven years and bore a child named William Rexford Fields Morris. After his relationship with Poole ended, he continued to have other multi-year amours. Fields, however, was not a licentious sugar-daddy but a lost, lonely, soul seeking companions throughout his life.

Before working for Hearst, Davies had completed the silent picture, *Runaway Roman*, in 1917. After seeing the movie, Hearst rewarded her with a $500 per week contract. "Silent pictures were right up my alley," she wrote. Recalling her stuttering since childhood, she confessed that they appealed to her because "I couldn't talk." Davies's films revealed her effusive charm, engaging smile, vivaciousness, and flair for comedy rather than drama. Hearst envisioned her playing Mary Pickford-like roles. Her talent for humor clashed with Hearst's penchant for extravagant dramatic costume spectacles. "I'm not going to let Marion be hit in the face with a pie," he once declared. She nonetheless appeared in only four costume pictures shot at the Cosmopolitan studio, one being *Janice Meredith*.[10]

In 1918, Hearst organized the Marion Davies Film Company and produced six features starring his new heartthrob by the end of the following year. Her initial pictures were box-office flops. Not until she made *When Knighthood Was in Flower* (1922) and *Little Old New York* (1923) did her films yield big profits and favorable reviews. *Variety* ranked Davies "among the leading players, those who can act—something mighty few beautiful women of the screen ever accomplish." In 1924, she was named the number one female box-office star and "Queen of the Screen" by theater owners. Fields's first appearance in a silent feature film therefore came at a time when Davies had reached a high point in her silent picture career.[11]

Hearst's ability to integrate his moving pictures with his nationwide newspaper chain was groundbreaking. "Making pictures is fundamentally like making publications," he said. "The same material is used more and more in both publication and picture." According to Richard Koszarski, "Hearst was, in fact, the first to recognize the tremendous possibilities of media synergy, cross-promoting his newspapers, newsreels, animated films, motion picture serials and general-interest story magazines." Hearst boosted Davies's image via photographs and stories in the Sunday drama sections of his newspapers and even featured her in his newsreels. He spent lavishly on his films and wanted to spend a million dollars on *Janice Meredith*. "I admit that our pictures are expensive," he wrote, "but that does not matter to me if I can make them sufficiently good."[12]

*Janice Meredith* was among the several American Revolution pictures being made in honor of the sesquicentennial celebration of the "War for Independence." The filmmakers strove to be authentic in the reproduction of historical scenes: the Boston Tea Party, the ride of Paul Revere, the battle of Lexington, Washington and his soldiers crossing the Delaware, the battle of Trenton, and the winter at Valley Forge.

The film's main competitor was D. W. Griffith's *America* (1924), a picture that recreated many of the same events, except for Washington's crossing of the Delaware. Rumors surfaced that Hearst made an agreement with Griffith not to film the historic event in return for promising good reviews and promotion in his newspapers. *The New York Times* felt the two films tied. *America* had better battle scenes and historical recreations, but the plot and performances in *Janice Meredith* were superior.

Winter scenes for *Janice Meredith* were shot on location in Plattsburgh, New York, where Hearst convinced the local military to grant Davies the title of "honorary colonel" and to film her reviewing the troops. Hearst's stunt backfired when the Secretary of War discovered that the newspaper magnate was boosting her image using American soldiers. He ordered the stoppage of awarding honorary titles to movie performers.

Washington crossing the Delaware was also filmed in Plattsburgh by first recreating the eighteenth-century town of Trenton by building forty houses on two large streets. The nearby Saranac River was so frozen that demolition crews needed to blast a huge channel so that the boat could get through. Fourteen hundred extras were used for the sequence. When the river's ice thawed, location shots were moved to Lake Placid, where the Battle of Lexington was filmed at a cost of $80,000.

A private screening revealed that *Janice Meredith* was dull and desperately needed merriment. After seeing *Poppy*, LeBaron realized that Fields was the perfect comedian to add hilarity to the American Revolution costume drama and love story *Janice Meredith* (1924), starring Marion Davies.

Thanks to LeBaron, Fields obtained a three-minute spot as a British sergeant. At the time Fields performed in *Janice Meredith*, Bill had been absent from the screen for nine years. It took Bill fifteen minutes to complete his role and walk away $1,500 richer. Given the freedom to do anything ludicrous in *Janice Meredith*, Bill performed some typical Fieldsian antics in a sequence in which he is guarding a British spy (Charles Fownes) in a mansion. He is decked out in a spiffy British soldier's outfit, multi-striped coat, and a three-cornered hat on top of a disheveled white powered wig. Fields does modified gags that stem from his vaudeville stunts. He lights a cigar with a candle and then foolishly places the cigar in the candle holder and the candle in his mouth.

When the elegantly dressed Janice (Davies) arrives, secretly plotting to free her lover, the spy being held prisoner, Fields's character removes his three-cornered hat, bows, and then mistakenly places his hat on a broomstick handle. To distract the guard, Janice flirts with him and gets him drunk, then unties the prisoner, a British Lord and aide to General Washington. British soldiers appear and discover that the detainee has escaped. They quickly depart, hoping to recapture him. Realizing he has been fooled, Fields rushes to follow, mistaking the broom for his musket in his haste. Discovering his mistake, he turns back to retrieve his weapon.

Although Fields's bit was short, he noticed that silent pictures had come of age. Frenetic physical humor—slapstick, knockabout comedy, and rough-and-tumble acts—that had dominated *Pool Sharks* was no longer in favor. He was not a gag jokester or smart-aleck monologist but a character comedian (lampooner, satirist, and parodist) who needed time to reach the point where he could deliver the punch line. During many years on the stage Bill had learned the important art of timing. His genius for pantomime, which he honed in vaudeville, was so innate that it seemed as if he was born with the expertise. In a silent medium he was unable to use his inimitable vocal intonations, expression, and modulations that later figured prominently in his sound films. By contrast, his talent to utilize facial expressions and body language provided him with the skills he needed in silent pictures.

*Janice Meredith*, which ran 153 minutes and derived from a Paul Leicester Ford novel, represented Fields's initial appearance in a feature. Due to Hearst's ambition to hire the best filmmakers for his huge Cosmopolitan studio, Fields was surrounded by experts in *Janice Meredith*: cinematographers (Ira A. Morgan and George Barnes); scenario writer (Lillie Hayward, a pathfinder woman screenwriter); film music composer (Deems Taylor, "the dean of American music"); a skilled director (E. Mason Hopper); screen actors (Harrison Ford, the handsome and popular male lead, playing a nobleman disguised as a bonded servant who becomes Janice's amour); and scenic designers (Joseph Urban and Everett Shinn, famous Ashcan School artist).

*Janice Meredith*, costing 1.5 million dollars, premiered at Hearst's New York's large Cosmopolitan Theater on October 27, 1924, where it had a record-breaking run. More than 2,000 fans without tickets lined the entrance "attracted as moths to the flame of lights thrown on the theatre." When the crowd became an annoyance to ticket holders, the police were summoned to remove the throng. The film drew crowds in cities, but box-office earnings were less in rural areas.[13]

The feature garnered mixed reviews. The picture received kudos for its recreations of American Revolution battle scenes and historic events such as Paul Revere's ride. Some reviewers felt the film was even better than D. W. Griffith's *America*, another American Revolution epic, which opened at the same time. Reviews in *Film Daily* were effusive about its patriotic theme: "Will be loved by every American who feels it is a pleasant homage to this great historical photoplay." It "should go on the list of things to see if one wishes to have a thrilling time," and "breathes the spirit of American independence in every sense." *Variety*'s critic felt that *Janice Meredith* was too long and suffered from "a jerky and often times illogical scenario." *Educational Screen*, however, listed the picture as one of "The Ten Best [Films] for 1924-25."[14] Wearing twenty gorgeous costumes throughout the course of the film, Marion Davies stunned the *New York Times* critic, who wrote, "She is enthusiastic, loving, mischievous, petulant, fiery, and imperious." The reviewer raved about her ability to use her eyes, mouth, and lips to display moods, including joy, anger, love, fearlessness, and defiance. *Moving Picture World* noted that "Davies stands as one of the finest achievements of the motion picture."[15]

When a fire destroyed much of the Cosmopolitan Studio, Hearst closed his New York facility a year after *Janice Meredith* and moved his operation to Hollywood, where in March 1925, he allied with MGM via a lucrative production and distribution deal. Davies made ten films under Louis B. Mayer, including Talkies starting in 1929, and four more movies with Warner Bros. before retiring in 1937. Among her 30 silent and 16 sound films, she left a mixed bag of flops and box-office winners. During her time Davies managed to sustain her reputation as one of cinema's most popular stars, who especially drew kudos for her comedy films. "One of the most delightfully accomplished comediennes in the whole history of the screen," wrote Orson Welles.[16]

Eleven months after the release of *Janice Meredith*, Fields left the 1925 *Ziegfeld Follies* to pursue a full-time film career. He realized that the Golden Age of the *Follies* was over. The 1925 *Follies* production climaxed the revue's heyday. The 1926 production did not occur due to the impresario's legal problems. Ziegfeld's 1927 *Follies* received mediocre reviews and was panned for its lack of originality. His last *Follies* in 1931 was nothing more than a trip down memory lane, with reproductions of scenes from earlier productions, causing it to close after five months. A year later The Great Glorifier, bankrupt and ailing, died. The showman, however, left a lasting legacy for producing the *Follies*, considered Broadway's best revue, and several outstanding musicals, including *Show Boat*.

Reviewers unanimously agreed that Fields was a big hit in *Janice Meredith*. His performance was "a tiny bit and one that he made so perfect that some producer has him signed up by now to do something bigger." "It was the funniest bit seen in a long time," extolled

*Figure 5.1 Three minutes with Marion Davies, who flirts with Fields playing a drunken British sergeant in* Janice Meredith *(1924). Author's Collection.*

another critic. "The movies haven't discovered Fields yet. But they will."[17]

In 1925, Fields stated how significant his role in *Janice Meredith* was in reviving his screen career: "I've been here in the *Follies* since 1914 [1915] and constantly during that time I have been trying for a movie chance. I never got a look until *Janice Meredith*. The bit I did in that was very small in the actual filming and much smaller in release. But it gave me my opportunity."[18]

**Notes**

1. *Smart Set*, November 1923; *Dial*, November 1923; *World*, September 4, 1923.
2. *Hollywood on the Hudson*, 45.
3. *Magnificent Rogue: The Adventures of W. C. Fields*, NBC Radio's Biography in Sound, narrated by Fred Allen, February 28, 1956.
4. *Hollywood on the Hudson*, 313.
5. Ibid, 116; David Nasaw, *The Chief: The Life of William Randolph Hearst* (2000; repr New York: Houghton Mifflin Mariner Book, 2001), 283.
6. W. A. Swanberg, *Citizen Hearst: A Biography of William Randolph Hearst* (New York: Galahad Books, 1996), 324.
7. Fred Lawrence Giles, *Marion Davies* (New York: McGraw-Hill, 1972), 62; unidentified clipping, August 6, 1924, scrapbook #10, WCFP.
8. Nasaw, *The Chief*, 253; Marion Davies, *The Times We Had: Life with William Randolph Hearst* (New York: Ballantine Books, 1975), 11, 28.
9. Nasaw, *The Chief*, 253; Davies, *The Times We Had*, 11, 28; Welles, foreword to Davies, *The Times We Had*.
10. Davies, *The Times We Had*, 33; Nasaw, 396.
11. *Variety*, September 22, 1922, 41.
12. *Hollywood on the Hudson*, 116.
13. Nasaw, *The Chief*, 346.
14. *Film Daily*, August 7, 1924; *Variety*, August 13, 1924; *The Educational Screen*, June 1925, 356.
15. *NYT*, August 6, 1924; *Moving Picture World*, August 23, 1924, 631.
16. Welles, foreword to Davies, *The Times We Had*.
17. *Variety*, August 13, 1924, 19; *Zit's Weekly Newspaper*, August 8, 1924, scrapbook #10, WCFP.
18. Ruth Waterbury, "The Old Army Game," *Photoplay* (October 1925), 68.

# PART II:
# A Rendezvous with D. W. Griffith

## CHAPTER 6

### *Poppy* on Broadway

After the famous director David Wark Griffith saw Fields's hilarious bit in *Janice Meredith*, he decided that the comedian should play McGargle in the silent screen version of *Poppy* (1923-24), a role that made him a star on the Broadway stage. When Griffith initially obtained the rights to direct the film, Fields's chances seemed slim to play the flamboyant con man, the leading male character in the play. After seeing Fields play McGargle on stage in *Poppy*, Griffith praised his performance. He even recommended a budding actress, Mary Hay, to study Fields's timing on stage if she wanted to improve her skill on the screen. That should have been enough to convince Griffith to sign Fields. The director, however, was hesitant about the comedian because of his limited experience on the screen.

Since Griffith was a perfectionist, he decided to give Fields a screen test. To perform on camera before Griffith, the virtuoso of the silent screen, created tension for the comedian. After the test, the director felt Fields needed to perform in more pictures. Griffith changed his mind, however, when he saw the comedian's role in *Janice Meredith*.

Fields's role in the Broadway play *Poppy* signified a defining moment in his stage career. "I have just the role for you to play," the theatrical producer Philip Goodman told Fields. "You are to be a country fair 'grifter,' the man who separates the yokels from their dollars." A newcomer to the Broadway scene, Goodman had obtained the rights to produce *Poppy Comes to Town*, a play by the well-known thespian Dorothy Donnelly. He was planning to turn it into a Broadway musical comedy and wanted Fields to take a leading part. "I have watched you work from the time I was a boy and I know that you are the one man in America for the role."[1]

Dorothy Donnelly belonged to a well-known theatrical family. Her grandfather was a prominent stage actor, her parents were also thespians, and her brother operated a repertory company at the Murray Hill Theatre, where Donnelly acquired considerable experience playing a variety of roles. Her stirring performance in the melodrama *Madame X* (1910) as a ravaged, yet noble, woman afflicted by alcohol and drugs gained her fame. When kidney ailments caused Donnelly to retire from acting in 1916, she turned to writing numerous plays, including the musical *The Student Prince* (1924), considered her best Broadway show.

Believing that *Poppy* needed changes to make it a hit, Goodman convinced Donnely to write a period piece depicting small-town American life in 1874. To strengthen the part of Polly's father, the producer hired the author Howard Deitz, who later became a famous lyricist. "I thought it would be a good part for W. C. Fields," Dietz stated, "who, while known only as a pantomimist, might be good with words, if they were the right words."[2]

Goodman signed Madge Kennedy, a noted stage and screen actor, for the role of the sweet-tempered adopted daughter Poppy McGargle. A pretty brunette with "brilliant brown eyes and a quaint little smile," Kennedy had starred in several Broadway hits before signing a movie contract in 1917 with producer Samuel Goldwyn, who featured her in twenty-one films. She was a natural talent. "I'm sure actors are born with an instinct," she once said. "You can't teach it. You have it or you don't. . . . I have an instinct for timing."[3] Having nonetheless never sung or danced on stage, Kennedy needed to audition before Goodman. After watching her perform, he became convinced that her winsome charm would captivate Broadway audiences.

Compared to Kennedy, Fields was a gamble. Although a celebrity in the *Follies*, he had never performed a major role in a play, something that would require him to recite numerous lines for three acts. During 1905–6 he had appeared in *The Ham Tree* as the ludicrous detective Sherlock Baffles, a secondary role compared to the stars, the blackface minstrels James McIntyre and Thomas Heath. In vaudeville and revues, he had mastered rapid short routines in which dialogue took a backseat to visual prop gags, spur-of-the-moment stunts, tricks, and socko endings. Along with Dietz, Emma Javier, a well-respected performer cast as the princess in *Poppy*, supported

Fields. Influenced by the two, Goodman became convinced that Fields was the best person for the role of Poppy's father, Professor Eustace P. McGargle, F.A.S.N. A flamboyant small-time con artist, McGargle operates a medicine show hawking a fake remedy guaranteed to cure all ailments.

Fields surprisingly balked when Goodman asked him to join the cast. "Oh, no," he replied emphatically. "I can never play a real role. You had better hire someone else." An avid ad-libber, Fields was petrified about sticking to memorized dialogue. "I haven't any memory," he told Goodman. A three-hundred-pound persuasive entrepreneur with an overpowering presence, Goodman refused to take "no" for an answer. As for his lines, the producer promised that he could ad-lib and would station two prompters at each end of the stage.[4] After much hesitation, Fields agreed to take the role. Looking back, his decision forged a new direction in Fields's character comedy. As McGargle, he played an endearing rogue, a colorful comic persona that Fields later immortalized on stage and screen.

Discouraged by his performance during rehearsals, Fields changed his mind and wanted to leave the show. "I told Mr. Goodman that I was wasting his time and money, and he should get someone else for the role. But he wouldn't let me resign. Madge Kennedy noticed that Fields was "terrified" about being a flop and encouraged him whenever she could. Fields fondly called her "daughter" and Kennedy dubbed him "Pop" both on and off stage. "Pop, wait till the opening night and you'll see how good you are." "We always had a lovely relationship," she recollected. "He was a very sensitive, gentle person." Encouraged by Kennedy and Goodman, I "decided to stick it out if only to collect my salary."[5]

Fields found the romantic melodrama written by the genteel Donnelly to be overly sentimental with mushy dialogue. "Daughter," he told Kennedy, "make them take away some of those lines."[6] He abhorred the false affectations in Donnelly's dated style. Fields and Donnelly, two strong-willed personalities, clashed. Finding Fields's alterations unseemly and improper, Donnelly fought against the changes he made to her lines.

Robert Woolsey, who played Mortimer Pottle, the estate attorney in the play, overheard an argument between Fields and Donnelly the night before the dress rehearsal. Fields wanted to include a stunt involving a swan, similar to his golf sketch in which a bird is shot from the sky and falls on his head. Donnelly overheard Fields telling his sidekick and foil Shorty Blanche about the scene "where I shoot the shot-gun off and it goes through the roof, and the swan comes through." "What do you mean, swan?" protested Donnelly. "You can't do this to my beautiful play! This'll ruin the thing." Despite her protests, the shot swan remained in the play. "That swan came through the roof and the audience laughed for five minutes," Woolsey said. "It never hurt the play."[7]

"You never knew what he would do" remarked Kennedy about Fields's talent to extemporize. In the scene in which McGargle is arrested by the sheriff, Poppy pleads with the officer, "You can't take him, look at him, he's like a child." One night Fields unexpectedly reached under his overcoat "to take out a lollipop the size of a cartwheel. Well of course the audience and the cast just convulsed."[8]

After *Poppy* opened, Fields continued to alter his lines. Near the play's climax McGargle steals a horse to escape arrest but is quickly caught. "I knew that mare was no good," he tells Poppy. "She succumbed right in front of the police station." The spectators never laughed. He changed Donnelly's script the following night: "I knew that horse was a bum. He dropped dead right in front of the police station." Laughter resounded from the orchestra seats to the balcony. "That went over big," remarked Fields. Although the genteel Donnelly found the expression "dropped dead" too provocative, she agreed to Fields's changes since the dialogue generated laughs. Fields improvised so much that the original script was unrecognizable by the end of *Poppy*'s long Broadway run. A dictum in Fields's comedy rule book read, "In comedy, as in almost everything else, it isn't so much what you say as how you say it."[9]

"The opening night I was frightened to death," Fields admitted about the sold-out gala premier on September 3, 1923, held at the Apollo Theatre on West 42nd Street. He faced a crowd of curious theatergoers who wondered how a *Follies* performer would fare in a three-act musical comedy. Standing in the wings waiting for his cue, Fields might have recalled his first make-or-break appearance at the Wintergarten Theatre twenty-two years earlier, when his nerves played havoc with his juggling. Bill was fortunately no longer a fledgling trouper, but an experienced thespian with a deep-rooted knowledge about timing, movement, gestures, and style. Equally significant, he knew how to capture the audience's admiration. His opening night butterflies consequently vanished after a few scenes. "Strange to say I never forgot a line," he recalled.[10]

Once Fields added his own lines to the script and improvised during performances, he created a story about a confidence man with a heart. Poppy, whose mother died at a circus, has been cared for by McGargle, her foster father. A medicine show trickster, McGargle travels with Poppy to county fairs and circus sideshows where he pitches his fake concoction, Purple Bark Sarsaparilla, guaranteed to cure all ailments. On the side he fleeces suckers in gambling games.

Landing the role of McGargle became a crucial turning point in Fields's career. *Poppy* provides Fields with his initial role as a con man, a part he will repeat many times in different disguises on the screen. He appears in several films as a fast-talking huckster hawking fake medicine, bogus inventions, and phony stock. These characters are not notorious swindlers, but within the confidence man lingo are called small cons. Fields impersonates small-time bungling con men with an additional dose of compassion that makes them more loveable than hateful. Their hand-to-mouth existence propels them to make a fast buck through shell games, stack-deck poker, petty thievery, and other fraudulent schemes aimed to outwit easy marks, suckers who don't deserve an even break. In the hands of Fields, most of his clumsy hoaxes become episodes in comic ineptitude. Only by luck do some of his shifty characters win a windfall at the end, but others, such as McGargle, wind up broke and alone, in pursuit of the next sucker.

"We produce such mountebanks in greater number than any other country," declared the legendary social critic H. L. Mencken, "and they climb to heights seldom equaled elsewhere."[11] Fraudsters come in various varieties: humbug, racketeer, schemer, trickster, speculator, imposter, counterfeiter, pitchman, card shark, huckster, and masquerader, among others. Charlatans are found worldwide, but the expression "confidence man" likely originated in the U.S.

According to legend, William Thompson (aka Samuel Thomas and Samuel Williams) encountered a stranger in lower Manhattan during May 1849 and pretended to be an old friend. After talking for a time, Thompson asked the man if he had confidence in him. Although the stranger could not recall meeting Thompson, he answered yes. "Have you confidence in me to trust me with your watch until to-morrow?" Thompson asked.[12] The man gave Thompson his gold watch. During the following days the imposter fooled two more victims. His luck ended when one of his suckers saw him again and called the police. Thompson was subsequently arrested and sent to Sing Sing prison.

A *New York Herald* newsman scooped city newspapers by first reporting the hoax. The reporter dubbed Thompson the "Confidence Man." Suddenly the rubric caught on as if Thompson had invented a new form of crime. Two weeks later a play opened in Manhattan called *The Confidence Man*. Rumors circulated that Thompson might have inspired Melville to write *The Confidence-Man* in 1857. Although this type of trickery had been around for centuries, it especially flourishes in the U.S. American history is rife with hustlers and swindlers whose stories of crime, fraud, and deceit are still found almost daily in the press and media. Con men thrive in American society due to people's strong belief in hope no matter how dire the circumstances. To succeed, the con artist needs the *confidence* of a gullible person. Without trust, the con man cannot achieve his objective. Desire, trust, and hope make naïve people easy targets for preying swindlers. "It's the oldest story ever told," wrote the psychologist Maria Konnikova recently in *The Confidence Game*. "The story of belief—of the basic, irresistible, universal need to believe in something that gives life meaning, something that reaffirms our view of ourselves, the world, and our place in it."[13]

The Confidence Man was first defined by the *National Police Gazette* in its 1859 *Rogue's Lexicon*: "A fellow that by means of extraordinary powers of persuasion gains the confidence of his victims. . . . The Confidence Man is, perhaps, the most liberally supplied with subjects; for every man has his soft spot. . . . This is just the spot on which the Confidence man works."[14]

The con scheme especially flourishes in the U.S., where unbridled individualism morphs into greed and the drive to make money no matter what means, especially through fraud. Society rewards entrepreneurs who succeed often without ever questioning and examining the way they made their fortune. As Amy Reading writes: "The stories of early American swindlers laid bare a terrible truth. Their country needed them. The new nation would never have prospered without imposture, speculation, and counterfeiting, because America was, from its inception, a confidence trick."[15]

In his novel, *The Confidence-Man, His Masquerade*, Herman Melville created the most insightful literary work on the American imposter. That Melville set his novel aboard the Mississippi steamer *Fidel* on April Fool's Day is not coincidental. Rootless travelers in limbo are an easy target for Melville's swindlers, who take advantage of their vulnerability and gullibility aboard the boat. Almost every chapter describes the abilities of the con men to deceive the passengers. The reader is left with the impression that American society is a sham populated with rogues masquerading as honest citizens.

Mark Twain was among Fields's favorite authors because he found in his writings so many con artists for his own portrayals. In *Life on the Mississippi* (1883), Twain describes numerous charlatans traversing America's longest river. There is a scene in which a professional gambler masquerades as a cattleman in a poker game, and by using a stacked deck wins a pot of money by holding four aces. A poker game occurs in Fields's film, *Mississippi*, but in this case Commodore Jackson (Fields) botches his cheating by dealing too many aces and nearly gets killed. In *Huckleberry Finn*, Huck and Jim find freedom sailing down the Mississippi, but on the shore they encounter a society where conning flourishes. They meet the duke and the king, slick con artists, who hoodwink townspeople with get-rich-quick scams. In *The Gilded Age*, Twain's target is land speculation, epitomized by Colonel Sellers, who dreams up wild schemes aimed to make him millions selling swamp property. (Land speculation becomes a theme in several of Fields's films, including *It's the Old Army Game* and *It's a Gift*.) In Twain's famous short story, "The Celebrated Jumping Frog of Calaveras County,"

Smiley bets that his frog, Daniel Webster, can out jump any frog in the county, but he loses because his opponent fills Daniel with quail shot. In *The Man That Corrupted Hadleyburg*, Twain tells the story of a stranger who corrupts a reputedly incorruptible town by exposing its best citizens' greed to win a sack of gold. Fields especially liked the exposé of hypocrisy and greed in *The Man That Corrupted Hadleyburg,* calling it "the greatest short story ever written."[16]

Fields enjoyed playing the con game by weaving tall tales about himself and relating them to newspaper reporters, studio publicists and movie magazine writers. He conned the public into believing all sorts of fabrications about his life. His hyperbolic accounts made good copy, beginning with the invention of running away from home for years. The stories of his drinking had a basis in fact but they were so overblown that they often gave the false impression he was a lush. Readers consequently became convinced that his persona on screen was identical to the real Fields off screen. If he was a child and dog hater in films, he was a child and dog hater at home, a myth that had no basis in fact. Bill let these stories run amok and delighted in conning the public.

Fields grew up during the time of the Robber Barons, when business and political corruption flourished. Twain called his book *The Gilded Age* after the era when the gulf between the newly rich and wretched poor widened. On one side of the tracks in Philadelphia lived Fields's family, in the row houses occupied by the working class; on the other side, industrial magnates resided in stately mansions in affluent areas like Chestnut Hill. In Fields's home town, larceny thrived, from petty theft to political graft. The muckraker Lincoln Steffens called "Philadelphia the most corrupt city in the country—a disgrace . . . to the United States and to the American character."[17] A political machine controlled voting, the police, public utilities, civil servant appointments, and other city government jobs. The populace, suggested Steffens, was too contented to make any serious effort at reform.

In *The Big Con*, David Maurer draws a distinction between the various types of confidence men. At the top are the big con type criminals such as gangsters, racketeers, and illegal stock manipulators, who swindle their victims over long periods, compared to the short con artists, who immediately seek to cheat their marks, as in poker games. Below these two types are thieves like pickpockets and professional gamblers. Next come the circus grifters, and last in the hierarchy are the small-time professionals. Fields primarily plays the carnival grifter, who cheats customers in various minor ways, compared to the big cons. He sells quack medicine, cheats customers of their money at his show's ticket window, hypes non-existent attractions, plays poker with stacked cards, and operates a shell game in which the gambler always loses.

Instead of portraying McGargle as a hard-edged malicious con man, Fields depicts the character as a tenderhearted mountebank. "[Confidence men] are human beings, manifesting salt-and-pepper mixtures of all the vices and virtues to which mankind is heir," wrote David Mauer in *The Big Con*. Despite his various schemes, McGargle is a benevolent huckster who cares for Poppy. "If a comedian doesn't excite your sympathy, you don't laugh at him," Fields declared. "No one likes the fellow who is all rogue," he commented, "but we'll forgive him almost anything if there is a warmth of human sympathy underneath his rogueries. The immortal types of comedy are just such men." The novelist and translator Ludwig Lewisohn called Fields a "Micawber with a touch of Barnum. He is the most delicious scoundrel imaginable. He is the astute medicine man, fakir, confidence man of the ages."[18]

During his youth Fields encountered various types of confidence men. Reflecting on his role as McGargle, Fields said, "I never dreamed then that someday I'd have a chance to use all the stuff I unconsciously absorbed from these guys. But when I started to rehearse the part, all sorts of things came back to me, things that I didn't even know I remembered. So if Prof. McGargle seems like a real person that is the reason why."[19]

"These guys" included the many rogues and sharpies he had met as a youngster. The "real person" could be any one of the familiar hucksters he knew, starting with his father hawking fruits and vegetables. While accompanying his father selling fresh produce from his horse and wagon, Fields learned the tricks of pitching unavailable goods in order to lure customers. To sell more papers as a neighborhood newsboy, he hollered fake sensational headlines.

Experiences working at other jobs gave him additional insights: the iceman who cheated his company by manipulating the profits; the cigar store owner selling inexpensive stogies as deluxe brands; the sales people hyping their wares at Sturbridge's department store; and the sharks in the Philadelphia pool parlors, who enticed unwary novices to play a game.

For the young Fields, petty pilfering resembled a sport to outwit an unsuspecting dupe. He indulged in the practice without remorse, stealing hay and fruit, swiping meringue pies, nabbing food from lunch counters, and snitching umbrellas. His mentor, Professor Bill Dailey, taught the youngster the army shell game at the Trenton Fair. Fields revered the elder Irishman as his guru who shed light on other con games to swindle the naïve. Dailey and McGargle share the same designation, "Professor," to gull the public into believing they were erudite experts.

As a vaudeville juggler Fields relied on deception, quick-hand actions that hoodwinked the audience. Spectators wondered how he performed his cigar box trick, which he completed by threading a string through the boxes so that they would not fall. Pocketing all the balls on his pool table with one shot was done by an assistant secretly pulling on a cord hidden underneath the table. Fields performed other tricks that relied on fooling his audience. Impersonating a small-time con man was a natural transformation for Fields because he had already mastered the art of trickery in vaudeville.

While working in the show biz trenches as a greenhorn, he stumbled upon numerous McGargle types. He saw pitchmen sell fake cures for diseases and other bogus products at fairs, carnivals, and circuses. In order to lure customers to see exaggerated attractions in a sideshow, a glib pitchman used hyperbolic sales talk, called the "bally," outside his tent. Fields also saw barkers hawk their sideshow oddities, archeological exhibits, and theater entertainment while working at two New York museums in 1899.

Popular outdoor amusements flourished during the time Fields began as a tramp juggler. Medicine show operators and an assistant traveled by wagon from one stop to another where they doubled as entertainer and smooth-talking snake-oil salesman. A larger medicine show consisted of several artists and shills, who enticed the crowd to buy bogus remedies. "If the 'sucker' didn't come quickly enough," recalled Fields, "the medicine man would say, *sotto voce*, 'shill in,' and the shillabars would heed the signal and proceed to buy."[20]

The expansion of railroad networks after the Civil War made it easier for outdoor entertainment companies to reach new locales across the country. In mid-America popular tent road shows proliferated, featuring repertory companies playing comedies, melodramas, and tragedies. In *Poppy* and its movie versions, McGargle is a medicine man who sells his remedies from a wagon at a carnival, but in the film *The Old Fashioned Way* (1934), the Great McGonigle's troupe of thespians travel by railroad.

Fields's experiences on the sawdust trail become the setting for several other films. Besides the two films adapted from *Poppy*, other movies about popular outdoor entertainment include the following:

- In *Two Flaming Youths* (1927, lost), Fields operates an impoverished carnival that travels via pickup truck and camper. As "Gabby" Gilfoil, he plays a "gabby" barker who lures customers to see his sideshow and wins money in a shell game.
- In *Tillie's Punctured Romance* (1928, lost), Fields plays a circus ringmaster, a conniver who unsuccessfully plots to kill the owner by feeding him to the lions. Friends again, they take their circus to entertain the troops during World War I, but mistakenly end up on the German line where their circus lions run amok, causing the German troops to flee and inadvertently helping the Allies win the war.
- In *The Old Fashioned Way* (1934), McGonigle (Fields) heads a bankrupt group of traveling troupers. As in *Poppy*, he has a daughter who finds happiness with a beau in town. After he leaves, McGonigle is last seen on a soap box ballyhooing a bogus remedy for hoarseness.
- In *You Can't Cheat an Honest Man* (1939), Fields plays Larson E. Whipsnade, a rogue who operates a small-time debt-ridden circus.

As soon as Fields went on stage, he experienced the cutthroat practices that ran rampant in show biz. To recap a few: the manager who charged Bill a thirty percent commission at Plymouth Park;

the jealous performers who backstabbed him, getting him fired after one performance in the Broadway musical *Watch Your Step*; and Ziegfeld, who gave more salary to his favorite comedians and criticized Fields's routines with little justification. The best model for McGargle was the scurrilous James Fulton, manager of the *Monte Carlo Girls*, who abandoned his burlesque troupe and absconded with the show's funds in the dead of winter in Kent, Ohio. This traumatic incident, which happened early in his career, awakened him to the quicksand that could easily sink a neophyte performer. He learned then and there to be always on guard for the snake-oil tactics of entertainment magnates.

*Poppy* (1923-24) was presented on Broadway during the time when fraud and crime monopolized the headlines. Prohibition had accelerated bootlegging and its association with gangsters and murders. One of the worst government scandals occurred between 1920 and 1923 during the Warren G. Harding administration. Called the Teapot Dome Scandal, it involved Harding's Secretary of Interior, Albert B. Fall, who accepted large bribes from oil companies in return for leasing Navy petroleum reserves in Wyoming and California at low rates. Fall was fined $100,000 and received a one-year prison sentence. With so much thievery in the news, the public was prepared for a play about a con man named McGargle.

*Poppy* begins on a September morning in 1874 outside the fair grounds at Greenmeadow, Connecticut. Theatergoers first glimpse McGargle clothed in a pearl-colored stovetop hat; a three-quarter length brown fur-trimmed frock coat, with large pockets and round bone buttons; black and white checkerboard trousers; a high collar with a black bow tie; and black spats. This attire, with slight variations, became the iconic regalia associated with Fields's portrayal of 1890s show-biz rogues. "Costumes are not funny, my keen-eyed friend," Fields said to a reporter. "They are only atmosphere. In *Poppy* I play a rascal who is old-fashioned even in the mauve decade, so I have to look the part. I am always in the mauve decade."[21] (This term describes the late nineteenth century, when the color mauve was widely utilized in fashion by applying an aniline dye.)

The initial dialogue between McGargle and Poppy reveals her need to end their days of trouping:

> Poppy: Why don't you let me get a job? I'm an elegant cook ... and you could do the chores.
> Prof: (*gasping*) What I, Eustace McGargle? I, who have fascinated thousands in my time....
> Poppy: I'm sick of this awful life, never knowing what minute you are going to be pinched.... In fact, I'm going out to find a good floor to scrub right now.
> Prof: So it has come at last! Deserted by my own child....
> Poppy: Pop, don't talk like that.
> Prof: Go, if you will, I shall not blame you. But some day, when you stumble over my emancipated deserted frame, laying in the gutter, say to yourself, 'this is my work,' and step over me.

They reach a compromise. McGargle agrees to lead a virtuous life, but only after they work one more time at the country fair. "Good" says McGargle, "one last crack at the boobs, and then Poppy, tomorrow a higher holier life."

Before long, McGargle has established his stand at the fair and is hawking his bogus cure in a burst of oratorical brilliance. The cadence of his sales pitch stems from hearing hyperbolic barkers outside Bowery museums and the rhythmic patter of his huckster father selling fresh fruits and vegetables, yelling, "pomegranates, rutabagas, calabashes!"

> Prof: Now, ladies and gentlemen, this stupefying secret of our presence before you has not been unveiled. It is purple bark sarsaparilla, the greatest discovery in the scientific world of medicine since Hypocrisies discovered the onion. ... Ladies and gentlemen, a wine glass full before meals will make the hair and teeth grow in any desired color. Who will be the first to try a bottle of the wonder worker? Step up! Step up! Shill in. Shill in.

"Shill in" are the code words for a prearranged person in the audience to be the first to try the concoction. When Bill, the man Poppy loves, asks for a bottle, she warns him not to drink the potion. "It might make you sick." Seeing few customers are buying, McGargle turns to an old sales gimmick: "Now, ladies and gentlemen, our stock is running low, who will take the few remaining bottles?" Desperate for more sales, McGargle tells the audience that his remedy will also cure hoarseness. Suddenly, his voice grows hoarse and is barely audible to the audience. He takes a swig from a bottle and his voice grows loud and clear.

Anxious to swindle the villagers in another con scheme, McGargle starts a three-shell or Army Game on the fair grounds. He is a sleight-of-hand trickster, eager to beat the suckers who are unaware that the game can be fixed. The first player is the pretentious Princess Tubbs, who asks if it is a gambling game. "Gambling?" McGargle replies, "Heavens no! It is a game of science and skill." To hoodwink the crowd into believing it is an easy game, he lets the Princess, who bets a dollar, win and double her money.

McGargle rambles off a sales pitch that Fields will use several times. "Remember," McGargle tells the onlookers, "it is not a game of chance. . . . It's the old army game. A boy can play as well as a man." Next up is Mortimer Pottle, McGargle's "mark" or sucker, who bets twenty-five dollars. McGargle shuffles three shells that are sitting on a table in front of the spectators. Pottle points to the shell he thinks hides the pea. He lets Pottle win, knowing that he will next raise his bet to one hundred dollars. By rapidly moving the shells around, McGargle's skilled hands can easily manipulate the pea, which falls through a hidden hole in the table. After Pottle picks the middle shell, McGargle lifts it. "You lose, Mr. Pottle. The pea is not there." Feeling that he has been cheated, Pottle accuses McGargle of rigging the game.

> Prof: Sir! You impugn my honor.
> Pottle: I've been laying for you. I've seen the swindle worked before. I'll have you sent to jail.
> (*enter Judge Delafield*)
> Prof: It is not a game of chance, your honor. It is a game of science and skill.

McGargle also plays poker with marked cards against two villagers. "The stud game in which he manages to deal himself four aces and to win a $1,000 pot without having undergone the burdensome necessity of putting up any money himself is the most hilarious minor episode of the new season," wrote the critic Alexander Woollcott.[22] The scene is the first time he impersonates a card shark, a character closely associated with his persona as a confidence man. Fields plays a card shark in the films *Tillie and Gus* (1933), *Mississippi* (1935), and *My Little Chickadee* (1940).

In the play *Poppy* Fields repeats numerous earlier sketches. He juggles tennis balls, sticks, and cigar boxes. With a bent cue he does trick shots on a pool table. From the *Follies* he recycles parts of his croquet scene. Repeating earlier stage material in a new undertaking became a custom, especially during his screen career.

McGargle plays a black ivory xylophone with a loose wooden bar that constantly whacks him in the face as he sings. His harsh voice reverberates across the auditorium to such an extent that it caused the composer Jerome Kern, sitting in the audience, to send a telegram to Paul Goodman. "THE FIELD OF COMEDY IS GLORIFIED BY THE COMEDY OF FIELDS BUT HE HAS THE ROTTENEST SINGING VOICE IN THE THEATRE."[23]

The plot thickens when McGargle learns that the deceased Jeremiah Foster, a wealthy citizen, has left his large estate to his daughter Kitty, who ran away to marry a circus performer and subsequently died. In an effort to give Poppy a better life, he forges a document declaring Poppy as Kitty's legal daughter and rightful heir to the inheritance. McGargle thus moves from petty pitchman to swindler.

During the final act Poppy proves she is the heir of the Foster estate by showing her locket which contains a picture of Kitty, her mother. McGargle reveals to Poppy that he is not her real father and that her mother and father had died while performing in a circus.

> Prof: I adopted you as my own. I thought you were promising material, but Poppy you'll never make a grifter.
> Poppy: Oh, no, Pop.

McGargle bids farewell, knowing that Poppy has finally found happiness and will marry her beau. Before McGargle leaves he offers "one word of fatherly advice" to Poppy. He pauses long enough to make the audience anxious to hear the advice her kindhearted guardian will give. "Never give a sucker an even break," McGargle says with heartfelt emotion. He is last seen on a soap box still ballyhooing a bogus remedy for hoarseness. "There was that unforgettable moment of gentle pathos and deep tenderness when Mr. Fields was about to make his final get-away," wrote the critic Charles Darnton. "Here the pain of parting from the girl to whom he had been a father through the years of struggle and flim-flam surged to his lips—choking back his emotion."[24] Fields's ability to express pathos surprised critics and fans. Due to Fields's fear of revealing his sentimental side, few knew that underneath his veneer hid a deeply troubled soul, a sensitive being capable of showing compassion to those less fortunate.

"I remember he was so good," said Madge Kennedy. Although Kennedy received good reviews for her charm and winsomeness, Fields' superlative notices suggested that he carried the show. Alan Dale, the critic for the *New York American*, who saw the premier, wrote that "Mr. Fields was so tremendously funny, and so outrageously clever, that he carried everything away from everybody. It was a W. C. Fields evening with a vengeance." The respected critic Alexander Woollcott best summed up the magic Fields conveyed as Professor McGargle: "It is difficult to imagine anything much more racy and engaging than his performance as the hopeless old mountebank who is the bogus father of Poppy in this retelling of the Cinderella legend by Dorothy Donnelly. As Prof. McGargle, the old time medicine man, . . . Fields is a delight."[25]

Since Fields was stealing the show, Kennedy graciously felt he deserved better billing. She telephoned Goodman, demanding, "Put his name up with mine. Put it right up there, please, he is magnificent." Thanks to Kennedy's largesse, he was now billed as a co-star.

Another break for Fields occurred when Kennedy left the show in May to return to the movies. His name was consequently highlighted on the Apollo marquee as the star. Once Kennedy departed, *Poppy* became a "one-man show." The forty-three-year-old trouper had been toiling for twenty-six years on the stage but never billed as a star.[26]

Playing the role of McGargle, the tenderhearted confidence man, greatly impacted Fields's career on the screen. The character becomes the archetype for every small-time mountebank he plays, albeit in different disguises. Fields's unforgettable portrayal along with the beleaguered husband (later solidified in 1925 in *The Comic Supplement*) formed the two pillars of his comic personae. In these roles Fields was destined to become an icon smasher, who used his comedic talents to slay venerated conventions that shackled individuality.

**Notes**

1. "Making a Juggler Talk on the Stage," *Boston Globe*, August 10, 1924, Shubert Archives, NYC; unidentified clipping, Shubert Archives.
2. Howard Dietz, *Dancing in the Dark: Words by Howard Dietz* (New York: Quadrangle, 1974), 64.
3. Anthony Slide, *Silent Players: A Biographical and Autobiographical Study of 100 Silent Film Actors and Actresses* (Lexington: The University Press of Kentucky, 2002), 193.
4. "The Story of Madge Kennedy," *NYT*, February 6, 1916, x6.
5. "Making a Juggler Talk on the Stage"; remarks by Madge Kennedy, "W. C. Fields: A Centennial Tribute," January 29, 1980, transcript p. 13, AMPAS; interview with Madge Kennedy, *W. C. Fields Straight Up*, unedited interviews, reel 2, 1985, UCLA Film and Television Archives.
6. Remarks by Madge Kennedy, "W. C. Fields: A Centennial Tribute."
7. "The Reminisces of Bert Wheeler," September 25, 1958, p. 13, OHCCU.
8. Interview with Madge Kenney, *W. C. Fields Straight Up*; remarks by Madge Kennedy, "W. C. Fields: A Centennial Tribute."
9. W. C. Fields, "Anything for a Laugh," *American Magazine* (September 1934), 129-30; James M. Cain, "The Gentle Side of W. C. Fields," *Washington Post*, September 26, 1976, L5.
10. "Making a Juggler Talk on the Stage."
11. Mencken, *A Mencken Chrestomathy*, ii.
12. Amy Reading, *The Mark Inside: A Perfect Swindle, A Cunning Revenge, and a Small History of the Big Con* (New York: Vintage Books, 2013), 24.
13. Maria Konnikova, *The Confidence Game: Why We Fall for It . . . Every Time* (New York: Viking, 2016), 4-5.
14. Reading, *The Mark Inside*, 26.
15. Ibid., 27.
16. Walter Blair, *Native American Humor* (1937; repr., Scranton, PA: Chandler, 1960), 86.
17. "Philadelphia: Corrupt and Contented," *McClure's Magazine* (July 1903).
18. Mauer, *The Big Con*, 178; Gladys Hall, "Have You Got the Makings of a Comedian," *Movie Classic* (December 1934), 30; Ruth Waterbury, "The Old Army Game," *Photoplay* (October 1925): 102; Ludwig Lewisohn, *The Nation*, vol. 117, no. 3037, clipping, scrapbook #10, WCFP.
19. "W. C. Fields Knew McGargle When He Was a Boy," *New York Sun*, April 3, 1924, scrapbook #10, WCFP.

20. *Boston Traveler*, August 21, 1924, scrapbook #10, WCFP.
21. Ida Zeitlin, "Life Begins at 20—says W. C. Fields," *Motion Picture* 50 (September 1935): 70.
22. Alexander Woollcott, "Shouts and Murmurs," clipping, *Poppy* theatre file, HTC.
23. Kern to Goodman, May 27, 1924, box 19, *Poppy* correspondence, WCFP.
24. Charles Darnton, *NYEW*, September 4, 1923, scrapbook #10, 1923-26, WCFP.
25. Interview with Madge Kennedy conducted by Anthony Slide, Paramount Pictures Studio, Astoria, NY; Alan Dale, *New York American*, September 4, 1923, clipping, scrapbook #10, WCFP; Alexander Woollcott, "Shouts and Murmurs," *NYH*, section 7, p.1, undated clipping, ca. September 1923, HTC.
26. Interview with Madge Kennedy, Astoria, NY.

# CHAPTER 7
## The Big House

Excited about the opportunity to work under the legendary director David Wark Griffith, Fields eagerly signed for a reported $250 a day to play McGargle in the screen version of *Poppy*. "I cut my salary almost in half to be in *Sally of the Sawdust* because I knew that I would get the benefit of the masterful direction of D. W. Griffith."[1]

Griffith had a fondness for the circus, which caused him to change the title of *Poppy* to *Sally of the Sawdust*. Numerous circus pictures were produced in the 1920s. They were popular due to their rich visual material and entertainment value, featuring daring acrobats, trapeze artists, and other thrilling acts. Circus films also featured a wide range of various characters, from lion tamers to tightrope walkers. They also appealed to a wide audience ranging from children to adults. "They touched a nostalgic nerve" by reminding moviegoers of their youth and an earlier time when the country was more rural. Circus movies featured an array of plots and appeared in various genres: dramas, romantic tales, comedies, westerns, tragedies, and crime, among others. The popular cowboy star Tom Mix made several westerns with circus backgrounds. Charlie Chaplin's *The Circus* (1928) stands out among the funniest comedies with its story of a tramp who becomes a popular clown performing hilarious skits.[2]

Griffith and Fields shared several experiences in common. They were born five years apart in the late nineteenth century (Griffith in 1875; Fields in 1880), making them both children of the late Victorian era. Both were shaped by the period's parochial customs and culture. Several of Fields's outdoor entertainment films in which he plays a mountebank are set in the late nineteenth century—the time he was an itinerant trouper primarily in burlesque and vaudeville shows. His oratory when he sells quack medicine is as rhapsodic and rambling as the long drawn-out prose found in Victorian literature. As he grew older, Fields became a biting iconoclast who attacked nineteenth-century shibboleths, especially the enshrinement of the family.

By contrast, Griffith held a lifelong nostalgia for the era that impacted his viewpoint and creativity, especially his flair for melodrama and sentimentality. The director recalled in 1938, "A scant half-century ago Queen Victoria was firmly seated on the throne of Great Britain and the world slid along nicely at three miles an hour." His Victorianism "influenced the florid and sentimental prose style of Griffith's intertitles which became one of the most distinctive features of his films," wrote Neil Sinyard.[3] Both shared a passion for Charles Dickens, especially the author's novels about orphans. The director desired to make a movie from the play *Poppy*, partly because the leading female character was an orphan.

Fields and Griffith had been unemployed itinerant troupers during their youth. Fields's experience involved burlesque, carnivals, and vaudeville shows. As an actor and playwright, Griffith barnstormed with travelling companies that staged melodramas, a genre he revered. Starting in 1891, he joined The Twilight Revelers, a troupe which crisscrossed southern Indiana. The experience gave Griffith a passion for melodrama, which impacted his films. "For ten years I led a miserable life, often shivering and sweating, always hungry. I slept in flophouses, did slob labor, and got stranded in tank towns without a cent or friend." Years later Griffith called his experience "a great apprenticeship for the work that lay ahead."[4]

In 1908, Griffith walked into the studio of the American Mutoscope and Biograph Company, located in a converted five-story brownstone at 11 East 14th Street, near Union Square, New York's early Rialto. Founded in 1895, Biograph produced one-reel shorts in its indoor studio relying on artificial light. When Griffith arrived the studio had lost its position mainly through poor management, lack of innovation, mediocre pictures, and legal battles with the Edison Trust. Having little interest in directing, Griffith instead was eager for the studio heads to read his scenarios or to get an acting job. As fate would have it, a director fell ill and Griffith was hired to oversee a one-reel short, *The Adventures of Dollie*, released on July 14, 1908.

At Biograph Griffith learned the syntax of filmmaking and experimented with new techniques that formed the foundation for his fascinating career. Here Griffith mastered the art of cinema by either creating new innovations or building on the work of earlier filmmakers: close-ups that dramatized facial expressions; moving and high angle camera shots to enhance action; parallel story development that interweaved narratives through cross cutting; the fadeout; and blending close-ups with medium and long shots to increase tempo and the range of the camera's vision. In addition, writes David Robinson, "he introduced realistic and expressive lighting. He used masks and irises to make the very shape of the screen an instrument for dramatic purposes. . . . He realized the screen image from a simply two-dimensional one and gave it perspective, foreground and background. He used the moving camera . . . for dramatic purposes."[5]

Here Griffith encountered performers who became stars of the silent screen, many joining his own stock company. Among them was Mary Pickford, who completed numerous Biograph pictures, including a short with Lionel Barrymore in *The New York Hat* (1912). Also among his actors were the legendary sisters Lillian and Dorothy Gish. Griffith was attracted to Lillian's "ethereal beauty" and Dorothy's "tender sweet charm." Lillian found Griffith "imposing; he held himself like a king . . . vigorous and masculine looking." He wore a "wide-brimmed straw hat . . . with a jaunty curve to the brim. His nose was prominent; his profile seemed to belong to a Roman coin, and he had the heavy lower lip and jaw of the Bourbons. It was an important face." In 1912, the two sisters debuted in his Biograph short, *An Unseen Enemy*.[6]

Griffith created an amazing record of directing about 450 Biograph movies, primarily one-reelers, as well as twelve two-reelers. To fulfill Biograph's needs, he made a picture every week in various genres. Subjects were regularly borrowed from classic and contemporary literature (from Tennyson to Tolstoy); U.S. history (the South and the Civil War); Westerns; farces; and domestic life bursting with melodrama and sentimentality His prodigious contributions made Biograph a leader in the history of early silent pictures. Pioneer film historian Terry Ramsaye writes, "Here was born the competitive force which was to make the motion picture a great industry ... to contribute more importantly than any other influence toward making it an art."⁷ When the studio refused to allow Griffith to direct feature-length pictures, he left Biograph in September 1913 for Mutual's Reliance-Majestic studio in Los Angeles. Here he enlarged his range of subjects: Biblical stories, European history, World War I propaganda movies, love stories, several social reform films, and sentimental pictures of rural America, as well as a silent feature that reflected his nostalgia for the South where he grew up.

That moving picture was entitled *The Birth of a Nation* (1915), Griffith's controversial 12-reel Civil War and Reconstruction epic. *The Birth of a Nation* reflected an antithesis between its significance as a milestone in the artistic advancement of film versus the picture's abhorrent racism against African Americans. Distributed by Griffith's own company, the Epoch Production Corporation, the film became exceedingly scandalous with its white supremacist and offensive racial stereotypes, especially its favorable depiction of the KKK. Although the film was a box-office success, opposition from the NAACP and other African-American leaders precipitated calls for the picture's suppression as well as nationwide riots. Joining the chorus of attackers was the African-American civil rights leader Booker T. Washington and the founder of the NAACP, Oswald Garrison Villard, who called the film a "deliberate attempt to humiliate 10,000,000 American citizens and portray them as nothing but beasts."⁸

Griffith's reputation plummeted with his classic epic. Hurt by the negative reviews, a distressed Griffith defended his film as a great advancement in cinema. Griffith was born in Kentucky, the son of a confederate brigadier general known for his heroism during the Civil War, and as a youngster he grew up during the racist era of Reconstruction. In defense, Griffith mentioned his 1911 picture, *Rose of Kentucky*, in which the Klan is presented as a villainous gang and the locals are saved by an African-American youngster. *The Birth of a Nation* continues to be afflicted by its dualism—a masterpiece of cinematic art versus its depiction of the country's sinful racism.

*Figure 7.1 Biograph Company's headquarters at 11 East 14th Street. Author's Collection.*

*The Birth of a Nation*, a long narrative film, premiered in 1915, the same year Fields was making his two one-reel shorts for Gaumont. Griffith's movie signaled that the film industry was embarking on making multi-reel features, and that even longer shorts were becoming passé. They were often relegated to being a less important part of a double bill highlighting a lengthy smash hit.

Griffith followed *The Birth of a Nation* with a number of outstanding features: *Intolerance* (1916), comprising four interwoven historical stories, and *Broken Blossoms* (1919), about a daughter abused by her brutal father. She is saved by a kind Chinaman, until her father discovers her and beats her to death, causing her rescuer to commit suicide. Adding to his accomplishments was *Orphans of the Storm* (1922), a dramatic French Revolution epic with the Gish sisters.

In 1919, Griffith left Hollywood to make his films again in the New York area where financiers, talented theater actors, and screen performers were located. He acquired a large estate in Mamaroneck, Westchester County, adjacent to Long Island Sound. The property, wrote Lillian Gish, was "surrounded by a sea wall of rocks and glorious old trees with branches chained together to withstand the sweeping winter winds." Griffith's output here suffered from an overdose of melodramatic sentimentality, a syndrome that had afflicted Griffith since his stage career. The assault on Griffith's films began in an article in the December 1924 issue of *Photoplay* magazine by James R. Quirk, who criticized his work as being out of touch with the real world. In his "Open Letter to D. W. Griffith" he scolded the director. "The time has come when, for the good of motion pictures, you should take an accounting of yourself.... Your refusal to face the world is making you more and more a sentimentalist."[9]

Fields encountered Griffith during the time he was facing serious financial problems due to box-office losses. He had borrowed money from banks hoping to repay his financiers through profits from his pictures. Instead, he lost money on some films. "When I work for someone else, I always make money for them. When I back my own ideas, I am bound to lose. I borrowed the money to finance *Isn't Life Wonderful*. I am still paying it back. I suppose I could have gone bankrupt, but I didn't. I'd rather do it this way."[10] Hoping to improve his financial situation, Griffith became a contract director in 1925 for Famous Players-Lasky (headed by film pioneers Adolph Zukor and Jesse Lasky) to direct four films at their Astoria studio.

Anxious to supplement their West Cost facilities and produce films in the East, Lasky and Zukor had opened their huge Astoria facility in September 1920. The name Astoria stems from Old Astoria Village, an early bucolic community, named after John Jacob Astor. The block-long structure is still located in Long Island City, a municipality in Queens. Linked to Paramount's corporate headquarters in Manhattan and its Hollywood studio, Astoria was considered the crown jewel of Adolph Zukor's Famous Players and Jesse Lasky's cinema empire. With its imposing façade topped by a dome roof and four huge Doric pillars, the building resembles a railroad terminal. Costing $2.5 million to build, the vast fourteen-acre structure was designated "The Big House" by performers and workers. A *New York Times* reviewer thought it had "the fittings of a palace."[11]

A writer in *Who's Who on the Screen* (1920) raved about the building: "From an architectural standpoint the new studio is one of the most interesting buildings in the metropolitan area. . . . Deviating from the familiar type of studio with its glass roof and sides, the huge building is well-lighted by many windows and a row of glazed openings in the clerestory, close to the roof." Found on the first floor were enormous stage spaces, various departments, and a fifty-seat theater for screening the studio's pictures. On the second floor were offices, a wardrobe department, luxurious multi-room suites for stars, and smaller dressing rooms for extras. The grounds outside included a versatile large back lot for outdoor filming. A separate building contained a laboratory for developing all Astoria films where six machines worked to thoroughly develop, wash, dry, polish, and tint prints. Astoria claimed that each week it processed three million feet of film ready for shipment to theaters.[12] Nearby was a nitrate film repository where old pictures deteriorated and were destroyed.

Some performers and directors complained about its facilities. Louise Brooks felt that Astoria lacked the amenities of Hollywood studios. It looked like "an old warehouse because in the winter the wind blew you off the sets in freezing cold and in the summer you simply dripped with sweat, and you went up and down in the freight elevator with electricians knocking you left and right." The film director George Cukor likewise felt it was "a rather klutzy place and ugly . . . not nearly as well known as the west coast [studios]—there was some rivalry."[13]

Nine months after its opening, a postwar economic depression forced the studio to temporarily close, causing filmmakers to criticize the facility. One individual labeled it a "Quixotic experiment." In June 1922, production resumed, and during the next five years

Astoria churned out 103 feature films. "Astoria filled a definite need as an adjunct to our facilities in the West," wrote Jesse Lasky. Its impressive record represented 40 percent of Paramount's entire output, proving that the company's East and West Coast facilities provided a valuable linkage.[14]

Astoria's atmosphere was charged with excitement. It attracted figures who felt Hollywood was a cultural wasteland compared to New York. Numerous writers, directors, and performers attached to Broadway preferred Astoria to Tinsel Town. Despite her reservations about its facilities, Louise Brooks raved about the studio's location near Manhattan. "Motion pictures did not consume us. When work was finished, we dressed in evening clothes, dined at the Colony or '21,' and went to the theater." In Hollywood "there was no theater, no opera, no concerts—just those god-damned movies." "The place was full of free spirits, defectors, refugees, who were all trying to get away from Hollywood and its restrictions," recalled Gloria Swanson. "There was a wonderful sense of revolution and innovation."[15]

Astoria belongs to the rich history of filmmaking in New York and its environs, a tradition that dates back to the first Kinetoscope parlor, which opened on Broadway in 1894. The studio was destined to achieve fame for the quantity and quality of its productions during the 1920s. During its first seven years, the studio created a thriving industry that produced 127 features in a prime location in the New York environs. About 65 percent of its releases were dramas and melodramas. Once a sleepy village with rural farms, Astoria became a burgeoning industrial and residential area. The locale was an easy commute: a fifteen-minute drive from Manhattan via the Queensboro Bridge (1909), an elevated railway line (1917), and a new BRT subway connection, which provided a twenty-minute ride from Times Square to a stop four blocks from the studio. The facility's accessibility enabled the studio to lure Broadway and film stars, cutting-edge directors, producers, and cameramen, among others.

One commuter described his trip to Astoria via subway. "Waiting for the train marked 'Astoria,' the platform was swarming with figures in various stages of half-awakedness, lugging huge suitcases. The Astoria sub came thundering in, and there was a surge forward.... One could not help wondering how many potential Mary Pickfords ... and Charlie Chaplins were there in that little coach." Upon arriving, "the company takes the beaten path, a well-worn cut that leads across open fields to where the white walls of the studio—Mecca to many hopeful hearts—looms up large before us.... At the studio the troupe holds at the office of the casting director, who hands out cards containing the name, length of time engaged, and space for assignment to dressing rooms."[16]

Astoria became Fields's home away from home. In addition to *Sally of the Sawdust*, he completed five more silent feature films here between 1925 and 1927: *That Royle Girl* (1925), *It's the Old Army Game* (1926), *So's Your Old Man* (1926), *The Potters* (1927), and *Running Wild* (1927). (Astoria is now a historic landmark multibuilding complex that houses the Museum of the Moving Image and the Kaufman Astoria Studios.)

Fields lived in Bayside, Long Island, which was near the Astoria studio. The town became a colony for numerous screen luminaries such as Rudolph Valentino and Mary Pickford, who lived in a stucco house next to Fields's home. "Live in an amazing house," Fields told the reporter Whitney Bolton. "It's got 3,200 panes of glass in it. It's like a roof nailed onto a lot of small pieces of glass." Fields invited Bolton to a party that lasted three days. "Thirteen panes had been used up in violent and sudden ways," recollected Bolton. "Like throwing shoes through them."[17]

William LeBaron, Fields's producer, related another anecdote about a formal dinner party at the comedian's abode. Bill asked LeBaron to help coordinate the gathering since he had never organized a large social event. The comedian hired extra servants, selected exotic food from a gourmet's guide, and bought cases of European wine. Dressed in evening clothes, Fields greeted his guests in a stiff aristocratic manner, which came undone half way through the dinner when he began to tell amusing farfetched stories. LeBaron found Bill terribly nervous and perspiring, but "proceeding with great fanfare." He ordered the butler to fill up his guests' wineglasses. By dinner's end the partygoers were soused and some began relating their favorite adventure tale. Retiring to the living room on a hot night, Fields loosened his collar. Other guests

*Figure 7.2 Zukor and Lasky's Big House—Astoria Studio. Author's Collection*

followed suit, including a man who took off his shirt and a woman who removed her shoes. Before LeBaron left at midnight, he found Fields without his shirt, feet on a table, and a champagne bottle on top of his head. LeBaron thought that the dinner party was a rare occasion for Bill. "He was not a really a gregarious man. He didn't seek people out; they sought him."[18]

Children in the neighborhood would peek through the holes in a wooden fence to eagerly spot the movie stars who were entering and leaving the studio. Thirteen-year-old Ethel Agnes Zimmerman, who resided near the facility, frequently stood by the fence watching the filmmaking and the stars. "The great and glamorous came to work in block-long cars, shiny with nickel. And we neighborhood kids stood there, stiff with excitement, and watched. I never saw Valentino. I would have remembered him if I had. But I did see . . . Adolphe Menjou, Gilda Gray, and to me, the most beautiful of all, Alice Brady. . . . Watching her, I decided to be not only a singer, but an actress too." She did become a star later, using her stage name, Ethel Merman.[19]

Visitors to Griffith's sets at Astoria were usually welcome as long as they did not offend Griffith. James Sibley Watson, Jr., a film buff interested in camera technology and later publisher of *The Dial* (a renowned literary socio-political journal) arrived one day at the studio. He entered a circus tent, the set of *Sally of the Sawdust*, where he spotted Griffith filming close-ups of a little girl. After meeting D. W. he noticed the "scenery, the lights, and the camera, the things he wanted to see." He got into an informative conversation with the cameraman about his hand-cranked camera and other technical issues. Upon leaving he wanted to thank Griffith for his visit, but to his surprise he "turned his back on me, evidently offended that I, a nonentity, had neglected him for his cameraman."[20]

Fields was apprehensive on the first day he arrived on the set of *Sally of the Sawdust*. He wondered what to expect. After all, he was only a novice, having appeared in two shorts ten years earlier, and a three-minute bit part in *Janice Meredith*. His worries were nonetheless offset by his excitement to work with Griffith. Fields failed to realize that he was in for a surprisingly rough roller coaster ride.

**Notes**

1. Harold Cary, "The Loneliest Man in the Movies," *Colliers*, November 28, 1925, 26.2.
2. Larry Langman, *American Film Cycles: The Silent Era* (Westport, Conn: Greenwood Press, 1998), 129-38.
3. Neil Sinyard, *Silent Movies* (New York: Smithmark Publishers, 1995), 20-21.
4. *The Man Who Invented Hollywood: The Autobiography of D. W. Griffith*, ed. James Hart (Louisville, KY: Touchstone Publishing:, 1972), 19, 26.
5. David Robinson, *Hollywood in the Twenties* (New York: Barnes, 1968), 49.
6. Lillian Gish, *The Movies, Mr. Griffith & Me*, (New York: Prentice-Hall, 1969), 35.
7. *A Million and One Nights: A History of the Motion Picture Through 1925* (New York: Touchstone Book, 1926), 328.
8. Ibid., 643.
9. Gish, *The Movies, Mr. Griffith & Me*, 223; Schickel, 508.
10. Sara Redway, "D. W. Griffith is Struggling to Pay His Debts," *Motion Picture Classic*, October 1925, in Anthony Slide, ed., *D. W. Griffith Interviews* (Jackson: University Press of Mississippi, 2012), 163.
11. *NYT*, November 7, 1920, 6.
12. Charles Donald Fox and Milton L. Silver, eds., *Who's Who on the Screen* (New York: Ross Publishing, 1920), 6.
13. Richard and Diane Koszarski interview with Louise Brooks, June 3, 1979, 1-2; Adamson interview with George Cukor, MMIOHP; Ethan Mordden, *The Hollywood Studios: House Style in the Golden Age of the Movies* (New York: Alfred A. Knopf, 1988), 44.
14. *Hollywood on the Hudson*, 31; Jesse Lasky, *I Blow My Own Horn* (Garden City, NY, 1957), 194.
15. *The Man You Loved to Hate*, Richard Koszarski, (New York: Dover, 1983), 9.
16. *Hollywood on the Hudson*, 31.
17. *NYMT*, December 7, 1956. *The Astoria Studio and Its Fabulous Films*
18. Robert Lewis Taylor, *W. C. Fields: His Follies and Fortunes* (New York: Doubleday, 1949), 191.
19. *Hollywood on the Hudson*, 33.
20. "The Films of J. S. Watson, Jr. and Melville Webber: Some Retrospective Views," *University of Rochester Library Bulletin* 28, no. 2 (Winter 1975).

## CHAPTER 8

### Sally of the Sawdust

The transition from stage to screen was a difficult challenge for Fields. He had been treading the boards since 1898, starting with two years in burlesque, followed by fifteen years in vaudeville, and ten years in the *Ziegfeld Follies* and other Broadway revues. After a time, Fields discovered that screen acting depended on a different set of skills. Once on the set he noted that distinct aptitudes were needed for the movies. He missed the presence of a live audience for his timing and to monitor his reception. "The hardest thing for a former stage player to get used to in movie work is to do your stuff minus applause or encouragement before a handful of cameramen and technical directors. You wonder if you're getting across, and there's no way of finding out." You have to depend on "all the people who stand around and watch you on a movie set!" The noise in the studio also distracted his performance. "The racket by the carpenters, the yelling for the lights to be switched on and off, the blowing of the director's whistle—gosh I thought those were some handicaps to doing my stuff right!"[1]

Fields believed that his years on the stage were excellent training for a movie actor. "Talk about the art of acting! What is there of art or acting, either, in simply responding to the director's orders like an automaton operated by a push button? ... If more picture actors had stage training they would not have to be told how to do every least little thing."[2] The theater gave Fields a great sense of timing, enhanced his remarkable talent for pantomime, and the opportunity to develop characterizations that he transferred to the screen.

While Fields was shooting *Sally of the Sawdust*, Louise Brooks was performing in *The American Venus* at Astoria. They were acquaintances since both had performed in the 1925 *Ziegfeld Follies*, in which Brooks appeared as a dancer. Although she had only previously played a bit part in one film, she felt Fields was a novice screen performer and acted as if he was still on the stage. While intensely watching Fields perform, she concluded, "He paid no attention to camera setups ... Long shot, medium shot, two-shot, or close-up, Bill performed as if he was standing whole before an audience that could appreciate every detail of his costume and follow the dainty disposition of his hands and feet."[3]

Brooks also recognized that Griffith's type of direction was wounding Fields's comedic style. Griffith's method of rapid cross-cutting, multiple camera angles, and fast-paced action was also at odds with the slower pace Fields needed to play a comic scene. "Every time the camera drew closer, it cut off another piece of him and deprived him of some comic effect.... As he ignored camera setups, he ignored the cutting room, and he could only curse the finished film, seeing his timing ruined by haphazard cuts."[4]

Fields faced another problem. Griffith's forte was mainly drama, romance, and spectacle. As mentioned earlier, he had gained experience with comedy as a Biograph director during his early years. Griffith once said that his first pictures "were comedies, regular slapstick comedies. I made the first comedy chase, the kind where they all pile up in a ditch at the end." Later, Mack Sennett, a Biograph extra, "took them over."[5]

"He was my day school, my adult education program, my university.... I began to learn how to make a motion picture," said Sennett. He soon learned that Griffith was not as "fascinated by comedy" as he was. "He went into silences when I brought up my favorite people, policemen. I never succeeded in convincing Mr. Griffith that cops were funny."[6] Despite Griffith's early contact with Sennett, he never evolved into a comedy director. This drawback would inhibit Fields's performances in the two pictures he did with Griffith. (Fields later made four sound shorts with Sennett during 1932-33 and presented him with an honorary Oscar at the Academy Awards in 1938 for his pioneering creativity in film comedy.)

Since this was his first feature, Bill was unaware of certain protocols in filmmaking. During one scene requiring two different shots, he appeared in two different costumes, causing havoc with the editing. An assistant was consequently appointed to keep an eye on him. Fields continued to use the fake mustache he had worn on stage despite being told that it appeared artificial on camera. Unsure of his ability to do a comic scene by himself, Bill brought along "Shorty Blanche," his favorite stooge from the *Follies*, to help perform a gag on screen or to give cues off screen.

Another unexpected problem for Fields was the presence of Carol Dempster cast as Sally, McGargle's adopted daughter or ward. Dempster was Griffith's leading lady and paramour between 1919 and 1925. Born on December 8, 1901, in Duluth, Minnesota, she moved with her family to Los Angeles, where as a teenager she enrolled in a school of dance operated by Ruth St. Denis, a famous prima ballerina and choreographer. Needing dancers for the terpsichorean Babylonian scenes in *Intolerance* (1916), Griffith visited St. Denis's studio, where he admired Dempster's graceful movements and lithe figure. "He asked me if I'd like to go into motion pictures," she recalled. "Since it was a chance to work with him, I went, of course."[7]

She appeared in the feast of Beshazzar scene in *Intolerance*, with hundreds of other dancers. Two years later he engaged her to dance with Rudolph Valentino in a prologue film shown before screening *The Greatest Thing in Life* (1918). During the rehearsal the stage was lit by blue and gold lights. "Mr. Griffith," recalled Lillian Gish, "incorporated the results into the final movie, by having sections of the film tinted in the laboratory." By 1919, Dempster had appeared in three silent pictures directed by Griffith and starred in several films during the 1920s. She represented Griffith's flair for discovering "new talent, sixteen or under, and molding them into something new and strange."[8]

Once Dempster became Griffith's leading lady, she faced a problem following in the footsteps of such luminaries as the Gish sisters (Lillian and Dorothy), Mae Marsh, Blanch Sweet, and Mary Pickford. Dempster was considerably less talented than these stars. By watching the Gish sisters and Mae Marsh, Dempster mimicked their acting styles, especially their gestures and movements. Dempster's predicament peaked when she replaced Lillian Gish, ill due to the flu epidemic, to star in *The Girl Who Stayed at Home* (1919), a picture about two contrasting brothers enlisting in World War I. Gish called her new rival "ambitious." Infatuated with his new starlet's looks, Griffith was "blind to all of Dempster's shortcomings." Colleagues felt she was sharp, stupid, and a third-rate actress. Karl Brown, an assistant to "Billy" Bitzer, Griffith's celebrated cameraman, described her as "narrow-faced with close-set eyes" with "a little protruding bump at the tip of her nose." He recalled Griffith saying, "To think that perfect beauty can be marred by one little bit of misplaced flesh. What a shame, what a crying shame. Otherwise ... perfection."[9]

Hearing Griffith speak through a megaphone, his performers became spellbound by his "hypnotic power of voice." "It was as effective as a musical instrument in its molding of the emotions. The tone, the resonance, the sudden harshness, the softening—all this had a profound effect on the performance." Griffith usually worked without a script. For *Sally of the Sawdust*, a shooting script was prepared, but the director ignored it. "I wouldn't read the script," he once said; "it might get you all balled up." Instead, "he blocked his scenes in long-shot and mid-shot, much as a painter sketches an outline."[10]

Griffith depended on rehearsals, during which he "was constantly altering, modifying, [and] polishing." The director often enacted each role for his performers, and he regularly insisted on retakes. Rehearsals for *Sally* occurred at a rented banquet room above Keen's Chop House on 44th Street. Griffith's work day followed a strict schedule. He started his rehearsals between 9:30 and 10 a.m., and his performers and crew worked six days a week. Actress Katherine Albert, who performed in *The Greatest Question* (1919), recalled that during rehearsal "Griffith's voice, a rich, deep, very beautiful voice, droned on, telling us what to do."[11]

On call twenty-four hours a day was young Frank Walsh, Griffith's assistant director, who did most of the grunt work. Griffith sometimes awakened Walsh at three in the morning with alterations for the next shooting. He often had conferences at Griffith's suite at the Astor Hotel. Walsh was also responsible for arranging the set for next day's shoot. "He was a gentlemanly guy, always," Walsh recalled. Even with the extras he was polite. "He would get mobs of people to do things for him that they wouldn't do for other people."[12]

According to Kevin Brownlow, "[Dempster] unconsciously put up a resistance to Griffith's hypnotic direction. It once took six hours for Griffith to induce Miss Dempster to cry." Anita Loos, legendary screenwriter and novelist, felt Dempster was "a bad actress and such a stupid girl, she certainly didn't do [Griffith] any good."[13]

When Lillian Gish wondered why Griffith added Dempster to his stable of leading ladies, he replied, "You don't know what it is to have a big nose." According to the young actor Richard Graves, the Gish-Dempster rivalry reached its apex in 1919. Dempster's replacement of Gish in Griffith's eyes "created quite a flurry. It denoted a change of viewpoint as well as a change of attention on the part of Mr. Griffith. Dempster's entry created jealousies and factions, as well as a feud among the staff members." Gish waited a few years hoping his passion for Dempster would wilt, but her hopes never materialized. Lillian left him in 1922, leaving a gaping hole in his future career. The journalist and screenwriter Adela St. John recalled seeing Griffith downcast and tipsy in a Hollywood restaurant during the 1940s. While discussing the past, he told her, "I never had a day's luck after Lillian left me." St. John replied, "Lillian didn't leave you! You chucked her out for that mediocre girl."[14] Griffith's movies in the early 1920s were afflicted with Dempsteritis, the excessive screen time he gave his amour. The director's obsession with Dempster caused her to monopolize *Sally*. Scenes of Fields juggling, for example, were partly cut in order to devote more time to Dempster's dancing. The Sally-Peyton schmaltzy romance is given far too much footage, to the extent that this sub-plot allows Griffith to frequently cut away from McGargle's comedic scenes. Rumors surfaced that Dempster complained that Fields had too many scenes and was stealing the picture. Griffith, consequently, reinstated Dempster's sequences that he had cut. After Dempster watched the rushes in the editing room, she still became irate that Fields was stealing the picture. She insisted on additional footage, which was reported to cost an extra $25,000. Her mediocre dancing is given more camera time than Fields's wonderful juggling exhibition. A long shot causes the heads of spectators to partially block the view of Fields's famous cigar-box routine. Several comic sequences with Fields ended up on the cutting room floor.

*Figure 8.1 Griffith directing Fields and Dempster in* Sally of the Sawdust. *Bison Archives/HollywoodHistoricPhotos.com.*

Griffith's obsession with Dempster was well known among the Astoria populace. His continual cutting in the studio's projection rooms caused delays in production of other films. According to Louise Brooks, "the standard joke around the studio was that you couldn't get into any projection room because D. W. Griffith was in there running film of Carol Dempster's legs. He was a big joke around the studio, which wasn't fair at all."[15]

To turn *Poppy* into a silent picture, Griffith junked the stage scenes he felt were too theatrical for the screen and created many new events to the extent that only the central elements of the play remained. Although the movie contains flashbacks to the period when Sally became a circus orphan cared for by McGargle, the silent feature is primarily set in the present. Griffith scuttled the play's suspense by letting moviegoers know at the beginning Sally's identity as the granddaughter legally entitled to an inheritance. McGargle thus takes Sally to Green Meadows to reunite with her family and claim her rights.

There are several different plot twists. The scenario transposes McGargle from a shady medicine show operator selling quack remedies at a fair to a side-show entertainer at a carnival. In an amusing scene he picks the pocket of a person but an elephant promptly takes the wallet out of his pocket with its trunk. Besides operating a shell game, he cheats suckers at three-card Monte, another sleight-of-hand scam, in which the dealer places three cards facedown on a table and the gambler (mark) must pick the right money card. After Sally allows McGargle to escape arrest, she is tried as an accomplice to his gambling. After a frantic car chase to avoid capture, McGargle appears in court to prove Sally's lineage and inheritance. She is acquitted, accepted by the Foster family, and marries a respectable citizen, Peyton Lennox.

Lennox was played by Alfred Lunt, who became a renowned actor with his partner-wife Lynn Fontaine. Most observers felt Lunt's performance was flat and lacked passion in his love scenes with Dempster. Lunt blamed his performance on Griffith. "He'd set up a scene and that was it. It was all ad lib and I never saw a script. It was quite paralyzing, to tell the truth. . . . I'd come from the theater, where I'd been brought up in a different way. Griffith was very pleasant, but he just didn't seem to bother. I remember in the grocery store scene I said, 'What do I say to the grocer?' And he said, 'Oh, say anything—ash cans, tomato cans, ketchup. Just keep talking.'"[16] Despite the experience, Lunt afterwards made a few more movies and received an Academy Award nomination for best actor in *The Guardsman* (1931).

Fields convinced Griffith to use the scene he performed in the 1917 *Follies* playing a peanut vendor who secretly sells bootleg liquor from his cart. Only this time the comedian used a baby carriage replete with a brass foot rail and sawdust scattered around the carriage. Filmed midway through the Prohibition era, the routine was more timely. The repetition of the scene eight years after Fields performed it illustrates his penchant to revive stage scenes from the past.

Two other scenes are worth mentioning since they derive from the early experiences of Fields and Griffith. To get to Green Meadows, McGargle and Sally sneak aboard a train and experience a rough ride on the "blind baggage" car where they cling together to prevent falling off the train. When they arrive at Green Meadows station, the conductor orders the engineer to open the tank spout, and the two get drenched. (This actually happened to young Fields when he hopped on a train's baggage car heading for the Trenton Inter-State Fair in New Jersey.) Sally and her foster father find a bakery shop (shot on location in nearby Bayside, a Long Island town used for other scenes depicting the fictional Green Meadows) where McGargle climbs into a kiln to keep warm. Sally, unaware that McGargle is inside the kiln, adds coal to the fire underneath. The sudden heat causes McGargle to nearly pass out, and he is almost burned to death until Sally drags him out with a long ladle. He looks with disbelief at Sally's bosom where unbeknown to him, she has stuffed bakery buns. "My you are growing up, Sally!"

Griffith derived the above scene from an experience he had as an indigent itinerant trouper. After being kicked off a train, he discovered a shop operated by a Dutch baker. The baker, seeing Griffith shivering from the cold, "let me toast my toes in his bake oven." When the baker wasn't looking, Griffith crawled completely into the hot oven. "Ách! Gott!" the baker shouted. "Years later, I employed the incident in W. C. Fields' *Sally of the Sawdust*."[17]

The film's finale differs considerably from the stage version. Near the play's end, McGargle becomes involved with bootleggers, which leads to an overly long sequence showing Fields racing in a car followed by the bootleggers. He ends up at the courthouse to save Sally, who has been put on trial for aiding her foster father. After saving her, McGargle walks out of town alone, swinging his cane down a long road, similar to the final scenes in Chaplin's tramp pictures. This conclusion was too bleak for Griffith. Rather, McGargle is suddenly confronted by Sally and her family, who convince him to return to town. The last sequence shows McGargle dressed in wealthy attire driving with Sally and her family past a huge sign that advertises his real estate business selling choice lots in Green Meadows. Although affluent, McGargle has not repented his habits and intends to fleece his customers in real estate. The adage "Never Give a Sucker an Even Break" is scuttled. Instead, a title card at the end reads "It's the Old Army Game."

*Figure 8.2 Entire company of* Sally of the Sawdust *(1925). Seated on chairs left to right: Fields, Griffith. Author's Collection.*

The conclusion of *Sally of the Sawdust* foretold the endings of numerous Fields films. They often conclude with the mountebank or beleaguered husband suddenly becoming wealthy. The characters strike it rich with gushing oil wells (*The Potters*); a profitable California orange grove (*It's a Gift*); invention of shatterproof windshields (*So's Your Old Man*); creating puncture-proof tires (*You're Telling Me*); earnings from expensive beefsteak mining stock (*The Bank Dick*); and Florida real estate (*It's the Old Army Game*). These happy-ever-after-endings were possibly tacked on to make the audience feel good when they left the theater. But there is often a deeper meaning. McGargle suddenly becomes a hero to his wife and family because of his newly found wealth. Fields's characters nonetheless reject the life of the nouveau rich, keep their lifestyle, and prefer socializing with old friends at a nearby bar such as the Black Pussy Café in *The Bank Dick*. The strike-it-rich endings parodied the Horatio Alger success story in which people are judged by their wealth and not by their character.

Before the movie's opening it was exhibited in venues outside New York City. Each time it was shown, Griffith made cuts. Despite the elimination of scenes, enough footage survives to display Fields's pantomime skills. The critic Richard Watts wrote, "W. C. Fields proves that he is a comedian of the first order. He brings to the part his enormous ingenuity and ingeniousness, his gift for humorous and racy characterization, his immense bag of physical trickery and ever present undercurrent of pathetic wistfulness."[18]

After Griffith previewed the film in towns outside New York for editing and cutting purposes, the 104-minute film opened at the Strand movie palace in Times Square on August 2, 1925. At the time, Fields was in the 1925 *Follies* at the nearby New Amsterdam Theatre, where the cast got word of the premier. About 250 *Follies* chorus girls marched down Broadway to attend the Strand opening. "Never have I heard such an ovation as [Fields] got on his first appearance," wrote the *New York Times* reviewer. "People who think he is about the world's greatest comedian constitute a cult. That he should be greeted with shrieks of laughter here is only to be expected.... For Fields is not only a great comedian—he is one of the most loveable people ever seen on the screen." The film then moved to the Rialto on September 3, 1925, and received similar accolades. "A great character that McGargle—another great character that will live on the screen, and how remarkably played by W. C. Fields."[19]

Some reviews suggest that Fields stole the picture. "Mr. Fields fairly towers in interest above Carol Dempster, above the photoplay itself, and—whisper it—above the great D. W. Griffith." The *New York Times* critic called Fields "the hit of the picture as Pop" and the *Film Daily* reviewer felt he was "easily the outstanding figure and carries the picture."[20]

The movie itself received mixed opinions in New York newspapers: "Among the finest of all motion pictures yet made" (*World*); "a glorious experience" (*News*); and "you'll regret it all your life if you miss *Sally of the Sawdust*" (*Herald Tribune*). By contrast, several critics lambasted the film. The *Screenland* reviewer derided Griffith as the "master of popular sentimental hokum." Leading the naysayers was the playwright Robert E. Sherwood, who in *Life* magazine complained about the overuse of subtitles and the director's inability to learn "that a movie camera can move by itself." Sherwood, however, felt Fields saved the picture with his comic performance. He believed Fields managed to "inject some of his own matchless comedy, and some of his own human warmth into this otherwise bloody story." Griffith felt the criticism was unfair. "I was surprised at the criticism of my new picture, *Sally of the Sawdust*. People seemed to think it funny that I had burst into low comedy. I didn't burst into it, I cropped out of it."[21]

By film's end Griffith and Fields admired one another. "If I could only act half as well as he directs I would be the greatest comedian of all time," Fields said. "It is his earnestness and sincerity that makes Fields great," commented Griffith. "He is the drolleries and the laughter of life itself. Two minutes in his presence and one is laughing. Yet he works as diligently and far harder than any bricklayer."[22]

The film, released by United Artists, yielded Famous Players-Lasky a profit of more than $200,000. *Sally of the Sawdust* premiered the same year as Chaplin's *The Gold Rush* and Harold Lloyd's *The Freshman*, two silent comedy classics. A critic from *Liberty* magazine who recognized this coincidence stated that "Fields has joined the ranks of Chaplin, Lloyd, and Keaton with *Sally of the Sawdust*." The *New Yorker* reviewer wrote that "Mr. Fields' pantomimic nature was meant for the screen. . . . His performance admits him into that marble temple with the custard walls which harbor Chaplin, Lloyd, and Keaton." (*The New Yorker*, which commenced publication six months earlier on February 21, 1925, would become noted for its film critics: Penelope Gillette, Pauline Kael, Stanley Hoffmann, and Anthony Lane, among others.)

The *New Yorker* critic also pointed out that Fields's humor was much different from the three leading silent comedy stars: "He plays about with the law in fine fashion, showing a remarkable aptitude for getting himself into foolish scrapes and just managing to extricate himself as the guillotine is about to descend." This comment addresses one of the poignant factors behind Fields's humor. He uses the intimidation people face from threatening objects and menacing individuals as the basis for his comedy. Another reviewer, Grace Kingsley, of the *Los Angeles Times*, noted the cornerstone of Fields's humor playing McGargle: "There are deep and saving humor, loyalty, courage and a droll and fatalistic sort of cynicism in this McGargle, whether he is jauntily accosting his betters or he is meeting the slings and arrows of outrageous fate with a shillelagh. And there is a sort of comic dignity more of the soul than the body. I don't know the equal of this Fields in this character. And I can imagine as great in anything he undertakes." During his film career, Fields embodied the Everyman confronting the travails of the human condition.[23]

Bill's success on stage in *Poppy*, followed by his favorable reviews in *Sally of the Sawdust*, precipitated different offers. One was an exclusive contract with Ziegfeld, who wanted him to play Capon Andy in a new musical he was producing, Jerome Kern's *Show Boat*. Having spent so many years under Ziegfeld's thumb, Fields turned down a binding contract with the impresario. He later regretted not appearing in the initial run of one of the greatest groundbreaking shows in American musical theatre. (He later played the role during April 1930 at an outdoor amphitheater in St. Louis.) Paul Goodman, the producer of *Poppy*, offered Bill a five-year contract guaranteeing a play each year. He refused, however, to sign a long-term deal that would tie him to Goodman. Both offers would bind him to the theater, whereas Fields wanted to escape from the grind of continual evening performances and grueling road trips. He had finally realized that the stage was declining in popularity compared to the film venues, which attracted large crowds. In movies, he said, the comedian "can use the whole world for his stage, while in the theatre, he has to be content with a couple of settings."[24]

A month after the film opened, an interviewer asked him if he would "like to leave the stage and make pictures?" "Yes, I think I would," Fields replied. "I've been on the stage a long time, and I'd like to try something else. Besides, I am tired of doing a set act." The writer wondered if Fields had ever previously tried the movies. "I have. In 1915 Pathé [Gaumont] was making comedies with one vaudeville actor a week. I made one [*Pool Sharks*]. There was one camera and fifteen hundred feet of film. If I missed my trick, I spoiled the picture, so after a couple of trials at this, I lost interest in the movies until now." Fields declared that he believed "firmly in the great future for the movies. There are no racial, language, time or distance barriers for them. That's why I'm so excited about having landed in them at last. I haven't had much experience in pictures, but I think they are wonderful."[25]

"I can't see myself as Eustace McGargle forever, though he's my favorite," Fields told a reporter after he finished *Sally of the Sawdust*. "I never was much for playing the same part steadily. It identifies you too much with one thing."[26] The chance to do a version in sound, however, was irresistible. In 1936, a Talkie entitled *Poppy* was made starring Fields, then 56 years old and in frail health. Since he was now a star, the film was largely constructed around McGargle, still a traveling trickster caring for his ward, Poppy (Rochelle Hudson). The plot mostly follows the stage play, but the new additions are often hilarious. For example, McGargle sells a talking dog to a bartender, but the new owner cannot get the canine to speak; at a fair he cheats customers playing the shell game; and as an avid inebriate, he delivers a marvelous oration about the evils of drinking. By the end, Poppy is discovered as a long-lost heir and marries the mayor's son. In a touching scene, revealing Fields's ability to exhibit pathos, McGargle says farewell to Poppy, warning her to "never giver a sucker an even break." With the famous maxim about suckers restored from the play, McGargle prepares to leave by himself. On his way out, he steals the mayor's hat and cane, grabs a handful of cigars, walks to the door, exits, turns right, and disappears as the film fades out.

Radio also gave Fields an opportunity to continue his role as McGargle. In 1938, a radio version of *Poppy*, with Fields as McGargle, was broadcast on CBS's *Lux Radio Theater*, hosted by Cecil B. DeMille. "Fields [was] superb and played for radio laughs rather than studio laughs," reported a spokesman for the J. Walter Thompson Company, the program's advertising agency.[27] Modifying his work from the past was a major factor that enabled Fields to appear in five different performing art mediums during the first half of the 21st century—stage; silent pictures; sound films; radio; and, in 1946, studio recordings, where, as a skillful raconteur, he recited two of his tall tales, *The Day I Drank a Glass of Water* and *The Temperance Lecture*.

**Notes**

1. Harold Cary, "The Loneliest Man in the Movies," *Colliers*, November 28, 1925, 26.
2. Neil Sinyard, *Silent Movies* (New York: Smithmark Publishers, 1995), 20-21.
3. Louise Brooks, *Lulu in Hollywood* (1984; Minneapolis: University of Minnesota Press, 2000), 79-80.
4. Ibid.
5. Anthony Slide, ed., *D. W. Griffith Interviews* (Conversations with Filmmakers Series, 2012), 164.
6. Mack Sennett, *King of Comedy* (1954; repr., San Francisco: Mercury House, 1990), 51-52.
7. Anthony Slide, *The Griffith Actresses* (New York: Barnes, 1973), 151.
8. Gish, *The Movies, Mr. Griffith & Me*, 221; David W. Menefee, *The First Female Stars: Women of the Silent Era* (Westport, Conn.: Praeger, 2004), 51.
9. Gish, *The Movies, Mr. Griffith & Me*, 203; Richard Schickel, *D. W. Griffith: An American Life* (New York: Touchstone, 1985), 387; Robert M. Henderson, *D. W. Griffith: His Life and Work* (New York: Oxford University Press, 1972), 257.
10. Kevin Brownlow, *The Parade's Gone By . . .* (Berkeley: University of California Press, 1968), 87.
11. Henderson, 257.
12. Brownlow, 87, 90; Anthony Slide, *Silent Players: A Biographical and Autobiographical Study of 100 Silent Film Actors and Actresses* (Lexington: University Press of Kentucky, 2002), 101.
13. Brownlow, 90.
14. Schickel, 413.
15. *Hollywood on the Hudson*, 53.
16. Brownlow, 91.
17. James Hart, ed., *The Man Who Invented Hollywood: The Autobiography of D. W. Griffith* (Louisville, KY: Touchstone, 1972), 55.
18. *NYHT*, August 4, 1925. Hart, *The Man Who Invented Hollywood*, 55.
19. *Theatre Magazine*, October 1925, 12; *NYT*, August 9, 1925, 23.
20. *New York Sun*, August 5, 1925, scrapbook #11, WCFP; *NYT*, August 3, 1925; *Film Daily*, August 9, 1925, scrapbook #11, WCFP.
21. Schickel, *D. W. Griffith*, 513; *Life*, August 27, 1925; *Screenland*, October 1925; Slide, ed., *D. W. Griffith Interviews*, 164.

22. *Sally of the Sawdust* Press Book, September 10, 1925, LC-MPD.
23. *New Yorker*, August 8, 1925; *LAT*, September 4, 1925.
24. *Brooklyn Times*, August 16, 1925, scrapbook #11, WCFP; *Sally of the Sawdust* Press Book, September 10, 1925.
25. *LAT*, September 4, 1925, A9.; *Sally of the Sawdust* Press Book.
26. Arthur M. Longworthy, "W. C. Fields—and Why?" *Park Avenue Social Bulletin*, August 1925.
27. David T. Rocks, *W. C. Fields—An Annotated Guide* (Jefferson, NC: McFarland, 1993), 17.

# CHAPTER 9

## "A Very Lame Idea"

Two weeks after the release of *Sally of the Sawdust*, shooting started for *That Royle Girl*, based on a *Cosmopolitan* story and a novel by Edwin Balmer, a Chicago-born novelist and *Redbook* magazine writer. Several directors had rejected the assignment, including Griffith, who initially refused to accept the picture because of its dreadful script and its theme, a Chicago underworld melodrama. "I begged Mr. Lasky to let me out of doing this picture, as I did not think I could make the right kind of picture out of it." Lasky tried to charm him by appealing to his vanity: "Only he could turn this drab material into a hit." Griffith had no choice after executives at Famous Players-Lasky coerced him by reminding the director that he was under contract.[1]

As production head at Astoria, William LeBaron was also under pressure to churn out over a hundred films annually for Paramount's large chain of film theaters. LeBaron convinced Griffith that despite the weak plot, the picture would be quickly forgotten "by the unending flood of films rushing through the world's theaters." LeBaron did not want Zukor or Lasky to storm "out of their offices, sniffing and snorting." As for Griffith, he depended on the studio's story department to have available projects suitable for filming. Unfortunately, all that was available was *That Royle Girl*.[2]

Nine years had passed since *The Birth of a Nation*. During that time, the leading Hollywood studios known as the Big Five (Paramount, MGM, Warner Bros., 20th Century-Fox, and RKO) had started to evolve into a vast industrial system dependent on profit rather than art. Standing at the apex with its large roster of stars, directors, and business executives, was Paramount, with its money-making vertical integration, a system that interlocked its production, distribution, and exhibition branches. A visionary, idealist, and creative artist, Griffith remained tied to his principles and was slow to recognize that he was now a cog in a machine.

During early September 1925 and after filming had started, Lasky announced that Fields had joined the cast of *That Royle Girl* (1925) under Griffith's direction. To add humor, Fields was employed to impersonate a pathetic dipsomaniac swindler—"a loveable old rascal of a father," said Griffith, "too weak to earn an honest living, but with a Micawber-like humor that could polish off the rough edges of life with laughter."[3]

After considerable squabbling with the studio, Fields was paid $2,500 per week, twice the salary he received for *Sally of the Sawdust*. A newspaper writer insinuated that his rise in salary was a "matter of conceit" and that he had been "slightly affected by his sudden rise to screen prominence." Fields set the record straight by writing a rancorous letter to the *Daily Mirror* that he cut his price for Sally "because I knew I would get the benefit of the masterful direction of D. W. Griffith, whom I consider the most patient and greatest . . . of any director living."[4]

In the letter he wrote flattering kudos that stand as the most exceptional praise he ever gave any director. "Any and all success I had in *Sally of the Sawdust* is entirely due to D. W. Griffith. I knew nothing of the screen and would never have the temerity to go to D. W. Griffith and ask him to take a scene, never again. To me, D. W. Griffith is the last word. If he is satisfied with the scene, why would I, who know nothing about the screen, and less than nothing about direction, ask to have a scene retaken."[5]

While filming *That Royle Girl*, Fields continued his performances at the 1925 Ziegfeld *Follies*. A movie magazine writer visited him at the New Amsterdam Theatre, the revue's splendiferous home. "I caught him in his dressing room . . . about 10 p.m." As the star, Fields occupied a premier dressing room where "the dazzling beauties of the chorus" ran "up and down the stairs that led by his door." Sometimes Bill would invite a few chorines in to visit for a drink from his homemade bar fashioned from his steam trunk. The writer was stunned about the setting. It "was mighty different from that in which I usually talk about pictures with a star." That Fields could do double duty appearing on the stage and a film set on the same day amazed the writer. "Fields intends to give about half his time hereafter to motion pictures, and half to the speaking stage," he wrote.[6]

In *That Royle Girl* Fields again plays the father of Carol Dempster's character, Joan Daisy Royle, described as a Chicago "jazzy, beautiful modiste's mannequin." Joan gets involved with a shady bandleader and jazz musician (Harrison Ford) in the Chicago underworld. The bandleader is accused of murdering his estranged wife, but Joan Royle successfully proves he is innocent, and a bootlegger is found guilty of the crime. Royle falls in love with the DA prosecuting the case.[7]

A visitor to the set of *That Royle Girl* witnessed Griffith's method of rehearsing his performers. At 9:00 a.m. the director discusses with his actors the scene that is to be filmed that day. "When he has a scene rehearsed to the point where everybody is following the story with close attention, he knows he has achieved perfection. Then the camera work is done. The process is slow, the results startling." In his autobiography Griffith remembers, "We wrote no scripts. I never did for any of my pictures. We would get the idea of the story, carry it around, eat over it; walk over it; drink over it; dream over it until every action and scene was catalogued in our minds. Then we would start rehearsing." It took two months to rehearse *The Birth of a Nation*. "Each actor knew thoroughly every scene he was to play, and there were four hundred separate scenes in *The Birth of a Nation*."[8]

Griffith shot *That Royle Girl* in Chicago, particularly in the Wilson Avenue district known for its vice and drug crimes. There are numerous exterior shots of Chicago, including the Loop, Lake Shore Drive, and the Cook County Jail, among others. Joan Royle is an idealist who worships Abraham Lincoln and often visits Saint-Gaudens' statue of the president in Lincoln Park. During the 1920s, Chicago was noted for its multi-facetted corruption: "its bawdry night life, gangsters, bootleggers, garish roadhouses, flashy men, and tawdry women." Griffith attempts to recreate a city that illuminates "ultra-modern jazz life." The picture depicts "roadhouses, restaurants, cafés, jazz bands, pistol shots . . . walking on roofs, a murder trial, and a hanging."[9]

To boost the film's flimsy plot, and to add to its drama, Griffith orchestrated a destructive cyclone effect. The whirling propellers of two dozen planes blew large amounts of water ejected from fire hoses in a windy spray over the set. Griffith had also used this type of dramatic spectacle in *One Exciting Night* (1922). For *That Royle Girl*, the cyclone scene was shot on a football field near the Astoria Studio, where stagehands built an entire village. Nineteen cameramen wearing protective goggles were employed for the sequence. "Whole buildings are blown away, houses, stores and churches collapse, pieces of roof and walls, as well as trees and telegraph poles fly through space, and the torrential rain takes on the proportions of a veritable flood." The cyclone sequence cost the studio $200,000, which caused the project to exceed its budget and add to Griffith's financial woes. The spine-chilling sequence typified the director's penchant to create a "cataclysmic act of nature" in his pictures. The cyclone was "the only elemental thing I could use that could carry on and culminate the fury of life in Chicago," declared Griffith.[10]

Anxious to see the cyclone since he was not in the scene, Fields found shelter by jumping into a peddler's wagon to escape the wind and rain. Hiding under a cover, he sporadically lifted it to see the cyclone, and on one occasion received a blast of dirt on his face. Believing Fields's actions were so funny, Griffith repeated the scene indoors by having a wind machine shoot water and dirt at Bill every time he peeked from under his cover. Afterwards Griffith asked Fields how he felt. "I'll be perfectly satisfied if I don't have to go through another cyclone."[11] It took four days to clean the dust and leaves.

Griffith was embarrassed to show the rushes to Lillian Gish. "May I see what you're working on?" Gish asked. "I'd rather not let you see it." She recalled "that his voice was hollow, and his eyes reflected despair." Griffith continued, "It isn't worth looking at." "It was a sad meeting," recalled Gish. "In the past he had always been so proud to show his latest rushes."[12]

After *That Royle Girl* premiered at New York's Strand Theatre, Griffith told the audience that his chief goal in making the film was to present enough entertainment to keep viewers from going to sleep. To reach his goal, he had enhanced his film with a "pleasure-craving flapper's adventure in the fast, rough, roaring jazz-belt and underworld of Chicago." He was embarrassed about making a picture for financial reasons. "Sometimes a director," said Griffith,

*Figure 9.1 Left to right: D. W. Griffith, William LeBaron, and Alfred Zukor. The three magnates presided over Fields's silent career at Astoria.*

"may indulge his art visions and creative dreams . . . but he has to square up at the box office on his batting average now and again."[13]

In a ten-page letter to Zukor, Paramount's head, Griffith explained his frustration. "I begged Mr. Lasky to let me get out of doing this picture, as I did not think I could make the right kind of picture out of it." As a Paramount contract director, Griffith was imprisoned in Hollywood's growing studio system interested in producing financial blockbusters rather than artistic classics. Paramount executives needed box-office winners for their large theater chain. Griffith apologized to Zukor by putting the blame on the material: "I was forced to do the best I could with a very lame idea."[14] But his so-called "lame idea" presented possibilities to direct a picture that revealed a significant chapter in America's social history.

Adding to Griffith's disappointment were the mediocre notices. Since the 114-minute ten-reel film is lost, reviews remain one of the only ways to judge the movie. After attending the film's premier on January 17, 1926, the critic for *Film Daily* wrote his review. "Griffith plays it straight to the box-office and hits the mark. The picture runs long, but the whirlwind climax is sure to send them out forgetting all about it." *The New Yorker* called Griffith "the grand master of moralistic-melodramatic balderdash." As for the nearly two-hour "long-winded" film, "there's nothing . . . worth saying about [it]." It is the "poorest thing Griffith has turned out in a great many years."[15]

Among the film critics was Carl Sandburg, the Pulitzer-Prize winning poet and author of more than forty books, including a six-volume biography of Abraham Lincoln, four books of poetry, several children's tales, and a groundbreaking study on folk music, *The American Songbag* (1927). On September 12, 1920, he wrote to Alice Corbin Henderson, co-founder of the journal *Poetry*, "I am the cinema expert, the critic of the silent celluloid for the *[Chicago] Daily News*." A fervent advocate of silent pictures, Sandburg wrote more than 2,000 columns published daily between 1920 and 1928, under the headline *The Movies Are*. He habitually saw many pictures on Sunday and then wrote his reviews, enough to fulfill his daily commitment. Sandburg took his job seriously, not as a theorist but as a newspaperman who recognized the importance of movies as a new art form. His goal was to point out the good pictures and criticize the bad ones.

A Chicago aficionado, Sandburg was obviously interested in *That Royle Girl* and its scenes of the Windy City. In his column he noted that this was Griffith's second film in six months, and that now he was under contract to Famous Players-Lasky to direct box-office winners. Consequently, he had lost his independence. "The time was when Griffith was doing his own producing, picking the stories

*Figure 9.2 Fields in front of the damage from the cyclone. Author's Collection.*

for his pictures and taking a year or a yefar and a half to finish one movie." Instead of art, Griffith's goal was now "getting the interest of the audience, holding the moviegoers in their seats, suspense, shock, thrills or melodrama." Sandburg judged a movie by the reaction of the audience. "An entertaining movie . . . held onlookers with the suspense of interest, the laughter and the thrills that they seek."[16] As a paid journalist, Sandburg avoided dissecting a film and instead mainly reported on a picture's appeal to an audience—its value as entertainment. In an earlier favorable review of *Sally of the Sawdust*, he called the picture "among the best of the year." He spent three paragraphs praising Carol Dempster's ability to merge "monkeyshines and majesty," while Fields received one sentence. In his review of *Sally of the Sawdust* Sandburg wrote: "W. C. Fields as Prof. Eustace McGargle, spieler, faker, and three-card man, is also a new development." Compared to *That Royle Girl*, Sandburg believed that Griffith was more at home in this picture. "Griffith still keeps his hand; he has superb qualities and maintains his leadership among the entertainers.... We recommend *Sally of the Sawdust* as entertainment."[17]

Another passionate film devotee stemming from Illinois was fellow poet Vachel Lindsay, a native of Springfield. He authored the pioneering book *The Art of the Moving Picture*, published in 1915. Both poets possessed romantic idealism that lured them to find beauty in the enchantment of film. But they differed widely in approach. Compared to Sandburg, Lindsay was much more interested in theory and the aesthetics of moving pictures. He developed three fundamental categories to analyze film: pictures of action (i.e. the chase), intimacy (i.e. the close-up), and splendor (i.e. the panorama). As pathfinders in early cinema, both Lindsay and Sandburg penned classic film discussions that remain in print.

Griffith had an opportunity to direct a film that recreated life during the 1920s in Jazz-Age Chicago. But he missed the mark. He preferred romanticism rather than realism, melodrama rather than drama, and idealism rather than actuality. Griffith once addressed Lillian Gish and other young players: "You are taking the first baby steps in something predicted in the Bible and called the universal language. When silent film reaches perfection, it could, combined with music, speak to the world without the use of words. Wars come about because people cannot clarify their issues. In future the difficulties could be filmed for all to see and understand, and even bring about the millennium."[18] Griffith had little interest in the film from the beginning. *Sally of the Sawdust* dealt with circus life and outdoor entertainment in rural America during the 1890s (a theme that attracted Griffith, an ex-itinerant trouper), while *That*

*Royle Girl* focused on Jazz-Age Chicago, the center of crime in America (a theme Griffith did not find personally compelling).

Lewis Jacobs, who authored one of the first histories of American film in 1930, felt that Griffith "clung to a moral code which was disdained and mocked as 'old fashioned'" after World War I. "Even when he chose up-to-date themes, his outmoded and deep-seated prejudices were obvious; all his films appeared stilted, forced, ludicrously colored by pre-war ideals. Griffith's great weakness was his inability to move with the times."[19]

The film was one of many during the mid-1920s that dealt with the Jazz Age and its offshoots: gangsters, bootleggers, liberating mores, sexual promiscuity, divorce, and sensationalism, among others. At this time the leader of pictures attacking the genteel tradition and flaunting promiscuity and the new morality was Cecil B. DeMille, who started the revolution with *Male and Female* (1919) and continued with a slew of movies about philandering among the wealthy. The silent screen became crowded with jazz babies, flappers, bathing beauties, speakeasies, night clubs, boudoirs, and petting parties. In addition, the silent screen exuded the worship of materialism found in the reverence for automobiles, furs, silk stockings, raccoon coats, and sterling silver flasks, etc.

Accompanying these changes were pictures about racketeers, bootleggers, hijackers, and gangsters committing unspeakable crimes and often envisioned as heroes escaping punishment. *That Royle Girl* was one of many films set in Chicago, known as the Mecca of crime. The city was ruled by gangsters who controlled specific areas and neighborhoods. Gangland leaders such as Al Capone made headlines during Prohibition by eliminating rivals in the illegal trades of bootlegging, gambling, and prostitution. Fights over territory led to gruesome murders, exemplified by the 1929 St. Valentine's Day Massacre, when seven gangsters associated with Capone's enemies were brutally murdered while facing a wall in a garage on the city's west side. Associated with protecting the mobsters were politicians such as Chicago mayor William Hale Thompson, and the city's police, listed on the gangs' payrolls. Fields's two pictures with Griffith released in 1925 coincided with the year Capone became Chicago's chief crime lord.

Among the numerous films depicting the city's crime spree was the popular picture *Chicago*, which featured all the accoutrements of the unlawful underworld, including a Jazz-Age free-loving bob-haired flapper. She leaves her poor husband for a rich playboy who provides her with all the luxuries she needs, until he is killed. Despite the crime she remains enamored by the exciting luxurious life she has led.

While at Biograph, Griffith had earlier completed several silent pictures about gangsters. Among them is *The Bandits Waterloo* (1908), about crooks' kidnapping a woman, whose fortitude enables her to escape with the gang's loot. More significant was Griffith's *The Musketeers of Pig Alley* (1912) shot in New York's crime-ridden Lower East Side and starring Lillian Gish, whose character is involved in law-breaking. The drama, which features a horrific gun battle, has been described by William Everson as "the first genre-oriented gangster film," which depicts crime as a "social evil," reveals "the significance of turf to the urban gangs," and shows various "examples of police corruption."[20] In addition, Griffith completed pictures about stock market manipulation, white slavery, prison reform, and political corruption.

By contrast, some critics felt *That Royle Girl* failed to bring to life the Jazz-Age sensationalism and violent crime found in Chicago. According to Lewis Jacobs, the director "could no longer satisfy the national appetite" for "speed, spice, and spectacle." Griffith's "reverence for Victorian morality had become outdated by the time he directed *That Royle Girl*." Since Griffith had earlier made movies about crime at Biograph, there is another reason for the movie's failure besides his "reverence for Victorian morality." At Biograph, Griffith was an independent director, free to choose his subjects. Griffith was now a contract director with Famous Players-Lasky and was assigned, almost forced, to do the picture. Once he lost his independence, he also lost his interest in *That Royle Girl*.[21]

Fields's notices were much better. Before the shooting he was fearful that his role would be shorter than in *Sally*. He wrote the actress Elizabeth Murray, whom he had met during his abbreviated appearance in the musical play *Watch Your Step* (1914): "I hope that I will be as successful in this as I was in *Sally of the Sawdust*. But I fear that Mr. Griffith will not give me as much opportunity in this picture."[22]

Fields plays a con man character with many other traits: a "dipsomaniacal slob," deadbeat father, drunkard, and swindler. Despite these contentious characteristics, "there is something loveable and super-pathetic about him," suggested a critic. Fields consequently "insinuates himself into the affections of the audience." Stills show him wearing his habitual pasted-on mustache and different clothes according to the situation. In one still he is standing in an office with his steadfast straight man "Shorty" Blanche from the *Follies*. He wears a zany costume highlighted by a large metal hat, thrift-shop blue coat, and a derby in his hand. Although limited to sporadic sequences, Fields performs some funny bits, including repeating his reliable stage stunt by placing a cigar in a candlestick and a candle in his mouth. Overall he depicts an inebriate blunderer and trickster character, a well-rounded portrayal that will mark his later films.[23]

The critics nonetheless noted his abbreviated role. "There isn't nearly enough of him," wrote the *Screenland* reporter. "He has nothing to do," agreed the *Variety* reviewer, "and does it just like a man with nothing to do would do it." Another critic wrote, "The redoubtable W. C. Fields prances in every little while as the drunken father, but he has, when all is said and done, very little to do with the story." *The New Yorker* warned that if Fields should continue working with Griffith, "he will surely be fired by Mr. Ziegfeld as being no comedian."[24]

Dempster failed to impress the critics. One reviewer called her "a mixture of hoydenish tom boyishness and wistfulness."[25] She changes roles at dizzying speed: manikin, dancer, detective (in order to prove that her boyfriend is innocent of a murder), and acrobat. To escape from pursuing gangsters, Dempster did seven retakes jumping twenty feet from a second story of a window to a ladder hanging from the next house. The studio crew found her difficult to handle and questioned why Griffith was infatuated with her. At age 51, the middle-aged director failed to see her shortcomings as a performer. Unlike the young nimble actresses he had discovered, such as the Gish sisters, Dempster was a bit more mature, set in her ways, and easily got Griffith to succumb to her demands.

Among her twelve pictures with Griffith, Dempster did manage several critically-acclaimed, standout performances. One was *Isn't Life Wonderful?* (1924), dealing with the problems of inflation in post-World War I Germany. In her last picture, *The Sorrows of Satan* (1926), Dempster delivers a convincing performance as Mavis, whose beau succumbs to the temptations of Lucifer, disguised as a prince. He accepts a life of riches, but in the end he returns to his amour. The way Griffith brought out her acting abilities was stunning, thought Kevin Brownlow. "Seeing ... this lovely face in close-up on the screen, you can still feel something of the electricity that passed between director and actress and generated this extraordinary performance."[26]

Despite her success in *The Sorrows of Satan*, she suddenly found it difficult to obtain any more roles. "I don't care to work for anybody but Mr. Griffith," she said. "When he has a part which he thinks is my type I suppose I will play it. I wouldn't worry if I never played in another picture." One day she suddenly burst onto the set of *Drums of Love* (1928) and informed Griffith, "I have something to tell you. I hope you will take it right. I'm going to be married." In 1929, she was wed to the New York banker Edwin S. Larson, and they settled in La Jolla, a seaside town in southern California. Interviewed after her retirement, she said, "I just never think of my days in pictures. I am always surprised that anyone remembers me. It was so long ago. So many of my movies were so sad. Maybe my fans would like to know that in real life Carol Dempster had a happy ending."[27]

Although there were rumors that Fields and Griffith did not get along after *That Royle Girl*, in reality their relationship remained unscathed. To squash the allegations, Fields called him "the best director I have ever had. He gives actors credit for having some brains. He is one of the finest men I have ever met." He liked Griffith's directing because "he lets the player feel his way through a scene. He sits by and watches and encourages. He has you do the scene over, two or three times to strengthen its weak points."[28]

Because they shared a passion for Dickens' works, they once talked of filming *The Pickwick Papers* together. "The more I think of Pickwick, the more intrigued I become with playing the character," Fields wrote Griffith. The comedian had a difficult time selling the idea to studios. "I had several people interested in Pickwick with you directing, but they blow hot and cold." At the time Bill had caught pneumonia, but he promised Griffith "to take the matter up again. I hope you will still be interested if I can interest them." Their proposal became an unfortunate pipe dream. Bill had reached the point in his life that he was only doing bit roles in movies due to his health. Griffith had not made a feature film since 1931. It was too late in their lives to revive the partnership between two virtuosos, one in the history of film; the other in the history of comedy.[29]

Griffith's record in sound films during the 1930s hardly compared to his creativity in the 1920s. Although *Abraham Lincoln* (1931) was well received, he had difficulty adjusting to the stark realism found in movies and film noir pictures during the Great Depression. According to biographer Richard Schickel, his last film, *The Struggle* (1931), a temperance drama, "was an unambiguous critical and commercial disaster. Griffith collected for it a set of notices that were not merely the worst of his career but may well be the worst that any director of his standing and past achievements ever had." His penchant for Victorian melodrama and romanticism had lost its appeal during the era's hard times. The factory assembly line of studio-produced films also alienated him. "Hollywood today is a sterile film—Detroit with emotions as standardized as automobiles," he declared.[30]

An urban legend relates that Hollywood forgot Griffith's innovations in the art of cinema and camerawork and bypassed him as a relic of the silent era. Yet in 1936, he received an honorary Academy Award for his contributions to filmmaking. Two years later, the Directors Guild created the D. W. Griffith Lifetime Achievement Award, but his name was removed from this honor in 1999, due to notoriety regarding *The Birth of a Nation*. For a short time, he worked as an advisor and general assistant to producer Hal Roach. Feeling that his role in Hollywood had reduced him to a has-been, he turned down other offers as a consultant. Hyperbolic stories about his bar hopping ran in film magazines, which related fist fights and landing drunk in jail. "He was out pursuing cheap bars looking for cheap little girls," said Louise Brooks. "Everyone in Hollywood saw him walking around. Of course, no one wanted to have anything to

*Figure 9.3 A disheveled Fields playing a drunken confidence man in* That Royle Girl *(1925). Next to him is William "Shorty" Blanche performing a bit part. Known as Fields's favorite foil on screen and the stage, Blanche was also his valet and all-around loyal assistant from the* Ziegfeld Follies. *Author's Collection.*

do with him."[31] His last marriage ended in divorce, causing him to retreat into a solitary life of self-pity and bitterness. Griffith retreated to Hollywood's fabled Knickerbocker Hotel (home of waning celebrities and nefarious scandals), where he lived alone and died from a cerebral hemorrhage on July 24, 1948. He was buried near his home town at Mount Tabor Methodist Church Graveyard in

Centerfield, Kentucky. In 1950, the Directors Guild of America provided a stone-and-bronze monument for his gravesite.

Fields never changed his mind about Griffith. Bill felt he was a "generous and unselfish character" and a "loveable great artist." Ten years after *Sally of the Sawdust*, his career at a standstill, Griffith told a reporter, "I am crazy about Fields. He has a sweet sadness, a gentility, a subtlety, something about his acting that I can't put into words. He is a great actor, an artist. I am going to get him in a picture where he is the whole thing a little later on. I have the greatest admiration for him." Bill never did another film with Griffith. Though he had the good fortune to work with other fine directors, none possessed the eminence of Griffith.[32]

Numerous directors remained indebted to Griffith for his groundbreaking achievements. "He was the teacher of us all," said C. B. DeMille. "No one can ever again create a film art," stated Frank Capra. "That honor belongs solely to the Master. . . . His concept of filmmaking . . . was so fertile that the concept spread and grew, and finally flowered in the Golden Age of Movies in the '30s and '40s. That Golden Age was Hollywood's real monument to David Wark Griffith. And every great picture made today adds yet another wreath to the memorial." Jean Renoir, the great French director, talked to him several times and came away with remembrances of an "authentic great man" who built "a non-intellectual world of feeling and sensation."[33]

The commencement of his silent picture experience in two features directed by Griffith was a major highlight in Fields's cinematic career. Working under the legendary director electrified him to pursue a new sphere of work as a screen actor. He discovered that the screen gave him more opportunity to develop comedy ideas. "You know, for years they wouldn't even consider me for pictures. Now I can take my choice. And I'm quite ready. I have a number of ideas. I have several scenarios tucked away—wrote 'em myself—many gags that have never been used, an idea for sub-titles that I don't believe have been used." Movies, he felt, also allowed him to play before many more people than the theater. "The eye of the camera," he said, "reaches everywhere."[34]

**Notes**

1. Schickel, 515.
2. Ibid.
3. Paramount Press Book, MPD-LOC; Henderson, D.W. Griffith: His Life and Work, 259.
4. "Mr. Fields Writes," *Daily Mirror*, November 4, 1925.
5. *That Royle Girl* Paramount Press Book, MPD-LOC.
6. Roberts, W. Adolphe. "Confidences Off-Screen: An Artist at Slapstick." *Motion Picture Magazine*, no. 5 (December 1925), 55.
7. Sara Redway, *Motion Picture Classic*, October 1925, in Slide, ed., *Griffith Interviews*, 167.
8. Griffith, *Autobiography*, 91.
9. Paramount Press Book, MPD-LOC.
10. Edward Wagenknecht and Anthony Slide, *The Films of D. W. Griffith* (New York: Crown, 1975), 219; *NYHT*, November 29, 1925.
11. Paramount Press Book, MPD-LOC; *The Films of D. W. Griffith*, 219.
12. WCFALOF, 33.
13. Lillian Gish, *The Movies, Mr. Griffith & Me* (New York: Avon Books, 1969), 291.
14. *The Films of D. W. Griffith*, 219.
15. Ibid; Robert M. Henderson, *D. W. Griffith: His Life and Work* (New York: Oxford University Press, 1972), 261.
16. Arnie Bernstein, ed., "The Movies Are," Carl Sandburg's *Film Reviews and Essays*, 1920-1928 (Chicago: Lake Claremont Press, 2000), 284-85.
17. Bernstein, ed., "The Movies Are," 272-73.
18. Lillian Gish, foreword to Edward Wagenknecht and Anthony Slide, *The Films of D. W. Griffith* (New York: Crown 1975), xi.
19. Lewis Jacobs, *The Rise of the American Film: A Critical History* (New York: Harcourt, Brace, 1930), 385.
20. Langman, *American Film Cycles*, 220.
21. Jacobs, 397.
22. Fields to Murray, August 26, 1925, correspondence, box 3, WCFP.
23. *The Films of D. W. Griffith*, 219; *Variety*, January 13, 1926, 40.
24. Ibid.
25. *The Films of D. W. Griffith*, 219.

26. Brownlow, 91.
27. Menefee, *The First Female Stars*, 57; Slide, *Griffith Actresses*, 162-63.
28. WCFALOF, 32.
29. WCFBH, 424.
30. Schickel, 560.
31. Brownlow, 85.
32. NYHT, November 29, 1935; MPW, November 21, 1925, 229.
33. *The Autobiography of D. W. Griffith*, xii; Schickel, 597.
34. "*Follies* Comedian Contemplates the Open Spaces of Movies," *That Royle Girl*, Paramount Press Book, MPD-LOC; *Stage and Screen*, November 1925, scrapbook #11, WCFP.

# Part III:
# From the Footlights to the Silent Screen

# CHAPTER 10

## *The Comic Supplement*

One day a talented writer, small in height, with waves of curly black hair and a bushy horseshoe shaped mustache, walked into Florenz Ziegfeld's office suite high up in the New Amsterdam Theatre building overlooking 42$^{nd}$ Street. Outside his window, Ziggy, his nickname known on Broadway, could see the theater's massive sign which at night flickered a rainbow of colors into his office. Beautiful furniture, modern amenities, and a large table displaying expensive collectibles, including Tiffany glass vases, adorned the impresario's headquarters. Across his cluttered desk paraded gold, silver, and jade elephant figurines, which he believed brought good fortune to his risky business. In an outer office sat his formidable secretary "Goldie," a potent gatekeeper who guarded the entrance by admitting only those who had appointments.

A notorious gambler at casinos, and a reckless spendthrift financing his productions, the impresario had recently produced a succession of hits and misses on Broadway. A few musicals that starred his favorite *Follies* performers, such as Marilyn Miller in *Sally* (1920-22) and Eddie Cantor in *Kid Boots* (1923-25), were box-office winners, while others starring his wife Billie Burke in *Annie Dear* (1924-25), and Leon Errol in *Louie the 14$^{th}$* (1925), were flops. The 1924 *Follies* had some good numbers, but as a whole, the revue lacked originality and pizzazz. Around Broadway, show-biz bigwigs from producers to critics were asking the question: Had Ziegfeld lost his touch? The impresario needed a new hit to remind the rumor mongers that he remained Broadway's top producer.

Needing a blockbuster, Ziegfeld wanted to talk to the writer who now sat across from his desk. The author was Joseph P. McEvoy, better known as "J. P.," who had recently written the hit Broadway play *The Potters* (1923-24), which ran 208 performances. Gene Buck had told Ziegfeld that McEvoy had an idea for a new musical. The author presented an impressive resumé. Born in New York in 1895, McEvoy first pursued a career as a journalist, and as early as 1919 had published a book of witty verses called *Slams of Life*. Its subtitle, *With Malice for All and Charity Towards None*, revealed the author's caustic worldview.

Looking straight at Ziegfeld, McEvoy told him about a revue he was writing. He called it *The Comic Supplement*, with actors resembling cartoon figures. "All the characters were to be dressed in those brilliant yellows, reds, and greens, and the sketches and dances were to reflect American life as it is lived in the Sunday funny papers." The libretto would feature "the America of the back porches and hawker-ridden alleys . . . bargain counters, lodge meetings, local beauty contests, drinking fountains, marriage license bureaus—in short the America that breathes and chuckles under our nose—is almost virgin ground for the comedy librettist."[1]

McEvoy's subject paralleled the craze for long-running newspaper comic strips read by millions. Among the most popular were family strips such as George McManus's *Bringing Up Father* (1913), Sydney Fisher's *The Gumps* (1917), and Frank King's *Gasoline Alley* (1919). Instead of portraying the ideal of a happy home, these cartoonists were realistically depicting families with everyday problems, conflicts between married couples and disputes with misbehaved children. Readers, who readily identified with their troubles, anxiously awaited the next installment of the cartoons' never-ending calamities. These comic strips might have influenced Fields to take up the subject of the dysfunctional family in his *Follies* sketches. McEvoy's interest in cartoons peaked in 1929 when he created the popular comic strip *Dixie Dugan* about a show girl modeled on Louise Brooks.

Fields's subject matter reflected both tradition and the social changes of his time. His portrayal of the horsewhipped husband hounded by a domineering wife dates back to the genesis of the theater. The beleaguered male spouse is a centuries-old comedic character depicted on stages far back in performance history. It is a "comic type that ranges from the classical Greek stage through the medieval tale, the restoration and Eighteenth century comedy down to modern times," wrote Donald McCaffrey.[2] In Greek mythology, for example, the supreme god Zeus is married to his sister Hera, a nagging and contemptuous wife. As soon as she harasses and manipulates her husband, their union evolves into a petulant partnership.

During the time he wrote his *Follies* scripts, major social transformations were occurring in American society. The power of the male-dominated society during the nineteenth century declined during the early twentieth century. Women began to join movements to assert their rights: suffrage, feminism, birth control, equal pay, and broadened job opportunities. The twenties flapper revolted against the conventions of Victorian mores, propriety, domesticity, and fashion. In its stead they created a new lifestyle: bobbed hair, short dresses, and sexual freedom. Women's liberation challenged the male power structure. The sacrosanct ideals of marriage and family began to be questioned. The dominant male in traditional marriages began to be replaced by the authoritarian wife.

Fields's depiction of the harassed male spouse in his stage and cinema oeuvre reflects these developments. Caught in a traumatic domestic experience with his exasperating wife Hattie and estranged son Claude, Bill underwent considerable anguish while in the *Follies*. Although Hattie did not fall in the category of "new woman," her irksome behavior toward Fields gave him enough ammunition to portray the besieged family man.

McEvoy felt that "The Great Glorifier," as the impresario was publicized, would never bankroll a realistic depiction of American urban life with cartoon figures. After all, Ziegfeld held a passion for creating escapist spectacles. McEvoy was shocked when the impresario declared: "All right, I'll take it. How much advance do you want?" "Three thousand dollars," replied the playwright. At that moment the Ziegfeld-McEvoy partnership, one of the oddest couples in Broadway history, was born. Not only did their philosophical views regarding the theater differ—romanticism vs. realism—but their motives collided. The venerable producer worked with dollar signs in his eyes; the avant-garde author strove to portray the true American scene on the stage regardless of criticism. Recalling McEvoy's disheveled bohemian appearance at their meeting, the suave well-dressed Ziegfeld told Gene Buck, "You should know that a fellow who looks like that couldn't write anything I would like." Ziggy's comment was a bad omen.[3]

In McEvoy's mind there was only one actor to play the lead, a performer who fit the role "like the proverbial glove." That was W. C. Fields. "I wanted someone to play the Great American, the good-humored, frustrated Man in the Street, whose feet wander casually into mishaps and humor ... who is the slightly bewildered and perfectly happy goat of our eccentric civilization. Mr. Fields strikes me as ideal.... [He] is forever raising his head out of what the alarmists call the debacle of modern civilization to crack a joke."[4]

McEvoy and Fields were two comrades-in-arms who shared similar views on the frustrations and absurdities of life. They felt that the only way to reveal the human condition was through razor sharp humor. "Bill's best comedy is gritty, grim, basically antisocial," wrote McEvoy seventeen years after their collaboration, in an article titled "W. C. Fields' Best Friend," a piece widely circulated in *This Week*, a syndicated Sunday newspaper magazine. "The character he plays is an old rogue and a rascal; always drinking, never drunk; always sinning, never saved. Fields is the resilient husband and father, unbroken by years in the marital yoke, uncowed, untamed, snorting defiance." Who is the comedian's best friend? McEvoy asked. "We'll give you one guess: It's W. C. Fields." "Dear Friend McEvoy," Fields wrote after he read the article. "Thanks for the many kind things you 'writ' in 'This Week'. An old-fashioned hug."[5]

Would Ziegfeld agree to Fields playing the lead in *The Comic Supplement* after all their disagreements? Realizing that Fields was now a Broadway luminary, the impresario readily concurred. Liking the idea of working with McEvoy, Fields put aside his animosity toward Ziegfeld, especially when the producer offered him $1,750 weekly on November 10, 1924. The contract gave the comedian considerable leeway in regard to his contribution. It ordered Fields "to aid and facilitate [McEvoy] and co-operate with him in every matter to the end that the parts to be assigned to you shall be adapted to your special talents and ability."[6]

McEvoy had already completed a script, which he copyrighted with the Library of Congress. Bill had at least two months before the Washington, D.C. tryout to his write his own scenes. By the time *The Comic Supplement* opened at the National Theatre in the nation's capital on January 20, 1925, numerous changes had been made to the original script that reflect Fields's influence.[7] The most significant addition is the Jones family, who appear from the plot's beginning to the end. The callous behavior of the Jones family resembles the Flivertons in his *Follies* sketches, which suggests Fields's impact on the revised script. Although he had earlier played spineless husbands in his *Follies* scenes, Fields's portrayal of the belittled spouse tormented by an overbearing wife in *The Comic Supplement* became a crowning achievement.

Heading the Jones family is the milquetoast "pathetic" father, a pharmacist, who is constantly nagged by his wife's badgering. Ma Jones is described as "a tall, thin, sour-faced person who is weary of life and continually throwing cold water on everything Pa wants to do."[8] Joining in the pestering of Pa is their young mischief-making young daughter, Gertie, played by the inimitable Ray Dooley, and their flirtatious daughter, Myrtle, along with her boyfriend, George. The play greatly enhanced Fields's characterization of the beleaguered husband, which along with the con man formed the two pedestals of his comic personae.

Four scenes in *The Comic Supplement* are especially significant: "City Alley," "Drug Store," "Joyride," and "The House by the Side of the Road" or "Picnic Scene." They are not only among Fields's best work on the stage but also form the basis for sequences the comedian will later transfer to the silent picture *It's the Old Army Game* (1926) and its reprise in the classic Talkie *It's a Gift* (1934).

Opening the revue is "City Alley," which can be attributed to Fields since it was not included in the McEvoy script and appeared initially in the dress rehearsal copy. "City Alley" contains one of Fields's most acclaimed routines, "The Sleeping Porch," which depicts Pa's futile attempts to nap due to incessant disturbances. The sketch recalls the time when Bill slept at his parent's house in Philadelphia after a vaudeville performance and wanted to sleep late. Despite his mother's attempts to keep the neighbors and sales people quiet, the noises in his home and the street constantly woke him up. One reason Bill chose a stage career was because he hated rising in the early morning. The deafening alarm clock that rang in his bedroom reminded Bill that he must go to work. "City Alley" draws on these indelible memories.

As the curtain opens on "City Alley," spectators see three floors of a back porch above a city alley as dawn approaches. Pa Jones appears on the second floor dragging his bed clothes, makes a bed on the swing, and attempts to get some sleep. Suddenly the milkman arrives to make his morning delivery and climbs the stairs wearing noisy wooden shoes that disturb Pa. The racket increases as dogs howl and alarm clocks ring. The iceman cometh next, a job familiar to Fields who in his youth assisted an iceman on his morning runs. "Ice! Ice!," the iceman yells loudly as he goes up the stairs with a large block. Hoping to mask the noise, Pa hides under his covers. The iceman drops the block of ice on the floor. Pa tries and fails several times to put it into the icebox. Finally, the ice slips over his shoulder and through a window.

Returning to his swing, Jones hears hucksters, including fish, vegetable, and coal peddlers, loudly hawking their wares in the alley. (This is a disturbance Fields knew from working on his father's wagon.) A grinder appears who makes harsh grating sounds while sharpening scissors, which prevents Pa from sleeping. Adding to Pa's frustration is his wife who wheels baby Gertie in her buggy to the porch and asks him to care for the child. Gertie is crying nonstop (superbly played by Ray Dooley). With the baby in his care, the infant screams so loud Pa stuffs some bed clothes in its mouth. But the infant is able to remove the clothing. Hoping to pacify the child, he gives the baby a mallet and mirror and returns to his porch swing to sleep. He is awakened when the baby conks him on the head with the mallet. (This scene foreshadows the many altercations Fields will have with babies and children in his films. The most well-known mischievous brat is Baby LeRoy.) A frustrated Pa brings the crying baby and the carriage downstairs to the alley and leaves her there.

Suddenly Pa's berating and bossy wife appears, setting off an argument between the parents. Ma angrily tells him: "C'mon, you're corruptin' the neighborhood. The very idea! Put some things on."[9] Trying to fall asleep on a hammock, he is disturbed by a newsboy hawking papers (another autobiographical remembrance from his youth selling newspapers). A housekeeper yells to a woman living in a flat above him. In frustration, he hurls a ringing alarm clock down the stairs. He returns to the hammock, lies down, and the hammock collapses, throwing Pa to the floor. After Pa readjusts the hammock, an Italian huckster appears, touting "ripe tomatoes, onions, potatoes," much like his father. Pa goes into his house to retrieve a shot gun, but the peddler is gone. Holding the shot gun, he lies down on the hammock, which falls to the ground, causing the gun to fire, a socko finale to a classic Fieldsian scene.

The next part is the "Drug Store," another milestone in Fields's career. Besides being castrated by his wife and badgered by his daughter, Pa Jones, a polite store owner, is confronted by haughty customers who take advantage of him. A "Proud Woman," played perfectly by the talented Elise Cavanna (a standout among Fields's stock company of character actors), gives the druggist five dollars to make a five-cent telephone call. Since it is early morning, Pa surrenders most of his change. A business man enters who wants to buy only a two-cent stamp (a hilarious bit that reappears in the film versions). Needing to make a call, he finds the telephone in use by the "Proud Woman." "Why don't you have more telephones put in here for the convenience of your customers?" he complains to Pa as he begins to leave. "It's an outrage that's what it is."

A woman arrives who wants goose grease for her child's cough. "Yes, yes, goose grease is good. We have good goose grease, nice goose grease," says Pa. "Oh, that's all right," she replies. "I have goose grease. Thank you ever so much. Goodbye." Another woman wants to buy some cold cream and hairnets, which Pa does not stock. "I don't think you have what I want anyway. Give me a glass of water please." A lady calls who asks for cough drops to be delivered and wants to know the correct time. A "Philanthropic Person" wants the druggist to make a ten dollar contribution to the Society for the Prevention of Cruelty to Armenians. A policeman enters carrying a woman who has fainted. "A Crowd of Regular Nuisances," hoping to aid the woman, grab everything off the shelves and wreck the store. Pa brings many drugs to help the woman, who finally awakens. "What happened?" she asks. "Where am I? Take me out of this awful place." The policeman takes her out through a revolving door. Still dizzy, she returns and falls into Pa's arms. Disgusted, he tosses her out of the store as the curtain falls.

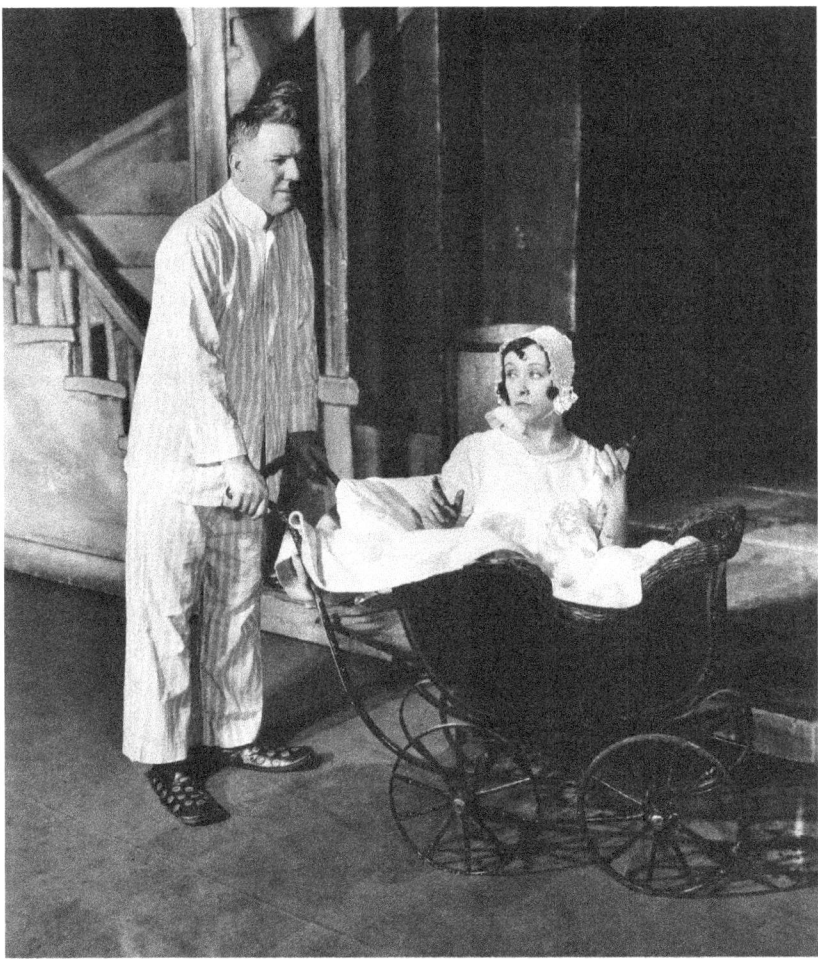

*Figure 10.1: Fields as Pa in the "Sleeping Porch" ("Back Porch") scene in* The Comic Supplement.

The "Drug Store" scene depicts a harassed kindhearted father and store owner under duress by his family and a hostile world. In his earlier stage work Fields played characters who were mostly assaulted by inanimate objects ranging from pool cues to cars. The "Drug Store" scene, by contrast, depicts an aggravated Everyman pestered by his fellow humans, a theme evident in much of Fields's future work.[10]

In the "Joyride" scene in Act 2, Pa Jones, Ma, and Gertie take a Sunday drive in their flivver intending to stop for a picnic in the country. McEvoy wrote a one paragraph synopsis without dialogue about a family who picnic on the lawn of a stranger's house. The picnickers wreck the property, break windows, litter the lawn, and decorate their car with flowers from the garden. The exasperated owner sits on his porch watching the destruction, but by the time he gets his shot gun, the family has left.

Using McEvoy's synopsis as a starting point, Fields wrote the dialogue and added more action. In so doing, he created one of the most hilarious parts in *The Comic Supplement*. While writing, he drew on the unpredictable events of his innumerable picnics. The subject gave Fields an opportunity to fully exploit the destructiveness of the Joneses. Pa becomes a pompous gatecrasher and housebreaker. Fields's hostile feelings about marriage and family reverberate in the exchanges between Pa, Ma, and Gertie.

Ignoring a no-trespassing sign, they decide to picnic on private property. They completely make a mess while there. Gertie enters the house to get some dishes. Returning, she falls on the lawn, scattering the objects everywhere. Pa refuses to clean the mess they have made. The owner arrives but does not complain. The family leave, waving goodbye to the owner.

McEvoy recalled watching a rehearsal of the porch scene, during which Ziegfeld suddenly yelled, "Off the stage, everybody. Stop it. I won't have it." McEvoy sensed "he was on a warpath." That night the two met at the impresario's hotel suite. "I've lost a hundred and seventy-five thousand dollars on pantomime," the producer fumed. "Pantomime comedy won't go." His deep-rooted dislike of Fields and his comedic style was once again bothering Ziegfeld. McEvoy said defensively, "Fields thinks it's funny and I think it's funny, and suppose we let the audience decide whether or not they think it's funny." Ziegfeld balked. "It's terrible. Nobody will laugh."[11]

The producer agreed to test the revue on the tryout's opening night at the National Theatre in Washington, D.C. on January 20, 1925. The program was called a "Public Dress Rehearsal": "Mr. Ziegfeld offers his new entertainment tonight in its entirety and will abide by the verdict of the Washington public as to its elimination." That evening McEvoy and Ziegfeld stood in the rear watching the porch scene. The milkman wearing wooden shoes ran up the stairs and back. "The house rocked with one of the biggest laughs ever heard in the theater," remembered McEvoy. Turning to the author, Ziegfeld replied "See. I told you." "But the people are laughing their heads off," retorted McEvoy. "They don't mean it."[12]

McEvoy had hoped that the usual revue additions to the show would be enough to appease the Great Glorifier's taste. Combined with the comedy were chorus girl dances; bouncy music and songs; a romantic kissing number; a cafeteria march by the counter girls; a city street and cabaret dance; a beach scene with "maidens in very sheer one-piece bathing suits;" a bathing beach tableau; and a scrubwomen's ballet! A team of talented assistants were hired for the music, costumes, choreography, and scenery. Cartoonist John Held, Jr. was employed to design colorful costumes of "brilliant yellows, reds, and greens [found] in the Sunday funny papers." The talented Norman Bel Geddes designed the scenery in "backgrounds of phantasmagoria as witty as they are vivid" and cartoons that illustrated characters "who fill up the colored sections of the Sunday papers."[13]

On the tryout's opening night, the play consisted of twenty-five scenes. As Pa Jones, Fields acted in ten of them, including his venerable pool game routine. In a lodge room Pa and Jake, a fellow lodge member, are discussing the club's upcoming parade as Fields goes through his entire pool routine. He shoots a ball into his hip pocket; catches a ball in his hat, flips it onto his shoulder, drops it to his leg, kicks it with his foot into his hip pocket; makes a massé shot as his cue pierces the table, and for the finale, pockets all the balls with one shot.

Despite some excellent scenes, the show needed considerable cutting and rewriting. Typical was the review in *Variety*: "This one comes closer to being a complete flop than anything Ziegfeld ever sponsored."[14] Fields generally received favorable reviews. "His Pa Jones was robustly comical . . . and at times his pantomime brought shrieks of laughter." Another felt Fields was "funny. But not in three-hour doses." The *Variety* critic agreed: "If ever a man labored loyally and faithfully it was Fields. But Fields for a solid three and one-half hours is too much Fields." But despite "being overworked he scored solidly." Geddes praised Bill's role. "Fields was much more than just a comedian. He was one of the great creators of theater humor as Mark Twain was of literary humor.... I think he reached the high point as a performer in *The Comic Supplement*."[15]

During the tryout's first night, Ziegfeld remained in the lobby, sulking and angry. The next day he sent a barrage of telegrams to McEvoy airing his critiques while the author defended the show. Ziegfeld threatened to close the production before it came to New York. Geddes offered to save the show by offering Ziegfeld one hundred thousand dollars. The impresario agreed to the terms but then reneged. Ziegfeld gave *The Comic Supplement* a second opportunity at a scheduled pre-Broadway tryout in Newark. The production was trimmed to twenty scenes plus the finale. A local newspaper reviewer noted that the show created a new type of revue that dealt with real American life, calling it a "theatrical event of a generation." One reviewer, however, noted the show's Achilles Heel. The revue lacked a "unified atmosphere.... The work of the author, composers, and directors did not seem to be carried out with mutual accord, and as a result the individual efforts frustrated instead of complemented each other... the material for the most part was just a widely assorted jumble of ineffective hokum." McEvoy tried to preserve his realistic portrait of an American family while Ziegfeld inserted uplifting songs and dances to counter the show's harsh reality. By working at cross purposes, McEvoy and Ziegfeld had sunk an innovative endeavor.[16]

Ziegfeld pulled the plug after the revue closed in Newark. The producer claimed he lost $120,000 to $200,000. Critics were stunned that the impresario ditched the show. They could not remember the last time he had closed a production before its Broadway debut. Rumors circulated that Ziegfeld and McEvoy, two incompatible hot heads, had refused to talk with one another. The closing "was brought about not so much by the quality of entertainment ... as by an unending conflict between the producer and the author," reported the *New York Times*.[17]

Ziegfeld might have saved the show, but he was ensconced in his own brand of spectacle and pulchritude. McEvoy's attempt to bring realism to the revue format was a valiant experiment before its time. The death knell of *The Comic Supplement* sounded the loss of a groundbreaking contribution to the Broadway revue. Geddes penned the show's epitaph: "All Ziegfeld could understand was his *Follies* formula. A show like *The Comic Supplement* was beyond him."[18]

Ziegfeld nonetheless agreed to inserting the four major scenes from *The Comic Supplement* in his 1925 *Follies*. "The Picnic," performed near the end of the show, received a raving reception from the audience and critics. A reviewer called the scene "a scathing piece of satire upon the American habit of littering up the face of the earth" and "ruining the premises of a vacant cottage." Finding the door locked, Pa in the typical Fieldsian tongue-in-cheek manner utters, "Why, the dirty rats, they ain't got no faith in human nature." When the pillaging ends Pa adamantly declares, "Why should I go around cleaning up these farmers' yards?"[19]

An important new bedroom scene, "The Nagger," subtitled "Late into the Night—Does Mama Love Papa," featured Fields as the beleaguered husband paired with the attractive blond comedian Edna Leedom as his wife. She is called "The Ball and Chain" for her ability to hamstring her henpecked husband. In the sketch Fields is unable to sleep because of his wife's continual nagging, which ranges from a mundane argument about turning out the lights to accusing her husband of infidelity with a woman named Bessie.

Although no script exists, *Follies* showgirl Louise Brooks, who saw the bedroom scene from the wings, fortunately wrote a description of this important sketch. Fields hears the telephone ring. "Bill turns on the lamp and gets out of bed, sodden with sleep, his hair on end, wearing old rumpled pajamas. He trots round the bed on his little pink feet to answer the telephone." He tells his wife that the call is from Elmer. "The telephone rings again. This time, when Bill says 'That was Elmer,' Edna sits up in a fury. She is lovely. Her blond hair is in perfect order and her lace nightgown exposes her lovely bosom and arms. . . . They fight over the identity of Elmer." His disbelieving wife thinks it's his paramour on the phone. "All the comic horrors of domesticity are revealed by the agonized Mr. Fields in this episode," wrote Charles Collins in the *Chicago Evening Post*. It is a classic repertoire of miscommunication and jealousy among couples. Fields took "The Nagger" sketch and repeated it in the film

*It's a Gift* (1934), with some modifications. The conversion represents another example of Fields's inclination to take a stage scene and transfer the material to the screen.[20]

Although *The Comic Supplement* had a short life as a play, it had an enormous influence on shaping Fields's persona on the screen. "The character I want to portray is the American husband, the boy of the newspaper cartoons," he told an interviewer. "He's so comic he's pathetic, and pathos is the true base of all laughter."[21] The "pathetic" husband became a major protagonist in numerous Fields films. The four main scenes in *The Comic Supplement* are the genesis for the silent *It's the Old Army Game*. Fields plays Elmer Prettywillie, an apothecary and humanitarian, assaulted by small-town folks, his family, and the material objects around him. The besieged character and the four sketches are revised in the sound film *It's a Gift* (1934), considered by many as Fields's best feature, in which he plays docile Harold Bissonette, hounded by his wife and son. In short, *The Comic Supplement* crystallized Fields's role as a beleaguered husband just as *Poppy* had shaped his persona as a benign confidence man.

**Notes**

1. "Ziegfeld Now to Glorify Native American Humor," NYT, December 7, 1924.
2. Donald W. McCaffrey, *The Golden Age of Sound Comedy: Comic Films and the Comedians of the Thirties* (A. S. Barnes: Cranbury, NJ, 1973), 165.
3. McEvoy, "He Knew What They Wanted," *Saturday Evening Post*, September 10, 1932, 110-11; Norman Bel Geddes, *Miracle in the Evening* (Garden City, NY, 1960), 307.
4. *NYT*, December 7, 1924.
5. J. P. McEvoy, "W. C. Fields' Best Friend," *LAT, This Week*, magazine section, July 26, 1942, box 9, clippings 1940-45; letter to J. P. McEvoy, August 8, 1942, correspondence, "M" personal file, WCFP.
6. www.ebay.com/itm, Ziegfeld to Fields, signed typed letter, November 10, 1924, accessioned July 24, 2013.
7. *The Comic Supplement*, 1925, typewritten copy on microform, submitted January 29, 1925, music division, NYPAL.
8. *The Comic Supplement* Script, Act I, box 19, WCFP.
9. *Comic Supplement* Script, 1925, copy, NYPAL.
10. *Comic Supplement* Script, revised 1925, copy, NYPAL; McEvoy, *The Comic Supplement* of 1924, copy, MDS-LOC.
11. J. P. McEvoy, "He Knew What They Wanted," *Saturday Evening Post*, September 10, 1932, 110.
12. *Comic Supplement* program, National Theatre, January 20, 1925, copy. NYPAL; McEvoy, "He Knew What They Wanted."
13. *Variety*, January 28, 1925, box 19, WCFP; McEvoy, "He Knew What They Wanted"; *New York Telegraph* critic quoted in Geddes, *Miracle in the Evening*, 310.
14. *Variety*, January 28, 1925, box 19, WCFP.
15. *Washington, D.C. Times*, January 21, 1925, scrapbook #10, WCFP; *Variety*, January 28, 1925; Geddes, *Miracle in the Evening*, 311.
16. *Newark News* as quoted in Geddes, *Miracle in the Evening*, 310-11; "*Comic Supplement* Flops at Newark," unidentified clipping, ca. February 1, 1925, scrapbook OS49, WCFP.
17. *NYT*, February 1, 1925, box 9, clippings 1920-29, WCFP.
18. Geddes, *Miracle in the Evening*, 310.
19. *NYEP*, July 11, 1925, scrapbook #10, WCFP; Washington, D.C. newspaper review, November 16, 1925, scrapbook #10, WCFP.

20. Brooks, *Lulu in Hollywood*, 78-79; *CEP*, December 21, 1925.
21. Ruth Waterbury, "The Old Army Game," *Photoplay* (October 1925), 102.

# CHAPTER 11
## It's the Old Army Game

After the curtain descended on the closing performance of the 1925 *Ziegfeld Follies* on September 19, Fields, age 45, walked out of Broadway's New Amsterdam Theatre, never to return. Over his shoulder he could see his name on the brightly lit marquee as the revue's star. Ten years earlier—June 12, 1915, to be exact—a nervous Bill Fields had entered the show's side door to begin his first *Follies* appearance as a principal on the playbill.

An invitation to join the *Follies* became a pivotal turning point in his career. He had earlier completed fifteen years as a vaudevillian, touring the world primarily as a juggler in various guises. Despite his never-ending squabbles with Florenz Ziegfeld, Bill managed to appear in seven *Follies* editions over a span of ten years. Fields's appearances in numerous sketches helped him evolve into a character comedian, impersonating beleaguered husbands badgered by nagging wives and misbehaved children, riotous types who surfaced in his films. This persona, the milquetoast husband and feeble father in a dysfunctional family, Fields revived in his films. The same could be said for his other persona from the play *Poppy*: McGargle-type rogues in circuses, involved in all manner of crooked schemes, ranging from selling worthless stock and fake medicine to cheating in pool and poker games. Sometimes Fields melded the two types into a single comic character, as exemplified by Egbert Sousè in *The Bank Dick* (1940). On a few other occasions, he played a completely different character, such as Dickens's Micawber in *David Copperfield* (1935), or Snavely, a Yukon gold miner, in *The Fatal Glass of Beer* (1933).

Fields signed a lucrative contract in November 1925 with Adolph Zukor's Famous Players and the Jesse Lasky Corporation, later renamed Paramount, its distribution arm. The agreement guaranteed three pictures annually for five years at a salary of $4,000 a week, a monetary windfall for Fields, whose starting salary with

Griffith was $400. The comedian signed a typical inflexible studio contract, with several options that gave the company the right to fire him before five years. "Fields is going to be the greatest comedy star in the world," said film magnate Jesse Lasky, an ex-vaudevillian and now the enterprising vice-president in charge of film production. Lasky called Bill "one of the really great finds of recent years." He promised "to give Fields vehicles that will permit full scope to his ability as a screen comedian." Adolph Zukor gave Fields some advice: "You hear a lot about people being helped to high places in pictures. But the only person who can really help you is yourself."[1]

Fields had been a stage performer for an astonishing 27 years when he signed his first long-term motion picture contract at age 45 with Famous Players-Lasky. By comparison, his film career from *Sally of the Sawdust* (1925) to *Sensations of 1945* lasted twenty years. Within the spectrum of Fields's lifelong seesaw career, he had now reached an initial peak period in his professional life, having achieved Broadway successes, good reviews in his recent silent movies with Griffith, a multi-year contract with a major studio, and his first starring role in his next picture, *It's the Old Army Game*.

As mentioned in the last chapter, *It's the Old Army Game* stems from four major scenes in the play *The Comic Supplement* and the 1925 *Follies*: the drug store, the sleeping porch, the joyride, and the picnic. Bill plays the small-town druggist, Elmer Prettywillie, one of "the most delicious scoundrels imaginable."[2] Fields got the protagonist's last name from a building sign he saw that read "Prettywillie's Lumber Company," but it could also stem from "Willie," a nickname from his youth. Prettywillie is one of the earliest examples of his penchant as a wordsmith to create inimitable witty names for his characters.

Compared to the druggist character's treatment in *The Comic Supplement*, he is presented with much more depth in *The Old Army Game*. The motion picture opens with an ironic title card: "This is the epic of the American druggist—a community benefactor. His shop is at once the social center, the place of countless conveniences, and the forum of public thought. It is the druggist we seek in hours of suffering and adversity, and day and night he is often the agency between life and death." Elmer Prettywillie is the antithesis of the ideal druggist. He is kindhearted and sometimes helpful, but he is a bungler who continually makes mistakes and is irritated by his small-town skinflint customers. Fields was so fascinated with the druggist as a comedic figure that he played the character in several other settings. In his riotous sound short *The Pharmacist* (1933), for example, he plays Mr. Dilweg, a henpecked husband and a meek store owner hounded by his small-town patrons.

Fields was on the Broadway stage during the time when writers from the Midwest were lambasting the small-time life where they were born. The group was once called "the revolt from the village school." An early exponent was the poet Edgar Lee Masters, whose characters in *The Spoon River Anthology* (1915) represent unflattering small-town types. Among them is "Trainor, the Druggist," who is the son of an evil couple, his father oxygen and his mother hydrogen, a combustible compound. Trainor, whom Masters calls a "druggist, a miser of chemicals," "live[s] unwedded," is known for causing "a devastating fire," and is "killed while making an experiment," revealing the character to be a malicious figure in small-town life. Another example is Sherwood Anderson's *Winesburg, Ohio* (1919), short stories about unflattering "grotesque" individuals in a small town.

During February 1926, Fields drove his large Lincoln car to Ocala, Florida, for location shots for *It's Old Army Game*. Accompanying him was the showgirl Linelle Blackburn, his newest amour. While performing in *Poppy*, Fields intently watched Linelle, a large buxom blond in the ensemble. At age nineteen, Linelle was on the rebound from a divorce the year before she joined the show. Bill was easily charmed by Linelle, a neophyte showgirl who was twenty-four years younger than he was.

Bill was ready for a new love affair. During autumn 1923, the relationship between Bessie Poole and Bill started to unravel. As Fields attained stardom in *Poppy*, his relationship with Bessie plummeted. Their careers were heading in different directions while they shared a plush suite in the ultra-posh 700-room Hotel Astor (1904) in Times Square. Bill was acclaimed "the toast of Broadway" in *Poppy*. Bessie's show biz aspirations stagnated as she found herself unable to find a job. As Bill's social circle widened, Bessie's narrowed.

Trapped in a downward spiral, she increased her habit of drinking. Her affair with Fields was doomed once Bill and Linelle started their romance.

Fields mainly avoided the Ziegfeld Girls as too challenging and expensive to court. He had a better chance with the ingénues in the ensemble. Linelle was thus the third showgirl after Hattie and Bessie in his amours. At age 43 he still looked slightly younger than his age due to his "baby face." Except for an emerging pot belly, the dire effects of ten years of heavy drinking had not yet ravaged his health. He complained mainly about the constant colds and coughs that had plagued him since boyhood. Bill stayed in physical shape motivated by his passion for sports—squash and handball in winter, and tennis, golf, and swimming in the summer.

Fields found it impossible to have long-term affairs. Since boyhood, wanderlust ran in his veins. As an itinerant trouper in the U.S. and a nomadic entertainer in Europe and the Antipodes, he kept traveling from one engagement to another on a nonstop whirlwind. Avoiding permanency, he preferred living a migratory life, moving from one rented house to another or from one woman to another—from Hattie to Maud (his first post-marital affair); from Maud to Bessie; and from Bessie to Linelle. After Linelle, he was rumored to have short-lived romantic attachments with the actress Judith Allen and his secretary Grace George, before hooking up with Carlotta Monti, a firebrand bit player. Bill and Bessie were together for seven years; about the same amount of time he lived with Hattie and Linelle. Only two women lasted longer than that, Maud (ca. ten years) and Carlotta Monti (sporadically for fourteen years).

Linelle was much different than Bessie. She was fun to be with and she was able to tolerate Fields's mercurial personality. While Bessie hailed from New England, Linelle grew up in a relatively poor working-class family in Houston, Texas, where her father John worked as a blacksmith on the railroad, and her mother, Tannie, reared six children, Linelle being the youngest. Embarrassed about her roots once she became a Broadway chorine, Linelle put on airs that she came from a wealthy Texas family. She hoodwinked Bill Grady, a flamboyant Irishman and booking agent who represented the comedian, who described her as "a Southern first-family belle, a college graduate who dripped with degrees." Linelle was alluring, but not the statuesque Ziegfeld Girl type. The director Eddie Sutherland called her "a rather plump girl with a beautiful face, but not a very pretty body." Louise Brooks described Bill's soul mate as "a large, plump blonde who wore ruffled pink organdy dresses with matching hat, gloves, shoes, and parasol." Brooks mistakenly identified her as Bessie, but the description matches Linelle.[3]

"Fields was a one-gal guy. I never knew him to two-time," wrote Grady, who recalled his first meeting with Fields in his *Follies* dressing room in 1916: "The introduction was a doozy. Fields gave me a 'wet fish' handshake, looked me in the eye and said 'Grady—I hate Catholics and agents' and I was both.... I realized that this was a sample of Fields' off-the-cuff humor. In spite of the remark I liked the guy, and from that time on began a friendship that lasted for many years." Grady's job was to settle his many disputes with producers. As Fields's right-hand man, Grady knew the ins and outs of his client's private life. He thought the seven-year itch ruled Fields's affairs of the heart. "I could always tell when a seven-year amour was ending," Grady recalled.[4]

Grady soon learned that Bill had a stubborn streak in regard to agents. "Fields was a very selfish man who lived for Fields and Fields alone. Any expenditure that did not contribute to his personal comforts was unthinkable." To avoid paying an agent ten percent of a contract, Fields usually did his own negotiations with producers. Grady believed he could have often gotten a better deal, "but Fields had this aversion, and stubbornly adhered to it.... He was very difficult to deal with once he had made up his mind." Grady was angry that Fields often did not pay him for his services.[5]

Grady first met Linelle in Billy Haas's Chophouse, a popular Prohibition era restaurant on West 45th Street, and one of Fields's favorite post-performance watering holes. Grady was sent there to keep Linelle company until Fields, who was taking Bessie home, arrived. The Irishman spotted the "belle" at a table in the back: "I thought there were three of her. She was wearing a big black fur coat that covered a pair of shoulders that could tote a half-ton cake of ice without strain." As Grady neared her table, he saw her smoking a cigar. "Yeah, Pokey told me a little old 'Irishman friend of his would sit with me," she said in her Southern drawl. "Who's Pokey?" Grady asked. My "pet name for Mr. Fields," Linelle replied. "What does Pokey call you?" "Putsie." Cute terms of endearment had already commenced as they had in Fields's other romances. "She was a doozy," Grady thought. "I didn't like this dame, and figured there is no accounting for tastes." He was relieved when Fields finally arrived. "I couldn't get away fast enough. Yup, the seven years started that night."[6]

Grady traveled with Bill and Linelle on their car trip to Ocala, Florida, located seventy-five miles from Orlando in the central part of the state. It was chosen for its mild weather during the winter months, year-round sunshine, and proximity to New York by train. The four-day journey turned out to be a nightmare on wheels. Nearly out of gas in remote Alabama, they pulled into a creaky old station run by an unkempt codger sitting on a rocking chair on his porch in front of his house perched on a hill. Fields stood up in the open car and kept swearing at him to come down. "Fields was at his most vituperative and used expressions that I had never heard before," remembered Grady. "The Belle," as Grady called Linelle, "was soothing him as though he was a kitten." As the grouchy owner started to pump gas, Fields asked him if there was a toilet for the lady. "Most people use the bushes there." As Linelle headed to the bushes, the owner started pumping gas so slowly that Fields told "Mattress Face" to hurry up. "Just for that language, Mister, you get no more gas." Linelle returned sobbing with a torn dress. Fields calmed her as if she were "a four-year-old child" while calling the owner "every name he could think of." After an hour, they finally left, and as the car turned the next corner there on the side of the road sat a huge gas station. That evening they discovered the water hose was leaking, and they had to stay overnight at a run-down hotel with "mattresses that had corn shucks for filling, and when you turned over it sounded like the cracking of walnuts."[7]

The next day the engine went dead just as they drove over a railroad track. Everyone panicked. Fields ordered Grady and Blackburn to run down opposite sides of the track to wave the train to stop. Fields began removing items from the car, starting with the bottles of booze, which he handled "like they were newborn babies."

He spotted a farmer clutching the reins of two horses affixed to a plow. Fields convinced him to use his horses to pull the car off the tracks. After the farmer hitched his horses to the car with a chain, the car moved off the tracks. A stranger, who arrived in a Ford, opened the car's hood and started the car. Before they left, the man told them this was a rarely used storage track; the main line was about a mile away. More frustration occurred when their car endured three flat tires. Fields wired the movie company's business manager: "The rubber had no chance to become acclimated to the nice warm weather of the sunny south."[8]

When they reached Ocala they discovered that the shooting had been temporarily postponed due to a barrage of rain and wind that had damaged the sets. So the trio set off on a sightseeing trip, since Fields had never been to Florida. Soon they were stopped at a railroad crossing with the gates down. After ten minutes the gates had not opened and Fields yelled to the gatekeeper "what are we waiting for?" The gatekeeper replied, "The 'regular' comes through every Tuesday, Thursday, and Saturday." To this, Fields angrily declared, "Well, goddamn it, this is Friday."

Fields bought a bunch of crabs and decided to have a picnic. He and Linelle had gone to a nearby river to get some water when Grady "heard the most terrifying scream and yell." Thinking it was a rock, Fields had stepped on the back of an alligator which hissed and opened it jaws. Terrified, they ran until they returned to the car where the two calmed their nerves by guzzling brandy. During another picnic a wild black boar with large tusks suddenly charged out of the woods, grunting and heading for a steak Fields was cooking. After trying a number of threatening gestures, Fields succeeded in chasing off the boar with a stick. By now, Fields had become a Sir Lancelot hero to Linelle, his Guinevere.

Heading back to Ocala, Linelle decided to ride into town with the car covered "with those beautiful little ol' dogwood blossoms."[9] While Grady watched, the two picked 105 blossoms to decorate the entire exterior. La Belle excitedly drove into town honking the horn. They were stopped at the courthouse where they learned it was against the law to pick dogwood blossoms. Their Ocala sightseeing adventure thus concluded on February 26 with $575 fine.

That evening, they checked into the modest Harrington Hotel, considered the best accommodations in town, where most of the cast was staying.

Fields found the entire crew already in Ocala. Excited about having a film company in town for location shots, its populace believed that the crew's presence would promote Ocala—lure "snowbirds" to settle in the locale, boost its mild winter weather, and drive up real estate prices. The local newspaper and the Chamber of Commerce advocated "that every assistance asked will be given to Mr. Fields and his company."[10]

On a Saturday morning nearly 500 locals gathered to see Fields christen the set. Although the film represented his first starring role, he was already well known to the citizens who had seen him recently in *Sally of the Sawdust* and *That Royle Girl* at Ocala's Temple Theatre.

The event was a publicity stunt organized by the Famous Players-Lasky Corporation. Newsreel cameras recorded the event and the pictures were sent back to New York to be shown in theaters. The audience applauded as Fields appeared in his pajamas, a costume he wore for The Sleeping Porch scene. Accounts differ regarding about what happened next. Fields either broke a bottle of wine over a bouquet of flowers, or smashed a bottle of ginger ale on a plank.

Eddie Sutherland directed *It's the Old Army Game*. The scion of a theatrical family, Sutherland seemed fated for show business. His father Al was a theater manager and producer; his mother, Julie Ring, a vaudeville headliner; and his great-grandfather, J. H. Ring, a well-known actor and playwright. Sutherland learned comedy starting as a Mack Sennett Keystone Kop in many silent movies, including *Tillie's Punctured Romance* (1914) with Chaplin, Mabel Normand, and Marie Dressler. "In those days," he recollected, "everybody did everything on a picture." He served as an actor, stuntman, prop man, cameraman, and editor, among other odd jobs. "It's the greatest background in the world." He called the Keystone Studio in Edendale, near downtown Los Angles, "the barest, most barren, most desolate-looking place you've ever seen—dirty old stages, tumble-down buildings."[11] Although he acted in numerous silent movies, he concluded that he was not a good enough performer to become a star. Deciding to become a director, he asked Chaplin if he could be his assistant, working with him on *A Woman of Paris* (1923) and *The Gold Rush* (1925). As Chaplin's assistant, Sutherland not only learned directing but the art of comedy.

Sutherland had directed four silent pictures for Famous Players-Lasky at Astoria before being assigned to *It's the Old Army Game*. "The atmosphere was just wonderful. I liked it better than Hollywood." The studio's executives picked him because he was a comedy specialist and was reputed to be tough on actors. They thought he could best manage Fields's temperamental outbursts demanding control of his lines during filming. "You can't be a comedy director . . . without a little ferocity," he said. "At least you have to get your own way once in a while, and you have to have a conception of the whole thing." When Sutherland first met Fields, he found him to be "an ugly man, and he was telling me what he was going to do and I was telling him what I was going to do, so we didn't like each other at all."[12]

Sutherland arrived on the set knowing Fields often fought with directors, especially when they rejected filming his sure-fire vaudeville routines. Behind his back they often cut his scenes. Sutherland believed that a funny antic on stage might flop on the screen, and he constantly reminded Fields that screen comedy differed from stage clowning. "Bunk!" Fields argued. "If a thing is funny, it's funny regardless of whether it is being laughed at by a stage audience or a screen audience." "In all the pictures I made with Fields, from nine in the morning till nine at night, we were bitter enemies—very polite to each other, but bitter enemies," said Sutherland, who directed six of his films.

Sutherland became one of Fields's very close friends after they moved to Hollywood, where they spent considerable time imbibing, playing golf and pool, partying, and attending boxing matches together. "Eventually we became, though still enemies in the daytime, pals and drinking companions from six at night till the following morning."[13]

After some time, he discovered that underneath Fields's façade resided a terribly wounded individual, traumatized by his experiences as a child, husband, and father—and that this pain lay at the root of his comedy. "He was a terribly funny man .... an earthy man.... a bright man, keen as a whip, self-educated, but a big reader. I loved [him] very much," he told an interviewer after Fields died.[14]

Sutherland took advantage of Ocala's small-town atmosphere for location shots. Six cameramen were employed in different units so that they could film simultaneously at various locations in the town. The Court Pharmacy on the southwest corner of Main (now 1st) and Broadway was used for the film's interior drug store scenes. In addition to the town's streets, other location shots included the train station, hotels, and magazine stands. For the sleeping porch scene, a three-story set was built behind the Hi-Way Hotel. To stage the fire scene inside the drug store, an old-fashioned, horse-drawn steam fire engine was bought from the Jacksonville Fire Department.

The citizens of Ocala welcomed the crew as a way of boosting Silver Springs, a nearby spa and tourist spot, but the party time interfered with the filming. "We were treated with so much hospitality that the script got lost and the shooting schedule wandered out of sight," wrote Brooks. Leisure time while shooting the film in the Ocala area ended up in an orgy of drinking. Brooks recalled that "nobody in Ocala seemed to have heard of Prohibition. And if ever there was a company that needed no help in the consumption of liquor, it was ours." Fields added to his stock by driving to Miami to pick up six cases of gin from a bootlegger. Near the back porch set, the crew played baseball, with Fields pitching for the Paramount Wildcats. Film production was already a week over schedule when producer William LeBaron saw the rushes in New York and wired back, "All second cameraman's rushes tilted. What are you doing? Sober up and come home." But the crew stayed on because the picnic scene had not yet been shot.[15]

In *It's the Old Army Game* the druggist Elmer Prettywillie resides in a small town in Florida where, according to the next card, "night spreads her sable wings o'er a fair countryside." An ironic statement given that the audience immediately discovers that the countryside is hardly pastoral. "Out of the silence there suddenly appears" on screen a woman accelerating her car, which almost collides with a locomotive. Meanwhile, the small-town folk and the out-of-town city slickers who enter Elmer's drug store are a breed of skinflints and scoundrels. Described as a humanitarian druggist, Elmer is a frustrated Everyman confronted by demanding customers, who want to buy stamps or use his telephone. Instead of selling more expensive products, the kindhearted Elmer caters to the needs of the town's citizens. Unable to make a profit, he is naïvely suckered into a bogus Florida land-speculation scheme.[16]

New characters appear in the film including Sarah, Elmer's nagging sister, who replaces Pa Jones's irksome wife in *The Comic Supplement*, a change that unfortunately eliminates Fields's role as a henpecked husband. Instead of the mischievous Gertie from the play, the film features Sarah's malicious son, Mickey, described as "a combination of Peck's Bad Boy, Gyp the Blood, and Jessie James."

In the film, Louise Brooks plays Marilyn Sheridan, Elmer's clerk. Brooks first encountered Fields during the summer edition of the 1925 *Follies*. She was a stunning eighteen-year-old spellbound

*Figure 11.1 Sutherland directing Fields at Astoria in* It's the Old Army Game. *Bison Archives/HollywoodHistoricPhotos.com.*

showgirl and specialty dancer with the show, her looks highlighted by her close-fitting bob, looking like a black helmet perched on her head. While in the *Follies*, she studied Fields's performances from the wings to learn how he generated laughter. "Fields never really left the theatre," Brooks wrote in *Lulu in Hollywood*. "I have never loved and laughed at W. C. Fields in films as I loved and laughed at him in the theatre.... On the stage, the crafty idiocy with which he attempted to extricate himself from ludicrous situations was unbelievably funny." Brooks was one of many admirers who knew the kind and charming side of Fields. "I adored him. He was a wonderful, kind man."[17]

After Fields and Louise Brooks left the 1925 *Follies*, they were reunited on the set of *It's the Old Army Game*. Casting directors and film producers habitually visited the *Follies* looking for gorgeous women among the dancers and chorines. With her stunning looks Brooks was one of numerous Ziegfeld showgirls to go straight from the stage to the screen. Before receiving a contract, she had to pass a screen test on a set resembling an old cellar in front of prominent director Allan Dwan. Brooks performed a dance that she had learned at a renowned avant-garde school operated by Ruth St. Denis and Ted Shawn, disciples of Martha Graham. She ran back and forth on the set, improvising vivacious uninhibited moves a la Martha Graham. "I didn't want to be a movie actress," she said. "I wanted to be Martha Graham.... Everything I learned about acting I learned from watching Martha Graham dance."[18] Brooks had completed three films at Astoria before she joined the cast of *It's the Old Army Game*.

A talented, expressive dancer, Brooks had recently toured with the avant-garde Denishawn (Ruth St. Denis-Ted Shawn) Dancers, known for their groundbreaking interpretative, free-spirited, and exotic repertoire. In the *Follies* Brooks's perfectly shaped long legs pranced wildly around the stage in gypsy and Apache dances à la Denishawn style. She "steps out like some wild creature of the woods and holds the eye as a magnet holds steel," wrote one critic. "She is tawny in coloring, svelte in outline, wicked in her steps and altogether, a fiery and dramatic young person to whom none can be indifferent." She played a tantalizing "Syncopating Baby" jazz

*Figure 11.2 The Court Pharmacy in Ocala used for scenes in Fields's store,* It's the Old Army Game. *Author's Collection.*

dancer in a boudoir setting and impersonated a seductive femme in the scene "The Paris Girls."[19]

Brooks and the vivacious *Follies* showgirl Peggy Fears regularly visited Fields in his dressing room, where Bill entertained them "with distinction." He offered them liquor from a trunk "which was planted as if it was an object d'art beside his chair," wrote Brooks.[20] After a few drinks Fields was entertained by the pair dancing joyfully around the room.

A prolific reader of masterpieces written by Proust, Ruskin, and Schopenhauer, Brooks had an eruditeness and free-spirited manner that alienated other showgirls, who believed she was a pretentious literary snob. When she arrived at the *Follies*, none of the chorines wanted to share a dressing room with her except her friend Peggy Fears. Lotte Eisner, the German film historian, felt that Brooks was "gifted with an unprecedented intelligence" and "lucidity in her observation of people and things."[21]

Later in life as a semi-recluse in Rochester, New York, she wrote about her troubled experiences in the film industry and the personalities she knew. She expressed her feelings about Bill in "The Other

Face of W. C. Fields," a 1971 article, which was included in her perceptive memoir *Lulu in Hollywood* (1982).[22] By the time Brooks authored *Lulu in Hollywood*, she had become a belated Jazz-Age cult symbol, with her photogenic looks from the twenties splashed on the pages of numerous movie and fashion magazines. Film critics and the public worldwide were simultaneously discovering her films. Topping the list was her intense and sensuous cinematic performance as the erotic, tragic prostitute Lulu in G. W. Pabst's German silent picture classic, *Pandora's Box* (1929).

As Elmer's assistant, Marilyn Sheridan, Brooks is described as "a counter attraction at the Prettywillie store." Every male who enters the drug store is attracted to her, including Elmer, who has a crush on her, but he is not her type. When she first arrives at the store Elmer tips his hat and smiles broadly. He can't keep his eyes off her while they converse at the drugstore counter. When he sees that she is in love with a city slicker, he kicks a door in frustration "This, in fact, was the only picture in which Fields allowed his character to be in love with the leading lady," wrote Barry Paris, Brooks's biographer. "It was as if he let down his vulnerable defenses just this once for Louise Brooks, whom he knew beforehand."[23] Eddie Sutherland, the film's handsome director, wooed Brooks during the filming, and about two months after the picture opened, they married, triggering a turbulent matrimony that evaporated within two years due to extra-marital affairs.

**Drug Store**

Moviegoers first see Elmer in bed awakened by someone ringing the store's night bell. He slowly arises, fiddles with his slippers, and over his white pajamas he puts on a morning coat and top hat, goes down a stairway, and trips on roller skates. The mishap is the first of numerous pratfalls and slapstick jokes. The extensive use of physical comedy reflects Sutherland's taste, and as mentioned earlier, his idea of humor was shaped by his association with Chaplin.

After recovering from the fall, Elmer opens the door, thinking the caller is a person in need of help. Instead, he comes face to face with a well-dressed snobbish woman who was driving the car that almost got run over by a train. "Quick, a stamp!" she bluntly demands. After the druggist obligingly gives her a two-cent stamp,

*Figure 11.3 Lobby Card showing Louise Brooks and W. C. Fields at the soda fountain in* It's the Old Army Game.

he yawns with his mouth wide open prompting the woman to quickly wet the stamp's back on Elmer's tongue. Mistaking a fire box for the mail box, she sets off the alarm, causing firemen to rush to Elmer's store only to find nothing burning. As a reward for their diligence, Elmer serves them free ice cream sodas, and while drinking, the firemen ogle the druggist's striking assistant.

Impersonating the stuck-up customer is the brilliant character actor Elise Cavanna, who had played the phone lady in the *Follies* scene. A fellow Philadelphian and former dancer, Cavanna belonged to Fields's faithful stock company of talented actors, whom he regularly called on for supporting roles as foils or bit players. The coterie included Shorty Blanche, Tammany Young, Sam Hardy, Johnny Sinclair, and Bill Wolfe, among others. Tall and lanky with long black hair and striking looks, Cavanna is best remembered as the sexy patient whose long legs wrap around Fields in an erotic sequence in *The Dentist*. She also played his wife in the Sennett shorts *The Pharmacist* and *The Barbershop*.

The two became lifelong friends. Fields corresponded with Cavanna regularly during the 1930s and invited her to his home several times. When Fields became seriously ill in June 1935, she wrote him asking if she could help in any way. "I love you and cannot bear the thought that you might not be as full of hell as usual." Fields wrote back, "I have a bad case of nerves, just one jump ahead of a nervous breakdown, and have thrown my sacroiliac out, which is the most painful thing that I have ever known of in my life, but I am beating it and in every way every day, I am getting better and loving you more. Your old sweetheart, Bill."[24] When Cavanna retired from the screen in the late 1930s, she had completed more than twenty films. Devoting herself to painting, she became a well-known California nonobjective artist known for her bright, flat-colored geometrical forms that seemed to permeate energy.

After the firemen leave Elmer finds a cigar box on fire. The frustrated druggist runs around the store looking for water in vain. A tube attached to his useless fire extinguisher only emits a weak stream, a water pail breaks apart, and he resorts to refilling a tiny eye cup and spitting on the flames. He finally stops the fire by closing the box's lid and then pilfers a lighted cigar from the remnants. Here Fields draws on his past experience as a sales boy in a cigar store where he pushed over a kerosene lamp and scalded his arm.

Many customers seen in the stage version arrive at the drug store. The haughty woman appears needing change from a ten-dollar bill to make a phone call. A man enters who wants a sanitized two-cent stamp from the middle of the sheet. "Can I interest you in Special Delivery?" asks Elmer, anxious to make a more profitable sale. Finding the telephone booth occupied by the snobby lady, the frustrated customer walks out, declaring, "This is a fine dump, dirty stamps, and not enough phone booths." Elmer receives a telephone call from a woman who needs a half box of Smith Brothers cough drops. "No, I'm sorry," says Elmer, "but we can't split a box—can't separate the brothers."

A new character is Tessie Gilch, a matronly railroad station agent ("one look at her and all the trains stop"). A spinster, she hankers after Elmer, a bachelor who cringes when he sees her. Tessie is played by the comedian and singer Blanche Ring (Sutherland's aunt), a veteran vaudeville and Broadway musical comedy star. A hilarious scene occurs when she asks Elmer to remove something in her eye. She takes the opportunity to flirt with the druggist but he resists her amorous advances. After Elmer removes the speck, he shows her the cotton swab. Seeing a cockroach perched on the end, she screams and flees the store.

The town's greedy citizens become ensnared in a real-estate get-rich-quick scheme. (At the time of filming, the Florida land boom and real estate bubble had just burst.) The sleazy salesman George Parker arrives to sell bogus New York lots to the naïve townspeople. "There's one born every minute," reads a title card, "the daylight saving law had provided Parker with sixty more suckers per day." Promising to share his profits, Parker convinces Elmer to join in the swindle by using his drug store to sell the lots.

Inside the drug store a crowd of naïve country yokels gather to buy the lots. Surrounded by a horde is a swindler making money in the shell game, "a game of skill where the hand deceives the eye." Spotting the action, Elmer approaches the operator and places a wad of bills on the table, well aware that the contest is rigged. Instead of picking the shell which contains the pea, he grabs two empty ones, then points to the other one and walks away with a handful of cash.

The shell game can be traced back to the Middle Ages and perhaps even further. A painting by the Flemish artist Hieronymus Bosch, "The Conjurer" (ca. 1502), portrays a trickster who stands behind a table with cups and balls trying to entice a possible mark to play. Working with the conjurer is a shill who pickpockets the sucker as he leans over the table. The shell game was also known as The Old Army Game, a phrase familiar to Fields who had ad-libbed the expression in the play *Poppy*. It became popular in New York, where newspaper writers used the term. Interested in its origins, one journalist wrote Fields asking about the source of the shell game. Fields told him, "My father informed me that immediately following the Civil War, the circus grifters and con men working the shell game or three-card monte all used the expression 'It's the old army game. A boy can play as well as a man.' The idea was to inspire confidence in the sucker. I really never got the lowdown from Pa whether he went against the game or was a worker, but he was well up on it."[25] The expression has also been used to refer to any rigged gambling game, including chuck-a-lug, a dice contest, or in a broader context any form of trickery and evading responsibility, passing the buck.

### The Sleeping Porch

"The Sleeping Porch" sequence repeats much of the action from *The Comic Supplement*. Trying to get some sleep on a porch swing, Elmer is assaulted by the same unending annoyances: a scissors-grinder, a vegetable peddler (reminiscent of his father), and an iceman (memories of helping Andy Donaldson deliver frigid blocks of ice as a youth). The iceman keeps asking Elmer where he wants to place the material. "Put it down the back of my neck," he suggests. The iceman replies angrily, "put it away yourself." After Elmer tries unsuccessfully to put the block in the ice box, he throws it into the garbage. He gets his rifle to prevent more intruders disturbing his sleep.

His care for his sister's crying baby leads to more frustration. He stuffs her mouth with a cloth, but the baby continues to wake him up. He gives a mallet to the baby who grabs it and beams him on the head. He threatens to drop the child from the second floor until his sister intercedes. When Elmer removes a large safety pin from her mouth, the baby pours milk over his head. He walks away with the threat, "Uncle will give you some nice razor blades to play with." The sequence ends when the porch swing collapses sending Elmer to the floor in a cloud of debris. A famous hilarious routine, "The Sleeping Porch" gave moviegoers the opportunity to see Fields's superb use of pantomime, physical comedy, and sight gags.

### The Joyride

The third scene in the quartet, "The Joyride" is completely changed. Elmer drives to New York in his new flivver in a panic. His customers have discovered that the land sale was a fraud and want their money back. He hopes to find the office in charge of the ruse but discovers the building is razed. He feels lost in the big city and realizes that people are rushing around with no time to help him. A card states, "Prettywillie was just one more Ford in the labyrinth of New York's traffic."

The setting depicts the disparity between small town and urban America. In the unfriendly noisy city, Elmer is a small speck amongst millions, while in his home town he is the neighborhood druggist willing to help people. Unfamiliar with city traffic, he drives his car on a one-way street, and after some narrow escapes, the auto's exterior parts come apart. His flivver stalls, and he is unable to restart the car. He meets a peddler with a horse-drawn wagon. Borrowing his horses, Elmer hitches the animals to the car, but they refuse to budge. He places some paper under their hoofs and lights it, causing the horses to take off with his car.

While in New York he learns that the sheriffs in Florida want to arrest him. He surrenders himself at a police station, but they are uninterested and toss him out. Exasperated by his wretched city experience, he returns to Florida expecting to be tarred and feathered by the people who bought lots. While Elmer was in New York they have learned that their deeds are not a hoax but have become valuable. Overnight Elmer has become the town's hero. In the sheriff's office he tells the officer that he knew all along the lots were priceless. "I never told a lie in my life," avows Elmer, as a portrait of George Washington falls off the wall.

## The Picnic

Before leaving Florida, Sutherland remarked that he "was well pleased with the work that has been done in Ocala. Ocala people have been very good and have given their services wherever needed to act as extras. The Famous Players are indebted to the town fathers for many courtesies." Linelle Blackburn, introduced as Mrs. Fields, stated that she "is very fond of Ocala," and hopes that she "may again have the pleasure of coming to the city." Even the town's citizens lauded the company: "The Famous Players have made many friends in Ocala, and Ocala will always welcome them."[26]

After 18 days of shooting, the crew moved to Palm Beach to film the picnic scene at El Mirasol, a million-dollar, forty-two-acre estate with thirty-seven rooms in a Spanish Colonial revival mansion owned by Mr. and Mrs. Edward T. Stotesbury (a J. P. Morgan partner). Incidents at the picnic sequence are a carbon copy of the stage version, except for Fields's destructive rampaging. On April Fool's Day, "a legal holiday in the Prettywillie household," Elmer

*Figure 11.4 Fields driving on the lawn of the El Mirasol estate for their picnic. Author's Collection.*

drives to the estate in his new flivver with his sister Sarah, her son Mickey, and Tessie, her mother-in-law. He is dressed nattily in a long jacket with a boutonniere pinned to its lapel, striped pants, tie, and a straw boater perched on his head. "A motorist has no rights anymore," declares Elmer when he sees the mansion. "Imagine a man building a house in the middle of a beautiful lawn like this!"

Sarah spots a no trespassing sign. "That's just to keep the bums out," he retorts. Driving full speed ahead, his car rips up the lawn, destroys the foliage, statuary, and other expensive objects. The picnickers find a spot near the mansion where they spread a cloth and begin to eat. Elmer uses a hatchet to break open a jar and the juice splatters all over his clothes. He consumes a mouthful of crackers spitting the remnants on his relatives.

The brat Mickey, one of Fields's naughty kids in his films, misbehaves. He makes faces, sticks out his tongue at Uncle Elmer, and grabs his leg. When the boy gets his hand stuck in a pickle jar, Elmer tells him, "good, put your other hand in." Annoyed by the child's naughty behavior, he pushes the child around. Elmer's manhandling of Mickey reveals another dimension to Fields's persona. Some characters he portrays in his films demonstrate meanness, bullying, or even cruelty. His adversaries, especially the women in his life, felt that his spitefulness sprung from the dark part of Bill's multisided personality.

Elmer encourages anarchy by giving the picnickers the green light to tear the place apart. They have no respect for private property. They toss tin cans, tons of paper, and other junk all over the lawn. Elmer hurls a rock at a woodpecker, which misses its target and instead breaks one of the mansion's windows. Louise Brooks saw the devastation: "During five days of shooting, the litter converted it into a garbage dump, and when the trucks and forty pairs of feet finished their work, it looked like the abandoned site of an old soldiers' reunion."[27]

The picnickers discover that they forgot to bring dishes. "I bet the guy in the house has a lot of dishes," declares Elmer. He and Mickey go to the mansion, but Elmer finds the door bolted. "Can you beat that, they've got the door locked. That guy's not got any faith in humanity. But I'll put a little love in his heart, believe me." He breaks down the door and tells the boy to go inside and take anything he wants. While waiting outside, a cocoanut falls from a tree and wallops his head. Finding a lamp, a grandfather clock, and a large bowl that Mickey discovers, Elmer breaks the items by tossing them on the grass. The boy appears carrying a heavy stack of dishes, but the tray tips and the pilfered goods fall to the ground.

"I guess we ought to clean up a little around here," suggests Elmer's sister. "Want do you mean—this place don't belong to us," replies Elmer. "Don't think I'm going around the country cleaning up farmers' yards." A butler spots the picnickers and orders them to leave. Elmer is indignant. "He's just a servant, isn't he?" The butler approaches the offenders angrily insists they vacate the premises immediately or face the consequences. Elmer starts the car, and on the way out, he crashes into a stone wall.

The picture has morphed from a Comedy of Frustration into a Comedy of Anarchy. The moral at the picture's end: "A bird in the hand is a hard pill to swallow. In a word, never give a sucker an even break–it's the old army game." In other words, cheating and destructiveness are permissible if the target is a sucker.

The Stotesburys, who watched the proceedings, could have sued Paramount for damages. Instead they enjoyed the excitement and attention. "Everybody in Palm Beach is driving by to see what is going on here!" Mrs. Stotesbury told Brooks.[28] She invited Brooks to tea and all the performers to dinner. The crew returned to New York to await the picture's release on May 24, 1926.

The film received mostly favorable reviews. Some New York critics complained about an incoherent plot with a series of sight gags stitched together. This was a repeated criticism in Fields's later films until it was pointed out that the comedian didn't give a "Drat" about a linear storyline. To Bill, comedy scenes made the plot. He felt different after he made *It's the Old Army Game*, which he admitted lacked a strong narrative. "I decided that a picture must have a plot. Picture audiences demand a consecutive story." "Airy Nothings" can get by in a musical comedy, but pictures need a plot. "On the stage a good actor can rescue a poor play; in pictures a good story can rescue a poor actor," declared Fields.[29]

By contrast, the *Variety* reviewer reported, "The succession of snappy gags make for a first-class laugh-provoker. W. C. Fields is first rate as the hero." Except for some New York critics who had already seen the *Follies* sketches, the city's mainstream presses were not bothered by their reuse in a silent picture. Not "a masterpiece of fun but . . . . a subject that will create plenty of amusement," wrote the *Times* critic. "Mr. Fields is busy throughout this production largely in episodes borrowed from his stage skits. The *Motion Picture News* reviewer agreed, "Here is W. C. Fields' first stellar comedy. He "borrows from his stage skits—and those who didn't see him in the *Follies* are certain to find plenty of laughs. He knows how to time his scenes—and he knows how to get the acme of the burlesque out of his comedy gags."[30]

*It's the Old Army Game* is the second stepping stone in the evolution of the four *Comic Supplement* scenes from the stage to a silent picture, and lastly to a Talkie. What the silent picture lacks, however, is acoustics—the din, racket, clatter, clamor, and other noises. Fields's multifaceted humor springs from the visual (pantomime, facial expressions, body language, sight gags, manipulation of props, etc.) and aural (the raspy grating voice, the mumbling sotto asides paired with acoustics, etc.). It was Fields's innate skill for pantomime that he had honed on the stage that shone in his silent pictures. Thomas Hart Ince, pioneer silent picture director and producer, recognized how critical the art of pantomime was to soundless movies: "To act a part an actor must feel it deeply, and so carry this feeling in his consciousness that, when he plays the scene, his reactions are instinctive. The pantomime of eyes, mouth, hands, and bodily movement will seem unconscious if the actor is thinking and feeling the part.... It is only when the screen actor has become a past master of the art of pantomime that the audience is lulled into the oblivion of illusion."[31] *It's the Old Army Game* proved that Fields's visual comedic skills were strong enough to propel him to stardom in silent pictures.

Several months after the film opened, Fields was ecstatic about the movies. "I love this work," he told a movie magazine reporter. "There's always something different here. I used to get sick of doing the same thing night after night, year after year. I don't want to go back to the stage, not for a long time, anyway. There's so many things I'll like to try out in pictures first. I want to do some slapstick comedies and also some work of a more subtle character." It was the latter ambition—"work of a more subtle character"—that Fields pursued as he began his next picture, *So's Your Old Man* (1926), as the harassed husband in a dysfunctional family.[32]

There was another reason Fields chose the screen over the stage: "An actor's art can be demonstrated far more broadly and more quickly through the medium of the screen.... And that's the reason I'm leaving the stage. The reason is to become better known by the public in greater numbers. Through the medium of the screen perhaps I can be so successful as to make three million people in the hinterland laugh. If I can make them laugh and through that laughter make this old world seem just a little brighter, then I am satisfied."[33]

## Notes

1. "*Follies* Comedian Contemplates the Open Spaces of Movies," October 4, 1925, HTC, Fields file; *NYR*, November 7, 1925, clipping, scrapbook #11, WCFP; *MPW*, November 21, 1925, 229.
2. Ludwig Lewisohn, *The Nation*, vol. 117, no. 3037, clipping, scrapbook #10, WCFP.
3. Grady, *The Irish Peacock: The Confessions of a Legendary Talent Agent* (New Rochelle, NY: Arlington House, 1972), 10, 21; *Interview with Eddie Sutherland, 1959*, CUOHP, 117.
4. Grady, *The Irish Peacock*, 21.
5. Ibid., 10.
6. Ibid., 21-22.
7. Ibid., 23.
8. Ibid.; Lisa Bradberry, *Lompoc Picayune Intelligencer*, issue #24, Winter 2005.
9. Grady, 30.
10. Bradberry, *Lompoc Picayune Intelligencer*, issue #24, Winter 2005.
11. *Interview with Eddie Sutherland*, 9, 29, 39.
12. Ibid., 71-73, 105.
13. *New York Telegraph*, October 28, 1928; Albert Edward Sutherland, CUOHP, February 1959, 105.
14. Sutherland, CUOHP. 105, 108, 119.
15. Brooks, *Lulu in Hollywood*, 81.
16. Quotes stem from *It's the Old Army Game* DVD, Hollywood Attic, 2008.
17. Brooks, *Lulu in Hollywood*, 78, 80; Richard and Diane Koszarsky interview with Louise Brooks, Museum of the Moving Image Oral History Program, June 3, 1979, 19.
18. *Hollywood on the Hudson*, 49.
19. "New *Follies* an Absolute Wow," *Zit's Theatrical Newspaper*, July 11, 1925, 8.
20. Brooks, *Lulu in Hollywood*, 78.
21. Lotte Eisner, "A Witness Speaks," *Lulu in Hollywood*, 114.
22. *Sight and Sound* 40 (Spring 1971), 92-96.
23. Paris, *Louise Brooks*, 155-56.
24. Cavanna to Fields, n.d.; Fields to Cavanna, June 20, 1935, box 1, correspondence, WCFP.

25. *WCFALOF*, 36.
26. Bradberry, 5-6.
27. Brooks, *Lulu in Hollywood*, 79.
28. Louise Brooks, "The Other Face of W. C. Fields," *Sight and Sound* (Spring 1971); www.psykickgirl.com/lulu/wcfields, p. 6, accessed August 9, 2013, 6.
29. *LAT*, July 31, 1927, C13.
30. Deschner, *The Films of W. C. Fields*, 46; Mordant Hall, *NYT*, July 5, 1926; *MPN*, July 24, 1926.
31. David Robinson, *Hollywood in the Twenties* (New York: Barnes, 1968), 46.
32. Helen Hanemann, "He Hated Alarm Clocks," *MPM*, August 1926.
33. *WCFALOF*, 41.

# PART IV:
# Milquetoasts

## CHAPTER 12

### The Henpecked Husband

Fields soon found his ideal role playing a different character loosely based on Julian Leonard Street's short story, "Mr. Bisbee's Princess," published in *Red Book* magazine and the recipient of the O. Henry Prize for the best American short story in 1925. A former reporter, well-known novelist and author of guidebooks, Street portrayed Bisbee as a Sinclair Lewis-Babbitt character, who is "among the city's captains of industry, the largest retail silverware and jewelry merchant in the southeastern part of the State." Conventional, boring and henpecked, he is ridiculed by his domineering wife as a "plain stick in the mud." Returning from a convention on a train, he meets a princess whose charm gives him the courage to live an unconventional life.[1]

Street's story was adapted for the moving picture *So's Your Old Man*. Fields plays Samuel Bisbee, a small-town ne'er-do-well glazier and inebriate inventor from Waukeagus, New Jersey, near Atlantic City. "The American glazier is one personage the movies have not yet seen to glorify," wrote a reporter. "But W. C. Fields has taken him out of obscurity and placed him in the cinema spotlight."[2] As a henpecked husband, Bill is nagged by his shrew-like wife and is viewed as an outcast among the town's uppity social set. Meek and subservient, he is a very different character than the shady carnival operator McGargle.

The role of Bisbee was tailor-made for Fields, who played in his *Follies* sketches a beleaguered husband-father (George Fliverton) in a dysfunctional family. Living in the poorest area, strapped for cash, and frowned upon by the town folks for his appalling manners, Bisbee personifies the antithesis of the American success story.

Thomas J. Geraghty, who had co-authored the screenplay for *It's the Old Army Game*, adapted Street's story for the movie. (Fields admired Geraghty's talent and the two became lifelong friends.)

Geraghty made Bisbee a ne'er do well who carouses with his drinking buddies in his cellar and fails to make money for his family.

The sixty-seven-minute *So's Your Old Man*, filmed at Astoria, become a biting satire on the American small town, with its smugness, class distinctions, hypocrisy, conformity, and stifling morality. Although he did not write the screenplay, Bill was able to put his own imprint on the character's development. He had created and performed several stage scenes in the 1925 *Follies* that lampooned small-town life, notably "Back Porch" and "Drug Store." As discussed in the previous chapter, these scenes became the centerpiece of *It's the Old Army Game*, which characterized numerous shallow-minded people in a small Florida town.

*So's Your Old Man* was released during October 1926 when the literary movement known as "the revolt from the village" was in full swing among a cadre of writers, many from the Midwest. Bill met Sinclair Lewis, associated with the school, while he was in the play *Poppy* (1923-24), through Philip Goodman, producer of the play. Fields wrote Lewis in the mid-1930s inquiring about his latest novel (probably *It Can't Happen Here*, about Fascism coming to America, 1935). "Our mutual friend Philip Goodman has just wired me you have written another of your yarns.... Is it published? I cannot find it out here [Los Angeles]. I am very interested."[3]

Goodman's New York apartment became a rendezvous for the literati. An historic encounter occurred here between two famous iconoclasts, Mencken and Fields. "Every time Mencken comes to my house he always asks to have Fields there," said Goodman. Like Fields, Mencken was a fellow curmudgeon and freethinker who attacked sacrosanct American values through trenchant essays. He coined famous words to define the country's Babbitts, calling them *booboisie* and *Boobus Americanus*. He was known for his scathing essays lambasting the bourgeoisie's stifling puritanism in small-town America. "Will you please give Fields my kindest personal regards?" Mencken wrote Goodman. "Tell him that he is one of the few artists I really admire."[4]

William LeBaron, now production head at Astoria, hired talented Gregory La Cava to direct *So's Your Old Man*. A handsome individual with penetrating eyes and a retreating hairline, La Cava at age twenty-four had already achieved a reputation as a skilled cartoonist. After studying at the Chicago Art Institute and the Arts Student League, he worked for Raoul Barré, a pioneer animator. In 1915, he was appointed head of William Randolph Hearst's animation studio, the International Film Service, at 729 Seventh Avenue in Manhattan. Hearst stole talented animators from other studios by doubling their salaries, and hired newcomers such as Walter Lanz, who later gained fame as the creator of Woody Woodpecker. During La Cava's reign he converted the magnate's newspaper comic strip figures into cartoon characters for the screen, among them *Krazy Kat*, the *Katzenjammer Kids*, and *Happy Hooligan*. The animated shorts were exhibited along with Hearst-Pathé's newsreels. The service was shut down on July 6, 1918, once exhibitors banned the shorts in protest of the tycoon's pro-German feelings during World War I. La Cava was undoubtedly involved in the early attempt at animation during the silent era.

He eventually moved to Hollywood, where he directed two-reelers starting in 1922, and live-action features starring Richard Dix. While working as a newspaper cartoonist and screen animator, La Cava developed a keen sense for comedy, a skill that led to his association with Fields and his long career as a successful director.

LeBaron was overly optimistic about a well-matched rapport between La Cava and Fields. La Cava was determined to stand his ground against the comedian's temper. During the filming the two constantly fought over scenes. La Cava believed that "incidents that cause a theatre audience to roar will sometimes fall entirely flat on a motion picture screen." When Fields rammed a car into a tree to demonstrate his shatterproof windshield, the employees roared. "Did you notice the laughter?" Fields asked La Cava. "That may not cause a giggle on the screen," replied the director. "But to get it over on the screen we'll have to break the sequence up with close-ups, and build the scene so that audiences will sense the impending disaster." "I don't see anything funny about that," declared Bill. "La Cava thinks in terms of pictures. I deal in terms of spontaneous audience reaction." Despite their disagreements, Fields learned more about film versus stage comedy from La Cava. "I know that his way is best, and believe me, I'm learning more each day."[5]

*Figure 12.1 Left to right: Marcia Harris (Mrs. Bisbee), Catherine Reichert (Alice Bisbee) W. C. Fields (Samuel Bisbee) in* So's Your Old Man. *Author's Collection.*

At the core of the sub-plot in *So's Your Old Man* is the pending engagement of Bisbee's angelic daughter, Alice, to handsome Robert Murchison, son of the richest person in town, Mrs. A. Brandewyne Murchison (Marcia Harris), the "belle cow of Waukeagus' social herd."

Discontent with the wide social gulf between the two families, Mrs. Murchison, a social snob, visits the Bisbee household intent on squashing the marriage plans. When Mrs. Bisbee shows her an album that proves she is related to the prestigious Warrens of Virginia, Mrs. Murchison agrees that the matrimony is possible.

The pretentious class divisions in small-town America are exposed when a disheveled Bisbee enters the living room wearing a straw hat, sleeveless undershirt, hideous clip-on mustache, and raggedy pants held up by suspenders. He proceeds to show Murchison his family album containing photographs of social outcasts, including himself in prison clothes. "I have never been so offended in my life," says Mrs. Murchison, who now forbids her son to marry Alice because her father is so vulgar. "I'll have you know my father is a gentleman," says Alice, one of several sweet daughters, compared to the many mischievous sons, in Fields's films. "No dame can pull that stuff on me and get away with it," Bisbee tells his family. (Quotes are taken from the titles found on the 16mm print housed at the Library of Congress.)

When Bisbee's uncouth behavior causes the engagement's break-up, Mrs. Bisbee angrily tells her husband, "Twenty years of you is enough to discourage any woman." She is among the numerous dominating wives who scold and browbeat their husbands in Fields's films. Samuel Bisbee belongs also in the long line of badgered henpecked husbands Fields will play on the screen.

Bisbee is a plebian inventor intent on demonstrating and selling his unbreakable windshield. He parks his car in front of the entrance to an automobile convention. Unaware that his car has been moved, Bisbee demonstrates his shatterproof windshield to executives on two similar-looking cars. He hurls a brick at one and hits the other with a hammer, but both windshields shatter. Feeling he is failure, Bisbee takes a train home and tries to commit suicide in the restroom by drinking a bottle of iodine. When he sees a man next to him shaving with a very sharp razor that could cut his throat, he trembles and now fears killing himself. Bisbee's emotional reaction to the man is among the movie's highlights. The sight of a cemetery from the train window reminds him of death, and he decides not to end his life.

As he returns to his seat, the train suddenly sways, and he is pushed into a private compartment occupied by the regal Spanish Princess Lescaboura, played by veteran performer Alice Joyce. She was a former top super-model who became typecast as a society woman in numerous screen roles. "Joyce's eyes were her most notable features: brown, large, and unusually wide-set. She had an aristocratic bone structure, a long nose and oddly-shaped mouth."[6] The character of the Princess, otherwise known as Marie, was supposedly influenced by the visit of Princess Marie of Romania to the U.S. in 1926.

Bisbee spots a bottle of iodine that the Princess is applying to her cut finger. This puts him in mind of his own earlier suicide plans, and, in a moment exemplifying Fields's ability to shift from comedy

*Figure 12.2 Left to right: Charles "Buddy" Rogers (Robert Murchison), Alice Joyce (Princess Lescaboura), and W. C Fields (Samuel Bisbee) in* So's Your Old Man. *Author's Collection.*

to pathos, he urges her not to poison herself, saying, "Don't do it girlie, it don't pay." Bisbee subsequently befriends the Princess and tells her about all his troubles at home.

Noticing a streak of kindness in Bisbee, she decides to help him by visiting his home town. Two Waukeagus gossipmongers spot Bisbee in the train compartment with the Princess, and when they return home they report rumors of an alleged affair. "He's not only drunk, he had a woman with him."

Returning to town despondent and afraid to confront his wife, Bisbee goes on a three-day binge with his drinking buddies. He buys a pony for his wife as a peace offering. Meanwhile, the Princess arrives and convinces the leading townsfolk, including Mrs. Murchison, about Bisbee's goodness of heart. "My dear Mrs. Bisbee—you're the luckiest woman in Waukeagus." "Is my husband dead?" she asks the Princess. Mrs. Murchison is impressed that the

Bisbees know royalty and agrees to the marriage. "By the end of the week the Bisbee home had become the stomping ground of Waukeagus society." Bisbee says to the Princess as she departs, "We certainly slipped that Princess idea over them, didn't we." Recognizing his sudden fame, the mayor selects Bisbee to inaugurate the town's new country club by playing golf.

Fields regularly dug into his bag of stage sketches to find his golf scene. After his pool game spoof, Fields's golf skit from the 1918 *Follies* was the comedian's favorite routine. The golf sketch is another illustration of Fields's penchant to take a stage act and transfer it to the screen. In his private life he was an avid, fairly good golfer, known to gamble against his opponents. Fields plays golf in seven films: four in which it is a sequence within a feature, two in which it is the main subject, *The Golf Specialist* (1930), and *Hip Action* (1933), and one as part of a newsreel. As mentioned earlier, stills from his short *His Lordship's Dilemma*, reveal that he did a golf routine as early as 1915. Its reappearance left him vulnerable to criticism that he was recycling worn-out stage material. If it were not for movie directors who felt it had no place in the storyline, the golf sketch might have emerged in more films. But Fields believed that his theater sketches could be modified and improved each time they were transferred to a new form—from stage to the silent screen and to sound film comedy.

Unlike a pool table or croquet layout, a golf game called for a much larger setting than the stage in order to attain its full potential. (The *Follies* scene occurred on the confines of a yacht!) The sequence was filmed on a golf course, which presented more opportunities to create additional action and to showcase Fields's versatile acting skills that ranged from subtle pantomime to physical tomfoolery.

The golf scene was shot at an unfinished country club at Great Neck, Long Island, where there was considerable dirt on the ground. Robert Lewis Taylor, Fields's first biographer, relates the anecdote that the director, Gregory La Cava, arrived at the club and spotted the cameraman filming Fields taking strokes that caused dirt to fly all over the place and blanket the scene. "You know the golf act won't fit into this thing," declared La Cava. "Why not?" asked Fields disdainfully. "It's not that kind of story," the director replied.

"What about the princess? We can use her as a caddy," retorted Fields. After several hours of angry deliberations, the director convinced Fields that the golf scene should not come in the middle but at the end of the picture.[7]

A still photograph shot on a hot cloudless day in August shows La Cava, cameramen, and others standing under umbrellas with their sleeves rolled up while assistants hold up reflectors to minimize the sun's glare. Standing on the first tee, Bisbee is clothed nattily in a bright blue coat, white flannels, spats, yellow gloves, and a straw hat, plus his habitual clip-on moustache. He is accompanied by his caddy, played by "Shorty" Blanche, Fields's long-term bit actor and general assistant, who had played the part in the *Follies* sketch. (One theory is that Fields purposely hired "Shorty" because Ziegfeld hated "midgets.") In nearly every golf sketch, the caddy is the foil, blamed for every annoyance that Fields encounters.

At the golf course is the youthful Charles "Buddy" Rogers (playing Robert, Alice's boyfriend), who later became a movie star and Mary Pickford's husband. Strikingly handsome at age twenty-two, lean and tall, he was then attending the Paramount Pictures School to develop new acting talent. Jesse Lasky called the school, which began in 1925, "the first step toward putting on a practical basis the motion picture industry's effort to augment its number of artists." Students were taught a range of subjects from fencing to dancing as well as how to fall down stairs and to hold a kiss for three minutes. Rogers was selected among the sixteen students to join the cast of *So's Your Old Man*.

The aspiring actor was told to dress in argyles, knickerbockers, and socks, and to be ready for a limousine that would drive him to a nearby golf course. Once near the course Rogers recollected, "I could see cameras, I could see action [and] people." Then "I saw this amusing, charming, beautiful man with those wonderful golf clubs." He found Fields easy to work with, pleasant, and a bit timid. "I just remember him being a funny, sweet guy."[8]

A *New York Times* reporter who visited the golf scene found Bisbee on the first tee with a large golf bag filled with numerous clubs. As in the *Follies* sketch, constant annoyances frustrate Bisbee. A gooey pie sticks to his club, and electric fans blow pieces of tissue paper in front of him. Bisbee's assortment of trick clubs become comic props for Fields. A driver wraps around his neck. A shot aimed at the second green lands on the eighteenth green by mistake. Instead of a putter, he uses a billiard cue to sink the ball. As a vaudevillian, Fields had used objects to generate laughter, and throughout his film career he continually relied on props and sight gags.

As he begins to tee off, he hears a sound and believes that that his trousers are ripping. When he discovers that the noise emanates from Shorty, who was tearing the lining from his cap, Bisbee becomes highly annoyed. The caddy becomes a scapegoat blamed for every annoyance. Bisbee resembles "an irritable golfer, the sort of player whose shot would be spoiled by a bird singing in the trees," wrote a reporter. "Behind the camera, players and extras were convulsed with laughter each time Mr. Fields, with a very serious face, went through his *So's Your Old Man* sketch on a real course before the camera." The *Variety* critic felt that the golf scene "proves funnier on the screen than on the stage."[9]

While on the golf course Bisbee learns that his unbreakable windshield is successful, and he receives a substantial financial settlement. The newly wealthy Bisbees now live in a mansion on the right side of the tracks. They befriend the Murchisons, and Alice and Robert marry. When the two families depart for a car ride, Bisbee's daughter tells her father that "I'm the happiest girl in the world." "So's your old man," replies Bisbee. "So's your old man" was then considered a longstanding remark employed as a comeback in response to an insult. Although Bisbee's statement has no relation with the phrase's original meaning, the expression was very familiar to the public and thus chosen as the movie's title.

Rather than take a Sunday drive with the haughty Murchisons and family, Bisbee rejoins his drinking buddies for a good time carousing. "If anybody wants me I'll be in the garage for the next two weeks," he says. Despite his new sudden wealth, Bisbee refuses to adapt to the town's stifling morality, prefers to hang out with his old friends, and remains true to his values. Several other films, including *It's a Gift* and *The Bank Dick*, have similar endings in which Fields's characters rebel against affluence and materialism.

The theme that runs through *So's Your Old Man* was quite common in American popular culture during the 1920s. An example is George McManus's very popular comic strip *Bringing Up Father*, featuring Jiggs and Maggie. Like Bisbee, the newly affluent Jiggs is more at home with his inebriate pals at his favorite watering hole than hobnobbing in polite society. By contrast, his bossy wife Maggie is a social climber indulging in the frills of her fortune.

*So's Your Old Man* is the first of numerous films in which Fields transitions from a pathetic milquetoast husband to the family breadwinner through ingenuity and often luck. Bisbee's wife becomes kind to her husband once he is a successful inventor. His refusal to accept the false values of wealth undermines the Horatio Alger rags-to-riches story, which promotes affluence as a panacea leading to happiness.

Although *So's Your Old Man* received mixed reviews, Fields garnered numerous kudos. *Variety* hailed the film as "the funniest picture he has made to date.... It is a series of humorous situations and laugh-compelling bits that follow along in an endless train from beginning to the end." "Fields is great," the reviewer wrote, but La Cava's direction is equally responsible for making the comedy bits go over. Mordaunt Hall, the *New York Times* critic, had nothing favorable to write about the movie, which in addition failed at the box office. The reviewer for *Motion Picture News*, however, felt that the film had its "comedy moments." but "Mr. Fields has yet to ring the Lloyd-Chaplin-Keaton bell." The critic praised La Cava for treating "considerable gags ... with a refreshing touch." *Moving Picture World*'s reviewer pointed out that the movie illustrated Fields's "ripening picture technique ... he is evidently finding that the purely picture getting gags get over better, and he is changing his style slightly to meet the changed conditions." The Fields-La Cava partnership led to one of Fields's best silent comedies.[10]

Lacking sound, Fields uses his wonderful pantomime talent and physical comedy to depict a multi-dimensional character in his second starring venture. Sam Bisbee is a henpecked husband, ne'er-do-well inventor, goaded golfer, and a rebel against small-town pettiness, phoniness, and class distinctions. *You're Telling Me* (1934), a sound remake of *So's Your Old Man*, provided the asset of hearing the various intonations of Fields's peerless voice, which escalated from barely audible mumbling asides to ear-piercing, grating sounds. Although the Talkie has numerous other virtues, it does not diminish *So's Your Old Man*'s reputation as a top silent movie to be judged according to the standards of a soundless medium. In 2008, *So's Your Old Man* was honored by being named to the National Film Registry at the Library of Congress.

**Notes**

1. Julian Street, "Mr. Bisbee's Princess," *Great American Stories: O. Henry Memorial Prize Winning Stories 1919-1934* (Garden City, NY: Doubleday, Doran, 1935), 302.
2. *LAT*, February 18, 1927, A8.
3. Draft telegram, ca. mid-1930s, Fields correspondence file. L Miscellaneous, WCFP.
4. *Boston Telegram*, October 9, 1924, scrapbook 10, WCFP; Mencken to Goodman, February 19, 1932, correspondence, box 3, M miscellaneous, WCFP.
5. "Stage and Screen Laughs Different," *So's Your Old Man* Press Book. MPD-LOC.
6. Eve Golden, *Golden Images: 41 Essays on Silent Film Stars* (McFarland: Jefferson, KY, 2001), 65.]
7. Robert Lewis Taylor, *W. C. Fields: His Follies and Fortune* (Garden City, NY: Doubleday, 1949), 196; *Hollywood on the Hudson*, 46.
8. W. C. Fields: "A Centennial Tribute," January 29, 1980, AMPAS, transcription, 15; Interview with Charles "Buddy" Rogers, *W. C. Fields: The Great Man*, Passport Video DVD, 2004; Anthony Slide interview with Charles "Buddy" Rogers, Museum of the Moving Image Oral History Program, n.d.
9. *Variety*, November 3, 1926.
10. Ibid; *NYT*, August 15, 1926; *MPN*, production file, AMPAS; *MPW*, November 20, 1926.

## CHAPTER 13

### "God Bless Our Home"

The milquetoast-breadwinner theme is likewise played out in Fields's next silent feature, *The Potters* (1927). This is his third starring picture after *It's the Old Army Game* and *So's Your Old Man*. It reflects Paramount's belief in Fields as a silent screen star and as a leading actor. The motion picture is the screen version of Joseph Patrick McEvoy's 1923-24 popular Broadway hit, *The Potters*, which ran 208 performances and starred Donald Meek as Pa Potter. The story originated from McEvoy's successful syndicated newspaper comic strip entitled *The Potters*, begun about 1922. A book was also published in 1923.

Fields and McEvoy were comrades-in-arms in their goal to spoof American middle-class marital life. As discussed earlier, they had previously collaborated on the writing of *The Comic Supplement* (1925), a play which never reached Broadway. Four of its comedy scenes formed the centerpiece of the 1925 *Ziegfeld Follies* and the film *It's the Old Army Game*. In these productions McEvoy and Fields created a formidable protagonist, the frustrated druggist Elmer Prettywille. By contrast, *The Potters* concerns Pa Potter (Fields), a milquetoast character constantly nagged by his family. Pa is described as "a pompously ineffectual man; solid citizen husband and father; with an alpaca office coat and a patch on the seat of his trousers."[1]

The influence of McEvoy is paramount in *The Potters*. A prolific writer and cartoonist, he published numerous books, magazine stories, plays, musical revues, and screen scenarios. In the area of illustration, his most famous work was the popular comic strip *Dixie Dugan*, featuring a show girl (Dixie) modeled on Louise Brooks, which ran from 1929 to 1966. During the 1930s he wrote a popular *Saturday Evening Post* column, "Father Meets Son" chronicling advice for a sibling about life's rocky road, topics ranging from work to women. McEvoy possessed a wry sense of biting humor in *Slams of s Life* (1919) with its theme cogently expressed in the phrase, "with malice for all and charity toward none." His ironic view of life surfaces in *The Potters*, in which Fields plays a middle-class office worker who suffers all types of indignities.

In particular, Fields was greatly influenced by McEvoy's portrayal of dysfunctional domestic life: the besieged husband, the berating wife, and their smart-aleck spoiled children. The latter solidified this theme in the comedian's mind to the extent that the conflict-ridden family was transferred from his stage sketches to his screen oeuvre. As mentioned earlier, Fields had already depicted domestic discord in his Fliverton sketches while in the *Ziegfeld Follies*. In the film, Pa Potter "tries to conceal his natural meekness beneath a cloak of assurance which is pierced too often by the reproaches of his nagging wife and the demands of his headstrong offspring."[2]

In the picture the ideal of the happy family household becomes a sham, a familiar theme that will dominate several of Bill's sound films. Both Fields and McEvoy shared a bleak view of marriage. Bill's feelings stemmed from Hattie, his hostile, pestering wife who refused to divorce him and caused considerable heartache for the comedian. Despite the lack of a marriage settlement, he paid her money during his life, although she and their son often complained that the sums were minimal for a successful entertainer with a lavish lifestyle. Fields was never the henpecked husband portrayed in his movies but just the opposite, a spouse who stood up to his wife and other women involved in his love affairs during his life. A complex individual, Fields possessed antithetical traits: temperamental *vs.* unflustered; amiable *vs.* disagreeable; generous *vs.* stingy; hard-edged *vs.* sentimental, among many other contrasts.

The movie closely follows the play in which Pa Potter, a middle-aged browbeaten husband, is constantly nagged by Ma Potter (played by veteran performer Mary Alden, known for playing motherly roles), described as a plump, controlling "housefrau." Joining the belittlement is Bill (vaudeville comedian Jack Egan), a teenage "wise-crackin', hard-to-manage son"; Mamie (junior star Ivy Harris), considered a "wholesome modern" daughter; and her "college-football-type" fiancé, Red Miller (Richard "Skeets" Gallagher, Broadway musical comedy star).

Playing a milquetoast character instead of a petty rogue as in *Sally of the Sawdust* was a difficult transition for Fields. He said, "In *The Old Army Game, So's Your Old Man*, and now in *The Potters*, my role is that of the dumb guy in the brown derby who always gets it in the neck. From slick and smooth to soft and snappy means an entire mental readjustment, not only in the aim of one's comedy effects, but in the manner of attaining those effects.... Making you laugh at the sucker is something else.... On stage I'd have played the swindler, but in the movies I have to make you laugh at poor, old ... Pa Potter.... There's a little kick, too, in being on the side of the misguided."[3]

By this point in his career he was starting to realize how important character development is in pictures. He declared, "If an actor or actress, comic or otherwise, can concentrate on the character they are portraying and refuse to be hurried or rushed, I personally believe they ultimately will be a success." As a comedian Fields also felt that timing was crucial to depicting a character. "Funny stuff is a failure unless it is timed correctly," he declared. "Timing comedy is like timing the explosions of a motor. A comedian must realize just exactly the right point at which a gag should develop and reach a climax. Otherwise its effectiveness may be lost."[4]

Another time, he noted, "The great thing for any actor, to my humble mind, is timing, which in turn means naturalness." Fields had developed this skill on the stage, where he often used pantomime. "Too many actors hurry their lines," he felt. Responsible for this problem are directors who are "palsie-walsie with the Front Office" where executives "sit in big stuffed chairs and suffer from intermittent, exaggerated ego.... So, if an actor can discriminate between a lunkhead director and a lunkhead executive and does not hurry his lines and is sincere, I feel he is bound to succeed in Hollywood." Fields had already become suspicious of the vast bureaucracy that ruled filmdom, an attitude that would later hurt his film career.[5]

A stage veteran used to audience reaction, Fields worried about the lack of applause during a filming. "The hardest thing for a former stage player to get used to in movie work is to do your stuff minus applause or encouragement before a handful of cameramen and technical directors. You wonder if you are getting across, and there's no way of finding out." He was also plagued by the many hours he had to spend at the studio. He had chosen the stage early in his career because it gave him an chance to sleep all morning after "getting to bed before two or three in the morning. It's hard as the dickens to turn up for work each day at nine." Now he rose at seven in the morning to report to the studio by eight-thirty. He spent his evenings walking in the Broadway area to find one of his pictures playing. "I drop in to listen for the laughter and applause I missed while making the film."[6]

The screen adaptation was directed by Fred Newmeyer, a former baseball pitcher and Shakespearean actor known for his work with Harold Lloyd. The screenplay closely follows the Broadway production. "From the very first entrance we are drawn to this poor struggling henpecked husband, and through his triumphs and failures are moved to smile and even sob, just a little." Pa (Fields) is a plodding, naïve stenographer costumed in a plain business suit and vest, and bow tie. For the character, also Fields sported his habitual glued on mustache, and smokes many cigars. "I used to smoke from twenty to

*Figure. 13.1 Advertisement for* The Potters. *Author's Collection.*

thirty cigars a day—before breakfast and when I went to bed. In fact, I've often been known to sleep with a cigar in my mouth."[7]

In the office Pa buys $4,000 worth of oil leases from a swindler with his mortgage money. He gives one of the leases to his teenage daughter. (The film was shot during the height of the Teapot Dome scandal when Secretary of Interior, Albert Fall, was accused of receiving kickbacks from oil companies.) When Pa learns that the oil leases he bought are worthless, his belittling wife declares, "You're a bigger boob than I thought you were. What did you do it for?" "Because you nagged me into it," Pa replies. "Day after day, morning and night that's all I've heard, money, money, money."

Pa Potter's wife orders him to visit the oil fields to see if they are really valueless. At the train station he enters an unattached Pullman car and falls asleep, later waking only to discover he has not left the depot. Although Pa's leases are worthless, the Potters receive a bonanza when the wells gush on Mamie's property, causing Pa to become a hero. "Pa, I'm so proud of you," praises Ma as she hugs him. "Well, I ain't such a terrible dumbbell after all—am I?" The movie poignantly depicts a family torn apart by the American dream of success and attached together only when the belittled father becomes wealthy. The book ends up mocking the Horatio Alger rags-to-riches tale that money cures all.

The film does have several original sequences that add to the comedy. Among them is Pa and his disrespectful son trying to shave in front of the same mirror. (Fields repeated this hilarious bathroom scene in *It's a Gift*, a good example of his habit of resurrecting an old routine from a silent movie to a sound film and making its reappearance look brand new.) At the breakfast table his inconsiderate son uses all the sugar and cream as his father looks on helplessly (also reprised in *It's a Gift*). Another is when Pa does handsprings in his living room when he learns that his daughter's property has gushed oil. The audience laughed heartily watching Pa chase a taxi for blocks only to discover that the driver has charged him since he began his pursuit. A still depicts Fields playing poker against four cronies, which anticipates the comedian's many future scenes as a card shark. The motto over the door that reads "God Bless Our Home" is completely at odds with the family discord. Fields stars in a movie that lampoons domestic bliss, which he considered a sham through his personal experience with a nagging wife and meek son.

The beleaguered husband who becomes wealthy appears in the plots of numerous Fields movies. In the silent picture *So's Your Old Man* (1926) and its sound remake, *You're Telling Me* (1934), the henpecked husband, Samuel Bisbee (Fields), strikes it rich at the end with his inventions. The same rich-in-the-end scenario is played out in the two film versions from *The Comic Supplement*: the silent *It's the Old Army Game* (1926) and its sound reincarnation, *It's a Gift* (1934). In the first, the druggist Harold Bissonette (pronounced Bis-o-nay) becomes wealthy by buying Florida real estate; in the second it's a large California orange ranch. In *The Bank Dick* (1940) Fields plays Egbert Sousè ("*Accent grave* over the e!"), a bungling ne'er-do-well dipsomaniac who by movie's end wins a three-fold jackpot: a profitable beefsteak mine, reward money for capturing a crook, and royalties from a movie he directed. The harassed husband becomes newly rich in each film, causing the protagonist to be treated as a beloved breadwinner. Bisbee, Bissonette, and Sousè reject the snobbishness and superficiality of the nouveau riche and remain true to themselves. By ribbing the affluent, the films satirize the Horatio Alger rags-to-riches theme.

*The Potters* was one of Fields's six silent movies made of flammable and perishable nitrate stock. Like all the others, it was lost, leaving an unfortunate gap in the record of his evolution as a screen comedian. Reviews, press reports, stock photographs, and memoirs fortunately remain as means to resurrect the lost treasure.

The film opened on January 31, 1927, at Adolph Zukor's new 3,664-seat Paramount movie theater at Broadway and Forty-Third Street in Times Square. The venue represented the flagship of Zukor's massive Publix theater chain, situated at the base of Paramount's high rise administrative building built in the shape of the studio's mountain-top logo.

According to reviewers, *The Potters* was the best film to date that showcased Fields's pantomime talent. "The role of Pa Potter fits Mr. Fields like the proverbial glove," wrote Mordaunt Hall in the *New York Times*. "I think that McEvoy is a realist," wrote the critic Heywood Broun after he had seen *The Potters* twice. "I think he is the sort of stout-hearted truth-teller that the nation needs." "*The Potters* is all Fields," wrote Sid (Sidney) Silverman, the son of Sime Silverman, the founder of *Variety* who had been the comedian's staunch advocate since his vaudeville years. "It's doubtful if his ability as a pantomimist has ever shown to better advantage on a screen.... If there is any doubt as to his ability as a screen subject, this performance should smother it."[8]

*The Potters* Press Sheet reported the final scene: "They discover that the oil gushed out on Mamie's property. Pa bursts into hysterical laughter.... Bill chimes in and another family argument starts with Pa merely listening in. He contemplates a motto hanging over the door: 'God Bless Our Home.'" The wide gulf between the flawed argumentative family and the sanctimonious adage exposes a potent clash in American life.

**Notes**

1. *The Potters* Press Sheet, MPD-LOC.
2. *NYT*, October 31, 1926.
3. *The Potters* Press Sheet.
4. *LAT*, October 4, 1925, 31.
5. Frederick James Smith, "Checking on Their Comments," *Silver Screen*, February n.d., copy, AMPAS.
6. *The Potters* Press Book.
7. *So's Your Old Man* Press Book. MPD-LOC.
8. *NYT*, January 18, 1927; *Variety*, January 19, 1927.

## Chapter 14
### "I'm a Lion!"

A year later, Fields and La Cava collaborated on their second silent feature at Astoria, entitled *Running Wild* (1927). Besides directing and producing the movie, La Cava wrote a bewildering story that gave Fields the difficult task of changing personalities in midstream. Fields plays Elmer Finch, who is hypnotized by a stage magician who transforms him from a mild-mannered meek husband and incompetent employee to a belligerent individual acting like a lion.

La Cava believed that Fields was perfect for the plot. The role of a beleaguered husband berated by his shrew-like wife and ridiculed by his obese, bratty stepson perfectly fit Fields's talent and familiarity with the character from his stage work and recent pictures. "He is only the head of the family on his income tax blank," reads a title card.[1] In the movie, Elmer Finch's character mirrors Fields's double-sided personality. During filming *So's Your Old Man*, La Cava encountered Bill's complex Jekyll-Hyde traits. He could be amiable, but suddenly become temperamental the next moment.

Completing the family quartet is Finch's sweet daughter Mary, played by the ingénue Mary Brian, a pretty, petite performer with blue-gray eyes and dark brown hair. As Fields's favorite screen sibling, she appeared in two other movies playing his daughter: *Two Flaming Youths* (1927) and *Man on the Flying Trapeze* (1935). During her career, she became a romantic leading lady from the mid-1920s to the late 1930s, and in total completed eighty-two films and TV appearances. Before her death in 2003 at age 96, Brian spoke at the Academy's tribute to Fields on his centennial birthday. "No day was ever dull working for Mr. Fields," she said. "I was very privileged to work with him and I adored him, and I think it must have been slightly mutual, because he was the one who would ask for me."[2] Her gracious remark was widespread among the ingénues in his films. Even Baby LeRoy (Overacker), who played mischievous brats opposite the comedian in numerous movies, held kind remembrances of Fields.

The domestic dysfunctional foursome in *Running Wild*—milquetoast husband, shrew-like wife, smart-aleck son, and adorable favored daughter—frequently reappear in other Fields's films. They were initially featured in Fields's sketches for the *Ziegfeld Follies*, "The Family Ford" (1920) and "Off to the Country" (1921), in which he impersonates the incompetent bungler George Fliverton. Fields certainly must have felt that Mrs. Finch in *Running Wild* mirrored his nagging wife, Hattie, and the mama's boy, Junior, may have brought to mind his only son Claude. (In the partial sound remake, *The Man on the Flying Trapeze* (1935), the sissy stepson is named Claude.) The sweet female siblings in his movies, who usually side with their fathers, represent Bill's unfulfilled longing for the daughter he never had.

When La Cava wrote the story, he might have been influenced by H. T. Webster's extremely popular cartoon series *The Timid Soul*, which began in 1924 in the *New York World*. As mentioned earlier, La Cava was a former newspaper cartoonist and screen animator. He might have been aware of Webster's strip, and especially its main character Caspar Milquetoast, a meek, submissive, and cowardly fellow. (Incidentally, the working title for *Running Wild* was *The Timid Soul*.) Webster's figure became so popular that the word "milquetoast," stemming from milk toast, an innocuous digestible food for people with sensitive stomachs, entered the American vernacular.

Elmer Finch is the paramount milquetoast until an incident transforms his personality. To evoke a little luck, he throws a horseshoe over his shoulder into a shop window, causing the police to race after him. He runs into an open door, which leads to a vaudeville stage where he finds the hypnotist Arvo. Thinking that Elmer would be an excellent subject, Arvo hypnotizes him. Arvo causes Elmer to knock out a husky truck driver in a boxing match, demonstrating that the procedure has been successful. The hypnotist tells Elmer he can go out and lick the world. Elmer now believes that he has been transformed into a violent, frenzied, and eccentric king of the jungle. "I'm a lion!" he roars. (Roy Briant, who did the screen adaptation, had recently written *The Adorable Lion*, a full length play on Broadway.) To portray his new persona, Fields discarded his old clip-on mustache that hung from his nose and replaced it with a large, bristly one that better fit his character. "I allowed the mustache to assume proportions befitting the king of the jungle," Fields declared.³

He returns to work, where Finch had previously been a sheepish clerk for twenty years without a raise. Elmer stuns his boss by getting a pig-headed client to pay his bills, obtaining a new $15,000 contract from a disgruntled former customer, and bursting into a directors' meeting, where he criticizes the group for their outdated business methods.

Arriving home, he interrupts his wife's tea party, shouting "I'm a lion!" He then smashes the portrait of his wife's first husband, and punishes Junior, chasing him down the street. These actions convince his family that he is now the head of his household. "From now on, I'm the big noise in this house!" Fearing that Finch will do

*Figure 14.1 Lobby card depicts Fields as Elmer Finch while stepping on a photograph of his wife's first husband, as his daughter Mary Brian (Mary Finch), Marie Shotwell (Mrs. Finch), and Rex the dog appear puzzled.* Running Wild. *Author's Collection.*

more damage thinking he is a lion, the hypnotist arrives and snaps him out of his spell. His transformation into a lion has garnered lucrative rewards. He learns that his boss will now give him a large raise, and other businessmen will offer him profitable contracts. Elmer is now a hero to his family, especially to his daughter, who becomes engaged to the son of Elmer's employer.

As suggested earlier, finding a pot of gold at the end of a Fields movie, which propels the lead character from anti-hero to hero, is a theme that runs throughout his numerous films. Whether milquetoasts or rogues, Bill felt that the characters he impersonated always "dropped their bluff and became human [once] they got around the corner."[4] In *So's Your Old Man* (1926) and its sound remake, *You're Telling Me* (1934), the henpecked husband, Samuel Bisbee (Fields), strikes it rich at the end with his inventions. The same rich-in-the-end scenario is played out in the two film versions from the musical play *The Comic Supplement*: the silent *It's the Old Army Game* (1926) and its sound reincarnation, *It's a Gift* (1934). In the first, the druggist Harold Bissonette becomes wealthy by buying

*Figure 14.2 Aerial photograph depicting location shots for* Running Wild *near the Astoria Studio. Fields's house (upper right); Fields walks to work (center); and Fields drives to work with boxing gloves (lower left). Author's Collection.*

Florida real estate; in the second he owns a large California orange grove. In *The Bank Dick* (1940), Fields plays Egbert Sousè, a bungling dipsomaniac who by movie's end wins a three-fold jackpot: a profitable share in the Beefsteak Mining Company, reward money for capturing a crook, and royalties from a movie he directed.

Despite their sudden affluence, Fields's characters reject the false snobbishness and superficiality of the nouveau riche and keep their original common-man values by hanging out with their friends, especially at the local bar. The transitions from milquetoast to affluence in these films transmit a message. For the protagonists in Fields's films, money is not the answer to happiness.

The reviews for *Running Wild* were mixed. The negative ones complained that Fields overacted as a "lion." "There are times when this comedy is really good, but quite often Mr. Fields overdoes the fun, with the result it falls somewhat flat," wrote Mordaunt Hall in the *New York Times*. "Mr. Fields manifests a fondness for returning to his extravagant actions, and plausibility is flung to the four winds." Although the *Los Angeles Times* critic felt some episodes were "rich in humor," he called *Running Wild* "an intolerably silly picture." The movie "does run wild becoming hokum plus" once Fields goes on a "ridiculous rampage." By overdoing his role as a vicious roaring lion, Bill lost the audience's empathy.[5]

*Motion Picture News*, by contrast, felt that Fields was refreshing, having "discarded his '*Follies* Tricks' . . . which were keeping him back. In this offering he demonstrates he has some different aces up his sleeve." "Excellent," raved the *New York Herald Tribune*. Even more complimentary was Sime Silverman's review in *Variety*, who called *Running Wild* "a laugh film. It will amuse all audiences for a week or two." Silverman lauded Bill as "a consummate pantomimic comic . . . who can handle the comedy, high or low. He classes with Charlie Chaplin in this." The film "needs a comic of Bill Fields' high caliber to make *Running Wild* the sure fire that it is." Silverman predicted that the movie would be a bonanza for Fields, giving him more starring roles and "a wider circulation than any or all of his previous picture productions have done."[6]

But the opposite happened! Box-office receipts were fair. Word of Fields's heated quarrels on the set with La Cava got back to his

*Figure 14.3 Cast and crew of* Running Wild. *In the first row Mary Brian is seated in the center, with Gregory La Cava on her right and Fields on her left. Bison Archives/HollywoodHistoricPhotos.com.*

Paramount bosses and gave him a reputation as a confrontational and quarrelsome comedian. La Cava refused to do another film with him. "I wouldn't direct you if you were the last actor alive," La Cava told him. They had continued their heated arguments on the set of *Running Wild*, especially when Bill changed the script. La Cava was not the easiest person to get along with either, and he was not afraid to challenge Bill's stubbornness. Possessed with a powerful personality, an insubordinate spirit, and a social conscience, La Cava had a reputation as a rebellious director who despised assembly-line filmmaking. He once said that the he preferred actors with a "red-hot, tobacco temperament." Fields fit that bill, and used it to his advantage in the role of the "wild lion." "Psychologically, the temperamental actor reveals a vivid imagination, a highly strung nervous system and animal emotions," continued La Cava. You "can arouse them to the necessary emotional pitch and feeling." Fields and La Cava were electrically charged personalities, so that when they clashed, fireworks exploded.[7]

If anyone knew Fields, it was La Cava. They became good friends later in Hollywood, where they continued their tirades on a golf course rather than on a film set. La Cava believed that pain was the wellspring of Fields's comedy. "The peculiar thing is that although he thought he was being pretty mean, there wasn't any sting in it," said La Cava. "It was only funny. Bill never really wanted to hurt anybody. He just felt it was an obligation. Nearly everything Bill tried to get into his movies was something that lashed out at the world." Fields later stated that La Cava had "a comedy sense not equaled by any other director." Fields admired La Cava's independent spirit. "He was born without fear. I have never known a guy who cared less for what the world thinks than La Cava."[8]

Their verbal tirades staged on the Lakeside Country Club greens, opposite Bill's Toluca Lake abode in southeastern San Fernando Valley, became notorious. Opened in 1925, the course was conceived by the legendary Max Behr, considered by golf aficionados to be one of the best designers in the game's history. Behr was awestruck when he first saw the undeveloped area, and felt it would be ideal for a layout similar to those in Great Britain courses. "The property had a rich variety of natural features," he recalled, "rolling sand dunes, mature walnut and peach trees, dried streambeds, and the moribund Los Angeles River itself that could be traversed to make for interesting play." Lakeside "stands out as his crown jewel" among the many courses he planned.[9]

On the greens, Fields and La Cava engaged in a tirade of verbal abuse, intensified by their high-stakes gambling at $100 per hole and bets on the final score. Liquor was the refreshment of choice as they tore up the greens. Fields nicknamed La Cava "Dago," a derogatory insult to people of Italian/Spanish lineage. The director thought that Bill extended fondness through innocuous ribbing. La Cava "called me wicked, vile names," Fields said, "made bad noises with his mouth by distending his tongue and blowing real hard."[10]

The director, in turn, accused Fields of cheating. "He would always question my score," recalled Fields. "If I got an eleven on a hole he would swear it was fifteen." Once, Fields's ball sunk in a river, and with a two iron he pitched it onto the green. La Cava failed to see the shot, doubted he made it, and called him a "fraud."

Fields constantly distracted La Cava by making noises behind him when he shot. "Listen you son-of-a-bitch, get the hell out from behind me!" exclaimed La Cava. "Is this all right?" queried Fields, just as the director began his backswing.[11]

According to one story, the two started the Fits and Convulsions Club, an informal fellowship of riotous irresponsible members, while together on a train. Applicants had to declare themselves mad, and possess a sense of humor. Initiation dues were a ten thousand dollar check that must bounce. Members were fined twenty dollars for having a sane conversation with an individual exceeding four minutes. The club drew the Hollywood crowd, especially those who enjoyed *joie de vivre*.

The passage of time, plus the fact that both went on to distinguished careers, tempered their feud. In 1937, La Cava told Damon Runyon that Fields was "a truly great artist. He has what all great artists must have, and that is soul. There is nothing synthetic or manufactured about him. He is completely human. He has a rare understanding of his art, and of all the business of acting. There is only one Bill Fields."[12]

Fields, in turn, wrote that "La Cava is, to my mind, the No. 1 director of these great and glorious United States of ours . . . with a comedy sense not equaled by any other director." Fields's view is prophetic. La Cava was known for continually rewriting scripts on the set, dialogue and improvisation that angered producers, but drew out superlative performances from his stars (e.g. Katherine Hepburn, Carole Lombard, Claudette Colbert, and Ginger Rogers), who greatly admired his professionalism. Possessing a social conscience, he completed several excellent Depression-era movies that critiqued political corruption (*Gabriel over the White House*, 1933) and economic inequality (*She Married Her Boss*, 1935). In 1937, he directed his comedy classic *My Man Godfrey*, about a hobo who has lost all his wealth and is saved by a socialite. A striking depiction of the wide gulf between rich and poor, the movie received six Academy Award nominations, including La Cava as Best Director. *Stage Door* (1939), which portrayed the tragic life of show girls in a boarding house, was nominated for Best Picture.

Ginger Rogers, who appeared in *Stage Door*, felt that La Cava "was kind and loving; as a director he was masterful."[13]

Like Fields, La Cava had an alcohol addiction that led to several stays at sanitariums to dry out. Ginger Rogers recalls that during the filming of *Stage Door*, he held a tea cup full of gin in his hand. His dissipation consequently shortened his career, and he only completed one film after 1942. He was fired from his last project by Mary Pickford, who discovered him filming without a script. A critic later spotted him on the beach at Santa Monica shooting sea gulls. After his death in 1952 at age 59 from a heart attack, his outstanding body of work became largely forgotten. Today, he is considered one of Hollywood's most underrated directors, an auteur deserving of rediscovery.

Midway through the shooting of *Running Wild*, Fields read some alarming news. "Paramount Will Concentrate Feature Production in West" was the headline on the front page of *Motion Picture World* on March 5, 1927. "In the future Famous Players will concentrate all production in its big new studio in Hollywood." (Once Astoria was wired for sound, production of features resumed, including *The Cocoanuts* (1929), starring the Marx Brothers.) Paramount, formerly the distribution arm of Famous Players-Lasky, had become the overarching trade name for the mega-empire, which also consisted of a chain of more than one thousand Publix movie venues.

Jesse Lasky, vice president in charge of production, announced that "transfer of activities will be affected as each unit finishes its current picture." The last movie to conclude at Astoria was *Running Wild*, and its director La Cava left for Hollywood on April 28. The reason behind the move was that the once friendly relationship between Paramount's eastern and western branches had collapsed. Problems had arisen from the beginning. "It was always a headache to our production department," recalled Jesse Lasky. "Overhead was higher in the New York area, the studio was limited in size and utility, weather destroyed sets on the back lot time and again, and locations for exteriors were more of a problem than amid the scenic variety of the West. Besides all this it was hard to keep the studio fully active when the West Coast studio had first call on story properties and when, indeed, most stories could be filmed more advantageously in Hollywood."[14]

Herbert Brenon's *Beau Geste* (1926) precipitated the breakdown. Initially a project supported by Jesse Lasky, the production, including the entire crew, was sent to Hollywood because the film's setting occurred in the desert. B. P. Schulberg, Paramount's associate producer on the West Coast, vehemently supported the idea. Lasky remembered: "The eastern personnel was sent west, and Schulberg was obliged to furnish studio accommodations for the interlopers and to watch the picture being shot in his own bailiwick under the Astoria banner." When Schulberg noticed that the film was credited to William LeBaron, Associate Producer at Astoria, he went berserk. Realizing that the connection between the New York and Hollywood studios was not working, he demanded that Lasky shut down production at Astoria. "I had hoped that forcing the two studios to co-operate on the same picture might ease the situation, but it worsened it, if anything," declared Lasky. "The only solution seemed to be to concentrate all production in Hollywood."[15]

Paramount's new 26-acre facility on the former United Studios lot had opened in 1926 on Marathon Street, off Melrose Boulevard in West Hollywood. The edifice appeared monumental compared to the Famous Players-Lasky studio on Selma Avenue and Vine Street, a horse barn converted to a production facility with an enlarged open-air stage. In 1913, Lasky and Cecil B. DeMille leased the studio, and by the end of the year production began on *The Squaw Man* (1914), one of the first Western feature films made in Hollywood. By comparison, the studio's new entrance on Marathon Street was highlighted by a large iron gate flanked by pairs of Doric Columns on each side; above, a sign spelled out "Paramount Pictures." The famous barn where *The Squaw Man* was shot was moved to the new facility because of its historical importance, or what Lasky called its "sentimental" value. "I thought it would be [best] never to lose sight of the modest way we started."[16]

The decision to close down Astoria meant that Fields needed to move to the film capital in order to complete the three films remaining on his contract. The stage had lost its attraction for

Fields. "I am going to stick in pictures as long as the public will let me," he declared.[17]

Fields had mixed feelings about leaving the city that had played a major role in his evolution as a comedian. He had been in New York for twelve fruitful years, during which time he had appeared on the Broadway stage in the *Ziegfeld Follies*, *George White's Scandals*, and *Poppy*. Between 1925 and 1927, Bill had completed six silent films at Astoria, a facility that churned out 127 soundless movies from 1920 to 1927. Although Fields received fairly good reviews for his last two films, *The Potters* and *Running Wild*, the movies were criticized for their flimsy scripts and muddled plots. Fields's rancorous altercations with La Cava on the set of *Running Wild* had become an albatross around Bill's neck. His reputation as a recalcitrant movie actor travelled with him to Hollywood.

Fields's status as a leading silent screen comedian was therefore in doubt when he left New York. He had no idea what lay down the road. Fields knew the perils of show business, up one moment and down the next. His chronic feeling of insecurity returned again with vengeance. It was as if all his achievements since 1915 meant nothing, and he was starting over again at age forty-seven in Hollywood. Moreover, the Talkie revolution had started during 1927, the year he departed for Hollywood. Fields needed to pull off a miracle with Paramount in order to survive in filmdom's ruthless milieu.

**Notes**

1. *Running Wild*, VHS tape.
2. "W. C. Fields: A Centennial Tribute," January 29, 1980, transcript, p. 16.
3. *Running Wild* Press Book, August 23, 1927, MSD-LOC.
4. *WCFALOF*, 165.
5. Donald Deschner, *The Films of W. C. Fields* (New York: Citadel, 1966), 55; *LAT*, August 1, 1927, A7.
6. *NYHT*, June 13, 1927; *Variety*, June 15, 1927.
7. Taylor, 201; Scoop Conlon, "W. C. Fields Speaks His Mind," *Screen Play* (February 1936), 8.
8. Taylor, 199; "Gregory La Cava Piece," Articles by W. C. Fields, box 220, file #1, WCFP, Conlon, 81.
9. www.lakesidegolfclub.com/history, accessed December 14, 2012.
10. Taylor, 199.
11. "Gregory La Cava Piece," Articles by W. C. Fields; Fowler, *The Second Handshake*, 101.
12. Damon Runyon, "The Brighter Side," *Daily Mirror*, October 25, 1937, box 9, clippings pre-1946, WCFP.
13. "Articles by W. C. Fields, WCFP; Ginger Rogers, *Ginger-My Story* (New York: Harper, 2008), 237.
14. Lasky, *I Blow My Own Horn*, 194-95.
15. Lasky, 195-96; *Hollywood on the Hudson*, 57.
16. Lasky, 196-97.
17. *LAT*, July 31, 1927, C13.

# PART V:
# The Hollywood Debacle

## CHAPTER 15
### Welcome to the Dream Factory

After packing his Lincoln, Bill and his amour Linelle Blackburn left New York in early June 1927 and drove to Hollywood. Unbeknown to Fields, Paramount had already decided on his next picture. Studio executives had viewed *Running Wild* and were disappointed about his performance. B. P. Schulberg, the studio's authoritative associate producer, had arranged a telegraph-phone conference with Jesse Lasky and Walter Wanger, who were en route to Hollywood via train. They decided that Fields should next be paired with Chester Conklin, a versatile and venerable funnyman known for his antics and walrus mustache, in a picture still to be determined.

As he drove westward, Fields had no idea about Paramount's decision not to star him alone in a picture, as he had done in his last four features, but to bill him instead in a two-man *silent* movie just as the era of Talkies was underway. If he had known about these developments and the noxious stink they emitted, he might have turned around and returned to Broadway. Nonetheless, he kept driving westward, believing naïvely that a bright future in Hollywood lay ahead.

After Fields and Blackburn arrived, they rented a house in the fashionable Whitley Heights area north of Franklin Avenue in the Hollywood Hills. The locale was named after the developer H. J. Whitley, known as the "Father of Hollywood," who owned 480 acres and built the Hollywood Hotel. Developed in 1918, Whitley Heights was a very popular residential locale where numerous movie stars such as Rudolph Valentino, Gary Cooper, and Marie Dressler resided. Legend has it that Whitley named the town Hollywood after he encountered a Chinese man who told him that his occupation was "I hollwood," meaning "I hauling wood." The meeting gave Whitley the inspiration to call the area Hollywood. A more plausible explanation is that Deidra Wilcox, wife of pioneer real estate developer Harvey Wilcox, named their vast acreage after she talked to a woman from Illinois who owned an estate named Hollywood.

Fields's Mediterranean-style abode offered a spectacular view of Los Angeles not only during the day, but at night when the city's lights sparkled. High above the house in the hills was the HOLLYWOODLAND sign with its huge, white-painted 50-foot-high metal letters. The marker was erected in 1923 by real estate investors anxious to sell property in the growing movie mecca.

*Figure 15.1 Newly constructed HOLLYWOODLAND sign. Author's Collection.*

Fields "was very proud of the house," remarked the well-known silent movie actor Chester Conklin, who visited regularly. "Now, I'm a real Hollywoodsman," Bill told him.[1] After Fields's death, Conklin testified at his probate trial about this visit, and revealed the comedian's remark. The judge used Conklin's statement to date Fields's initial residence in California (1927), a time that made his will subject to the state's community property law.

Fields had first visited the area in 1904 when he was on the Orpheum Circuit performing his vaudeville juggling act at the 1,500-seat Grand Opera House on Main Street in downtown Los Angeles. He had married his wife Hattie a week earlier in San Francisco, where he entertained at the 3,500-seat Orpheum Theatre, then considered the most famous vaudeville venue in the West. Hattie assisted her husband by handing him juggling props that sat on a table: cigar boxes, matches, hats, rubber balls, and a big hat. Compared to staid Los Angeles, San Francisco had boisterous showplaces that offered a diversity of amusements, from raucous honky tonks and concert saloons to stately theaters and opera houses. Given the strong evangelical religious tradition in Los Angeles, the Grand Opera House prevented smoking and drinking and banned lewd entertainment.

Bill and Hattie took a lovely trip on a rented horse and buggy to nearby Pasadena, then a small town, health resort, and retirement community. On the forested hillsides of the Arroyo Seco were abundant eucalyptus trees and flowering plants. Fields enjoyed looking at the verdant gardens and orange orchards. He loved nature and the outdoors. The smell of fruit trees ripening in the balmy air might have reminded him of the time he had helped his father peddle fruits and vegetables; the mesmerizing scenery may have transported him into musing about his future and thoughts of retiring in the area. Fields later spent considerable time in Pasadena sanitariums recovering from severe ailments and alcoholism. He would die fatefully at Las Encinas Sanitarium in Pasadena on Christmas Day, 1946.

After Hollywood was incorporated as a municipality in 1903, it was eventually consolidated with Los Angeles in 1910. The town's initial few buildings were surrounded by vineyards, barley fields, and citrus groves. When Fields arrived, the bustling locale had forty-one banks, sixteen movies houses, and two newspapers. By the year 1927, "motion pictures had become the fourth largest industry in the world, and the first of California's thirty-five top industries," reported the historian Kevin Starr. "In 1927 a heroic $103 million was spent making movies." To lure tourists and new residents to southern California, Hollywood was promoted as the land of "material dreams."[2]

Filmmaking evolved during the first two decades of the twentieth century. Silent screen companies initially moved west to escape the Edison Trust patent suits that prevented their use of necessary filmmaking equipment. Equally important was the need to find a milieu that offered a year-long sunny climate, in contrast to shooting indoors with artificial light. In addition, Southern California offered a variety of scenery for location shots. A reporter praised Hollywood as a site for filmmaking: "Clean air and sunshine are available three hundred days out of the year, perfect conditions for picture making. The scenic advantages are unique. From the heights of Edendale [the site of Mack Sennett's Keystone studio] one can see the Pacific Ocean and the broad panorama of southern California with its fruit and stock ranches, its snow-capped mountains and its tropical vegetation to the east, north and south."[3] Its amenities were a major reason D. W. Griffith moved west to make his Biograph shorts, *In Old California* and *Ramona*, in 1910. Enchanted by the environment, Griffith made the region his headquarters, filming several of his masterpieces there. In October 1911, the Nestor Company built the area's first studio in a roadhouse on Sunset Boulevard. In 1913, Jesse Lasky leased land on Selma and Vine Streets and built a barn-like studio. When Lasky's company combined with Zukor's Famous Players, the genesis for Paramount was created, a merger that resulted into an extraordinary studio that played a major role in Fields's cinematic career.

The diverse population moving to Los Angeles resulted in a hybrid populace. The city had been inhabited by conservative Evangelical Protestants, upright people from rural towns in the Midwest, wealthy and snobbish health seekers, and social and political leaders whose affluence stemmed from controlling interests in real estate, oil, and local newspapers. New arrivals and old-time settlers held negative stereotypes of actors. "Hollywood inherited the suspicions of immorality that had traditionally focused on the stage actors," wrote an historian. "The movie colony was widely reputed to be a source of licentiousness and corruption."[4] These negative views changed during the 1920s, as moguls built large studios and the public began to idolize and adore movie stars.

The area supported a population of about 150,000 people in 1927, the year Fields arrived in Hollywood. On the boulevards below Fields's house were all the trademarks of a commercial city. Leading citizens and movie moguls invested twenty million dollars into Hollywood's development in 1925. On nearly every corner of Hollywood Boulevard, large banks, such as A. P. Giannini's Bank of Italy (later Bank of America), had a board of directors that read like a who's who in the movie colony, comprising producers, theater owners, and famous actors. Hollywood Boulevard featured the I. Magnum luxury department store, advertised as the "Fifth Avenue of the West" and "Style Center of the World." A multitude of swank hotels lined the boulevard and its side streets with names such as the Knickerbocker, Plaza, Regent, Recto, and Roosevelt. At the Ambassador Hotel on Wilshire Boulevard, the Oscars were awarded at its lavish nightclub, the Coconut Grove. Movie palaces arose with exotic names and interiors such as Sid Grauman's Egyptian Theatre (1925) followed by his spectacular Chinese Theater (1927). Popular restaurants abounded, such as the Pig 'n' Whistle and Musso & Frank, where famous novelists, now screenwriters, frequented (i.e., Faulkner and Fitzgerald). Near Fields's residence was the nearby Masquers club, a premier actors' association, located in a large house off Hollywood Boulevard.

Fields found that the city had mushroomed into a hectic metropolitan area. There were already traffic jams on its main boulevards, where automobiles, streetcars, and outmoded horse and buggies fought for space. Real estate speculation had propelled subdivisions practically everywhere, creating a patchwork of spatial communities that stretched from downtown to the Pacific Ocean. New oil money had generated millionaires who controlled the city's finances and other entities. On Hollywood Boulevard numerous automobile dealerships offering easy financing were established. Los Angeles was already destined to become a car city due to its immense and sprawling layout, accessible only by gas-guzzling vehicles that, in time, spoiled the air with smog.

*Figure 15.2 Hollywood Boulevard, 1927. Author's Collection.*

The writer Budd Schulberg (son of B. P. Schulberg), who grew up in Hollywood during the 1920s, described Los Angeles in a nutshell: "Downtown Los Angeles had spread out in all directions, determined to turn its back on the architecture of its Hispanic past. The new conquistadors were devoted to money rather than to tradition or beauty; their aim was to build as rapidly and as profitably as possible."[5]

Boosters with shady schemes lured small investors into dreams of prosperity. On September 5, 1924, in the newly constructed Hollywood Bowl, oil tycoon C. C. Julian addressed thirty thousand potential investors pitching stock in his local wells. A year later his enterprise was exposed as a pyramid scheme. The Julian story read like the screenplay from *The Potters* (1927) or *The Bank Dick* (1940), W. C. Fields's rogue movies in which frenetic oil stock buying occurred.

The timing of Bill's trip to Hollywood was problematic. Fields arrived just when studios were going through a major transition from producing silent pictures to sound film. Due to its revolutionary implications, the introduction of sound systems sent earthquake-like reverberations across the film industry. In 1926, Warner Bros. led the way by using its Western Electric sound-on-disc system to produce Vitaphone shorts featuring music and other entertainment, including many vaudevillians performing their acts. In May 1927, exuberant moviegoers watched Fox's *Movietone News* in sound, including its most celebrated event: Charles Lindbergh flying across the Atlantic and returning to a jubilant homecoming parade. On October 6, 1927, Al Jolson's *The Jazz Singer*, a partly-sound feature produced by Warner Bros., premiered. Its synchronized songs and dialogue rocked the Hollywood studio moguls and performers. A year later Warner Bros. presented its first all-talking film, *The Lights of New York*. Other studios soon followed with their own systems and wired theaters to produce Talkies. The transformation to sound propelled astounding changes in every area of filmmaking.

These groundbreaking events occurred while Fields was in Hollywood making silent features for Paramount. Sequences in his three films were shot at the studio's new facility in West Hollywood on Marathon Street. Compared to Astoria where "complete freedom" thrived, Paramount's Hollywood operations, according to Louise Brooks, were a "factory" run like a "police state."[6]

Brooks recalled that Paramount faced the transition to Talkies in 1928 by cutting salaries. She was summoned to Schulberg's office on the day her option was up for renewal. He told Brooks that she "could stay at her old salary or quit." Brooks refused "to take what amounted to a cut" and left Hollywood. She travelled to Germany to work with G. W. Pabst playing Lulu in the classic *Pandora's Box*, considered her best role.[7]

Production at Paramount was divided between the old soundless formula and the new Talkie format. After the studio made an agreement with Western Electric for its sound system, Paramount decided to reopen its Astoria facility for Talkies, where shooting began on its first sound feature during October 1928, *The Letter*, with Jeanne Eagels. Paramount also wired its large treasure trove of nationwide Publix movie theaters. Also equipped for sound was its flagship venue in Times Square, the 3,650-seat Paramount Theatre (1926), situated on the ground floor of the studio's spectacular, thirty-nine-story pyramid-shaped skyscraper.

When Fields arrived, Paramount was still headed by its long-term tycoon Adolph Zukor, a resourceful and crafty empire builder who turned the studio into a gigantic bureaucratic corporation. Its numerous departments were overseen by specialists, many of them "yes men" who feared higher-ups. A Hungarian by birth, Zukor exemplified the Horatio Alger American success story. Immigrating at age sixteen, his rise from a fur salesman to amusement arcade owner and to head of the Famous Players Film Company (1912), featuring stars from the legitimate stage, was breathtaking. Needing a partner, Zukor's company merged with Jesse Lasky's Feature Play Company (1916), forming Famous Players-Lasky, the producer of Fields's films at Astoria. A ruthless fighter and a financial wizard in a cutthroat business, Zukor was small in height, but huge in influence, as an ambitious potentate who ruled over a powerful show-biz empire. Zukor possessed a dual personality; quiet and reserved one minute and suddenly verbose and temperamental the next. Through clever maneuvering, he snatched his partner's (W. W. Hodkinson) movie distribution business named Paramount. Zukor eventually adapted the catchy name for all his studio operations. He also pilfered Hodkinson's logo, a snow-capped mountain crowned by a halo of stars. Over time he forced out most of his early partners, including Samuel Goldfish (Goldwyn), Cecil B. DeMille, and Jesse Lasky. "Mr. Zukor enjoys power," wrote DeMille. "There would come a time when he would put his two clenched fists together and, slowly separating them, say to me, 'Cecil, I can break you like that.'"[8]

Zukor's sovereignty was cleverly built on vertical integration, a three-part business operation combining film production, distribution, and exhibition. The studio's exhibition control featured block booking, a system that required movie houses to present a large chunk of Paramount's movies. These innovations helped the studio to become a powerful member of Hollywood's "Big Five," which included MGM, Warner Bros., 20th Century Fox, and RKO. Paramount reigned supreme by ruling over a long roster of celebrities in its star system and through unfair, one-sided contracts that tied actors to the studio and exposed them to termination. Fields had three more films to do under his contract, after which the studio could either renew the agreement or fire him. This *modus operandi* was labeled "a treadmill to oblivion" by radio star and film actor Fred Allen.[9]

Fields faced another problem. William LeBaron, Fields's mentor, had departed Famous Players-Lasky in 1927 and was now vice president overseeing production at the Film Booking Offices of America, headed by Joseph P. Kennedy, the president's father. Once LeBaron left, Fields lost his number one supporter. Without a VIP booster at the studio, Fields was given mediocre screenplays and relegated to co-star status. When LeBaron later returned as a producer at Paramount Pictures, he played a major role in Fields's success in Talkies during the 1930s.

The general manager at Paramount when Fields arrived was Benjamin Percival Schulberg, better known as B. P. Schulberg, a headstrong former journalist and publicist described as "a roughneck with his broad nose and wide mouth." In 1912, Schulberg joined Famous Players-Lasky as an assistant assigned to finding screen scenarios that merited a movie and as a publicity manager spewing out long flowery words about motion pictures: "You bring light where there is darkness. . . . You banish ignorance; you cheer and comfort. . . . You are the agent of the age, the messenger of futurity."[10]

Schulberg left the studio after losing a power struggle over United Artists' formation. He founded Preferred Pictures in 1921, a company with lavish offices on Broadway. His main goal as studio chief was "discovering talent," the "keystone of this burgeoning business-art." He first focused on making Katherine McDonald, "a strawberry blond with limpid blue eyes," a star by wining and dining her at Manhattan's most luxurious restaurants.[11] After Schulberg snared a contract with McDonald, he featured her in numerous mediocre money-losing pictures.

She was soon replaced in 1923 by a more sensational catch, Brooklyn-born Clara Gordon Bow, "The It Girl" considered the "first mass-market sex symbol." Schulberg exploited her vivacious energy in eight cheap Preferred Pictures and loan-out movies in 1924. Not all of them were box-office winners. A lack of exhibition theaters caused Preferred Pictures in late 1925 to file for bankruptcy owing $820,774.

With Bow under contract, Schulberg returned to Paramount in 1926 as the studio's associate producer. Paramount was controlled by the star system that promoted leading celebrities as the key to making their films box-office winners. A grand master of the system, Schulberg developed new celebrities, including the sensational sexy Clara Bow, whose 1927-28 movies were huge box-office hits. Bow was the archetypical 1920s flapper figure embodying "It," defined by writer Elinor Glyn as "that quality possessed by some which draws all others with its magnetic force."[12] At Paramount, Bow's career took off, included many blockbusters, and capped with the film *It* (1927). By the age of twenty-five she had completed forty-eight films. By 1933, however, with Talkies on the rise, her Brooklyn accent became a liability to her career.

Schulberg quickly moved up the chain of command with the backing of Zukor, who admired his youthful vigor. As general manager, Schulberg now reigned supreme over the studio's genres: dramas, gangster films, woman's films, musicals, adventure films, and comedies. Besides promoting a bevy of starlets, he hired many of the studio's famous directors, including William Wellman, who made *Wings* (1927), winner of the first Oscar for Best Picture. The picture starred Clara Bow and Buddy Rogers, who, as mentioned earlier, began his career in *So's Your Old Man*. When Fields arrived at Paramount, the studio had under contract leading dramatic performers such as Adolphe Menjou, William Powell, Gary Cooper, Richard Dix, Ronald Coleman, Bebe Daniels, and Marlene Dietrich, among others.

Fields's chief competitor in comedy on the Paramount lot was Harold Lloyd, who made two excellent hit films, *The Kid Brother* (1927) and *Speedy* (1928). Paramount also churned out popular situational comedies such as *Behind the Front*, a World War I spoof starring Wallace Berry, the studio's best box-office draw in 1926. Anxious to present new comedic performers, the studio signed the Marx Brothers, who completed their first feature, *The Cocoanuts*, in 1929. Once the Paramount brass focused on younger comics, the studio lost interest in Fields, who would turn fifty in 1930.

During 1927-28, not one studio executive recognized Fields's unique voice for sound films. His *Ziegfeld Follies* colleagues outpaced him. After appearing in several sound shorts, Eddie Cantor did a 96-minute Talkie in 1928, *Glorifying the American Girl*, a homage to Ziegfeld. Will Rogers made fifty silent pictures before starring in his first Talkie feature in 1929, *They Had to See Paris*. Cantor's belting voice and Rogers's folksy humor, which depended on "accent, intonation, and phrasing," perfectly fit the sound film medium.[13] Stuck in silent features, Fields had to wait until 1930 to film his first Talkie, the twenty-one-minute short, *The Golf Specialist*.

During his trip to Hollywood, he was pigeonholed into three mediocre silent pictures just as that medium was fading. With mixed reviews on his last two Astoria movies and a reputation as a difficult performer on the set, Fields arrived in Hollywood when myopic Paramount executives had lost faith in him as a screen star. Unwilling to chance another Fields flop, they cast aside the milquetoast *Running Wild* formula in favor of the *Poppy* con-man caricature, giving him a McGargle-type role as a scheming operator of an itinerant carnival in a film tentatively entitled *The Sideshow*. Although Fields often worked best as the sole star, the studio was uncertain of his popularity at the box office as a stand-alone comedian, and insisted on double billing him with Chester Conklin.

Schulberg, a potentate at Paramount, did little to support Fields. He had backed the closing of Astoria, which he felt was a tame rival compared to Paramount's new studio in Hollywood. He was known for his ability to discover beautiful young flappers for licentious Jazz-Age films, and he habitually used the casting couch to bed some of his starlets. His affair with star Sylvia Sydney destroyed his marriage to one of Hollywood's top agents, Adeline Jaffe. Most important, he had little interest in comedy when the screen was dominated by flaming youth, flirtatious flappers, short skirts, bob hair, bathtub gin, and numerous other manifestations that mirrored vast changes in morality during the 1920s.

In *What Makes Sammy Run?* (1941), Schulberg's son Budd, a well-known writer, penned a disguised portrait of his father, a notorious gambler and reckless spendthrift, "a strange mix of drinking-wrenching-studio-intellectual." His description of Hollywood during the 1920s exposed "outsized characters in all their venality, charm, pettiness, and vindictiveness." Budd also authored *Moving Pictures* (1981), an autobiographical account of his boyhood growing up in shallow Hollywood, in which he remembers his father as a "unique combination of intellectual curiosity and robust joy, [superior] to the moguls I knew as tough, selfish, ignorant and mean."[14]

On June 11, B. P. Schulberg confirmed that "W. C. Fields and Chester Conklin will form a Paramount comedy team."[15] Schulberg chose Louis Lighton, a specialist in Westerns rather than humor, to oversee Fields's three films with Conklin. Comedy teams were once again in vogue, including Stan Laurel and Oliver Hardy, who were making two-reel comedies for the Hal Roach Studio.

Fields also found himself at a studio with a host of stars, celebrated performers who could carry a picture by themselves. The star system was now thoroughly entrenched in Hollywood, where well-known celebrities dominated the industry. In the area of comedy, Fields needed to compete with well-established humorists such as Chaplin, Keaton, and Lloyd, whose famous personas were known to fans nationwide.

Since Fields had developed his reputation at Astoria in the East, Hollywood's film moguls viewed him as newcomer. The type of prickly, unrefined comedic films Fields made in New York differed from the slick comedy pictures Paramount churned out during the 1920s. During that decade, "comedy was judged by the glossy, professional standards that Fields's East Coast-manufactured films could not match," wrote film historian William Everson.[16] At Astoria, Fields imitated a browbeaten husband who challenged the sanctity of marital bliss, and a confidence man who whipped naïve suckers, thereby exposing the country's massive fraud schemes. In short, the themes and characters in Fields's silent pictures were antithetical to Paramount's production of glamorous and sexy Jazz-Age films.

By the late 1920s Paramount stood out as a big business studio tied to Wall Street interests that caused films to be produced according to standardized assembly-line formulas. The moguls exploited "proven success with formula pictures and cycles of any particular genre which temporarily sells," wrote David Robinson. The studio "was notoriously economy-conscious, often reducing the more exciting potentials to a mere programmer level," believed Everson. A programmer picture "lies midway between a 'B' picture and an 'A' picture. It is short and economical, but usually is just long enough or possessed of a sufficient plot, star, or other values to find its own level in a theatrical program." This was the type of Paramount film to which Fields was destined to be relegated, not once but three times.[17]

## Notes

1. Harold Cary, "The Loneliest Man in the Movies," *Colliers*, November 28, 1925, 26; box 39, probate trial, May 9, 1949, p. 526, WCFP.
2. Kevin Starr, *Material Dreams: Southern California Through the 1920s* (New York: Oxford University Press, 1990).
3. David Robinson, *From Peep Show to Palace: The Birth of American Film* (New York: Columbia University Press, 1996), 115.
4. Neil Sinyard, *Silent Movies* (New York: Smithmark Publishers, 1995), 20-21.
5. Budd Schulberg, *Moving Pictures: Memories of a Hollywood Prince* (1981; Chicago, Ivan Dee Paperback, 2003).
6. Brooks, *Lulu in Hollywood*.
7. Ibid, 96.
8. Cecil B. DeMille, *The Autobiography of Cecil B. DeMille* (Englewood Cliffs, Prentice-Hall, 1959), 211.
9. Fred Allen, *Treadmill to Oblivion* (New York: Little Brown, 1954).
10. Neal Gabler, *An Empire of Their Own: How the Jews Invented Hollywood* (1988; New York: Anchor Books, 1989), 203; *Moving Pictures*, 80.
11. *Moving Pictures*, 100.
12. Lawrence Napper, *Silent Cinema: Before the Pictures Got Small* (London: Wallflower Press Book, 2017), 87.
13. Larry Langman, *American Film Cycles: The Silent Era* (Westport, Conn: Greenwood Press, 1998), 129-38.
14. *Moving Pictures*; 131, 138, 261, back cover.
15. *LAT*, June 11, 1927.
16. *American Silent Film*, William K. Everson, (1978; New York: Da Capo Press, 1998), 270.
17. David Robinson, *Hollywood in the Twenties* (New York: Barnes, 1968), 30; Ibid, 12, 30; Everson, 12.

## Chapter 16

### Not Once, but Three Times

"There will certainly be no dearth of comedy teams this season," wrote a reporter in 1927. "It seems that all the studios have at least one fun-making duo, while others are going in for it as a wholesale business."[1] That duo for Paramount was W. C. Fields and Chester Conklin. To emphasize the pairing in their first co-star picture, the studio changed the title from *The Sideshow* to *Two Flaming Youths*. As if that were not enough, Paramount added nine popular two-man acts from vaudeville and the movies to perform their specialties in *Two Flaming Youths*. The duos included Joe Weber and Lew Fields, Mack and Moran, Bert Savoy and Jay Brennan, and Wallace Berry and Raymond Hatton.

Hiring walrus-mustached Chester Conklin, a well-known silent screen comedian, appeared to be a sure bet. A veteran performer, Conklin had already created a long resumé, listing many appearances in different forms of entertainment. He caught the show-biz bug early when he received an ovation at a childhood comic recital. Feeling that his intolerant pious father would never tolerate his becoming an entertainer, he ran away from home and found work in Des Moines as a bellhop, the first of many odd jobs. After being inspired by seeing Weber and Fields perform their ethnic comedy routine in St. Louis, he decided to do a character act based on his employer, a Dutch baker named Shultz, who had a walrus mustache and a thick accent. The walrus mustache became Conklin's iconic trademark, which he used to trigger laughter. He also used a hangdog look and highlighted his small and hefty physique as part of his comedic appearance.

Like Fields, he earned his acting credentials as an itinerant trouper. As a "Dutch" (German) ethnic comedian, he travelled the sawdust trail for numerous exhausting years with stock companies and vaudeville troupes and as a performer in circuses and various tent shows. "The combined careers of W. C. Fields and Chester Conklin has taken them ... to every city of more than 60,000 inhabitants in every State of the Union," claimed one reporter.²

In 1913, Conklin was hired by Mack Sennett as a Keystone Kop, earning three dollars a day in slapstick and roughhouse silent moving pictures. He performed in more than a dozen shorts with Charlie Chaplin, who became both a friend and later an employer. Conklin appeared with the Little Tramp in the first *Tillie's Punctured Romance* (1914), performing a bit part as a singing waiter. At Keystone he also teamed with comic Mack Swain in numerous "Ambrose and Walrus" comedies, playing the villain. He gained a reputation as a versatile actor with boundless energy, performing madcap pie-in-the-face comedy parts and as a victim named Droopington. A quarrel with Sennett over his contract led Conklin to sign with Fox in 1920. After freelancing, he entered into a three-film contract with Paramount in January 1927.

The Fields-Conklin partnership was based on their diverse physical appearances. Chester was smaller and stockier than Bill and played a hayseed in their first film, compared to the taller, slick swindler performed by Fields. Conklin was also a gifted pantomime artist who showed emotion by fiddling with his walrus mustache, using his expressive eyes, and playing with his eye glasses precariously perched on the rim of his nose. He took advantage of his amusing facial features while impersonating an impish mischief maker in *Two Flaming Youths*.

Conklin and Fields had contrasting mustaches which they used for comic effect. "My mustache denotes comedy and at the same time, it helps a lot in expressing pathos," asserted Conklin. "Being just a slight model, built low on the ground, the big mustache gets many a laugh. But then again, it is realistic. One sees many a sympathetic little fellow with such a growth. Getting a mustache that is applicable to both comedy and drama was a hard task, and it took me years to work it out."³

Fields used his much smaller, artificial clip-on mustache for humor. "I can get just as many heartthrobs and laughs out of the bit on my upper lip as Chester can get with his great, blooming home-grown whiskers." During routines, his mustache wiggled in all directions and hung precariously from the end of his nose to his mouth. "Furthermore, it's easy to put on," Fields continued. "Just a dab of spirit gum and it's there for all day long. It's not uncomfortable and hot. It is economical and it has personality. I'm just as loyal to mine as Chester is to his."[4] A prop from his late vaudeville and *Follies* shows, Fields's mustache affected his appearance, added years to his baby face, and offset his large, high brow and thinning hair.

Compared to the screen veteran Conklin, who had fourteen years' experience in the movies, Fields was a neophyte. Bill therefore respected Chester's vast background in early cinema. "On the screen they're bitter enemies, but off they are the greatest of friends," noted the director Charles Reisner. "Although they are represented as being at sword-points all the way through the picture [*Fools for Luck*], they were continually together while off the scene." Conklin and Fields teamed together in three silent films during 1927-28, all unfortunately considered lost. Existing reviews, stills, and scripts fortunately help to evaluate the movies.

In their first, fifty-five minute silent feature, *Two Flaming Youths*, Fields plays Gabby Gilfoil, a debt-ridden rogue who operates an itinerant small circus, while Conklin performs the role of Sheriff Ben Holden. Gabby is accompanied by his daughter, Mary Gilfoil, played by the lovely and photogenic nineteen-year-old Mary Brian, who appeared as Fields's daughter in *Running Wild* (1927). Mary yearns for a better life than as a traveling circus entertainer, a character similar to Poppy, as well as the Great McGonigle's daughter in *The Old Fashioned Way*. A title card reads, "Born in a tent, [she] had longed all her life for a home that wouldn't fold up." Like the other daughters, she finds a husband who provides a life of stable domesticity by the film's end.

In an interview, Brian later expressed fond memories of Fields. "I enjoyed him thoroughly, and luckily he liked me, cause he used to request me whenever they had a father and daughter story [*laughs*]. . . . He was really something to see cause he was really much more serious about his work than most people ever [gave him credit for]. He lived across the lake from me in Toluca Lake and every so often, he would shout across the lake and say, 'You're going to be my daughter. . . . I have a script and I'll send it over for you. . . .

The father and daughter are great friends and they do so and so.' No day was ever dull working with Mr. Fields." Brian remembered the way Fields wanted her to act. "He would tell me certain lines that would be the identifying line for me to say whatever he wanted me to say. He also made suggestions about what to do between my lines. 'You try to get me to do whatever the thing is and no matter what I say, you just keep after that one point.'" Mary also referred to Fields's comedic art as "spontaneous." "He would ask me to go and do something that we never rehearsed. The thing is, he knew he could count on me to do certain things and never look as if I don't know what it is." The entire process, Brian recalled, "gave him enough leeway" to do a comic routine. Called "the Sweetest Girl in Pictures," she made a successful transition to Talkies, playing, innocent nice-girl parts, including Fields's daughter in *The Man on the Flying Trapeze* (1935).[5]

In *Two Flaming Youths*, an opening title sets the scene: "Gilfoil's Nonpareil Circus attracts bad weather, sheriffs, and bill collectors—everything except cash customers." The troupe arrives at Arkosa, Kansas, where Gabby encounters his nemesis, the town's sheriff Ben Holden (Conklin), who, seeing the ragtag group, orders them to leave town and to "keep going till you hit the horizon!" The sheriff and Gilfoil are rivals for the affections of Madge, the town's debt-ridden hotel owner, a plump blond woman they mistakenly believe to be rich.

The sheriff orders Gabby to stay away from Madge: "She's my fiasco—If you'll pardon my French!" Gabby tries to entice the sheriff to play the shell game: "a game of skill and science! The hand is quicker than the eye." The sheriff refuses to play, asserting, "I know you city slickers! I played that once with a fellow and he won my sheriff's badge!"[6]

Lost to posterity is valuable footage showing Fields doing his vaudeville stunts, including juggling balls, glasses, and salt shakers. Outside the circus tent Fields exhibits his skill as a bally, standing on a platform while bellowing his spiel about the attractions inside. "Atlas, the strongest man in the world—he will take this horseshoe of solid steel and bend it like a pretzel!" Gabby again wears a late nineteenth-century sideshow pitchman's garb: top hat,

*Figure 16.1 Chester Conklin (Sherriff Ben Holden) and Fields (Gabby Gilfoil) are rivals for the attention of Cissy Fitzgerald (Madge Malarkey).* Two Flaming Youths. *Bison Archives/ HollywoodHistoricPhotos.com.*

cutaway coat, checkered vest, watch chain, and string tie. Behind him are colorful canvas banners advertising the attractions: "the strongest human in the universe," a person thirty-four inches high, and an eight-foot-nine-inch giant. On the platform Fields does his famous cigar box tricks, including balancing them on his chin. When someone loudly blows his nose, the boxes fall to the ground.

The sheriff believes Gabby is the wanted criminal Slippery Sawtell, worth a $1,500 reward. To avoid arrest, the circus owner puts the sheriff in a cage with a boxing kangaroo. Gabby gives a spiel urging the crowd to see the sheriff fight the kangaroo. Tickets sell fast, and he lures enough customers to pay off his debts. In the meantime the hotel owner has married the wealthy Simeon Trott. Annoyed about the marriage, Gabby and the sheriff lure Trott to play the shell game, and the two win substantial money.

*Figure 16.2 To attract customers, Gabby Gilfoil (Fields) displays his talent as a bally advertising his attractions inside his sideshow.* Two Flaming Youths. *Author's Collection.*

During the final sequence in *Two Flaming Youths* (1927) the sheriff still believes Gabby is Slippery Sawtell, and is intent on capturing Gabby and winning the reward money. To evade the officer, Gabby quickly mounts a bicycle and peddles as fast as he can. While filming the chase sequence, Fields collided with a truck, falling off his bicycle and fracturing his third cervical vertebra.

The driver, unable to see Fields as he lay motionless on the road, began to back up. Fortunately, Johnny Sinclair, a stuntman alert to the accident, reached Fields in time to grab his legs and pull him clear of the truck, likely saving his life. (Fields hired Sinclair as a stuntman and gag writer in numerous movies he made during the mid-1930s.) While recovering in the hospital, Bill received a card from Will Rogers, who quipped, "If we could only call back the old times. I knew you when no truck living could catch you. Are you sure Ziegfeld wasn't driving the truck? Want to see you soon."[7]

Fields contributed an amusing piece about his experience, "The Art of Breaking a Neck," in Frank Scully's edited volume *Bedside Manna: The Third Fun in Bed Book*. "While cavorting before the camera on a bicycle," Fields wrote, "a truck backed into me. It not only upset me—it broke my back.... So I held my head (for once in my life) until my doctor arrived. The doctor announced something in Latin. The accident thus received no publicity.... All the while I was in the hospital I carried my head in an upward position. Like a fellow counting the stars."[8]

Accounts in the press publicized the accident. "Fields Actor Will Survive Injuries," was the headline in the *Los Angeles Times*; the article noted that although there were no further complications, Fields's physician estimated that the comedian needed hospital rest for five weeks. Another story in the *New York Times* reported that Fields had collided with the truck after turning his head to look at the pursuing Conklin, and had broken his neck.[9]

The accident-prone Fields kept experiencing calamities all during his screen career. Returning home from the hospital, he immediately experienced another accident. "While thus gazing at the heavens with a cocktail in my hand, I missed the first step of a stairway," he said. "The back of my spine caught it.... When I reached the bottom of the stairs, I still gazed upward, as in all that commotion my head had not moved, and neither had my cocktail spilled.... Isn't life the song, though?"[10] While the tale that his cocktail never spilled was probably exaggerated, the story about the stairway fall is true. His back was out of alignment and his coccyx was broken. In his next film, *Tillie's Punctured Romance*, Fields was almost eaten by lions, and received shrapnel wounds while running through a minefield. Like a cat with nine lives, Bill managed to recover each time.

*Two Flaming Youths* received mixed critiques and failed at the box office. Fields and Conklin, however, received good reviews. "The comedy has a minimum of slapstick," observed a reviewer. "It attains its humor by characterizations of two definite types. Both Fields and Conklin [are] excellent." The *New York American* called them "the best comedy team in filmdom." The *Chicago Herald Examiner* reviewer felt the picture was a "long scream." Mordaunt Hall in the *New York Times* called Fields "a resourceful promoter" and "a good pantomimist, one who does not have to pretend that the rest of the world is deaf because he is acting for the silent screen." Hall felt it was "a funny picture, obstreperous in some places, but quite diverting."[11]

The negative reviews, however, outweighed the positive ones. Hall believed there were too many "catapults, mud, water, and other old reliables" in the film. He blamed the young director John Waters, who "ought to have been able to do more with the ability of these . . . comedians." Others, like Pare Lorentz, the film critic and later renowned documentary filmmaker, believed that the editing was poor and the story "meaningless and dull." Paramount was likewise unhappy with the result. So, too, was Fields. He wrote a tongue-in-cheek letter of apology to the studio suggesting that his accident inadvertently helped the picture: "I only did it to lighten your burden. I had not been able to give you a good story up to now, so I just had to do something." All was not lost, since Fields recycled some of the film's material to better reception seven years later in *The Old Fashioned Way*.[12]

By the time Fields finished shooting the movie, he had developed a negative opinion of Hollywood. On the positive side, he found film work easier than vaudeville—less time to do a picture plus a larger salary, $45,000 a film. He was nevertheless shocked to experience Paramount's factory-like system. He became irked about how stories were developed by hordes of studio screenwriters, continuity writers, and gag men, and manufactured on the set by studio hacks. Hoping to write his own scripts as he did in the *Follies*, he found his craft assumed by others. Any suggested changes Fields wanted had to be approved by Paramount executives. Thinking he had little knowledge of comedy, the studio heads felt that his job was strictly to carry out the direction of others. The studio ran a highly efficient system, churning out a multitude of films featuring their stars. Distribution of its output resembled a well-oiled structured process guaranteeing its theater chain first-run films, reaping box-office profits. In Hollywood, Fields felt like a cog in this bureaucratic, mass-production operation.

As he began to realize that it was futile to fight the system, Bill gave up his earlier combative tendencies, a surprising turn for an actor who regularly battled Florenz Ziegfeld over his salary and changes to his sketches, and successfully led the strike by chorines demanding better wages. A reporter noted Fields's new demeanor, writing, "W. C. Fields has settled down for peace and quiet in Hollywood. The smell of the boards might be all right in its way, but Hollywood is the place for a good rest when a man comes to need one. Fields, completely dazed by the habits and customs of the Hollywood screen lords, has decided to let well enough alone and do just as he is told. The peacefulness and security of his new existence is wonderful to him after a lifetime of continual movement from one place to another."

As he waited for his next film, he nonetheless started to feel insecure. Worrying about the uncertainty of his future in show biz had overwhelmed him numerous times in vaudeville. Furthermore, not one producer had offered an opportunity for him to do a Talkie, although the format had grown significantly in popularity since *The Jazz Singer*, a part-sound film, had opened at the Warner Theater in Manhattan in 1927. Fields's prospects as a screen comedian remained "in the laps of whatever gods there is watching over the destinies of motion picture production," declared a reporter. "It is a trifle sad to see the superb theater personality of W. C. Fields wilting under the influence of the upstart movies."[13]

By November, Fields was on the Paramount lot shooting his second film, *Tillie's Punctured Romance*. The feature was not a remake of Chaplin's famous 1914 Keystone comedy with a similar name, which derived from the musical Broadway farce, *Tillie's Nightmare* (1910). Fields's film was produced by the brothers Al and Charlie Christie, Hollywood pioneers. Al Christie had operated the Nestor

Studios, the locale's first movie company, formed in October 1911, and located at Sunset Boulevard and Gower Street. A year after opening, Nestor merged with the newly formed Universal Film Company, where Al oversaw comedy films until 1916, when he and his brother formed the Christie Film Company, specializing in the two-reel silent Christie Comedies. The brothers owned the rights to *Tillie's Punctured Romance* while Paramount would distribute the picture. The production of *Tillie's Punctured Romance* by a noted comedy film team was a good omen.

Two more talented comedians were added to the cast. Louise Fazenda, an ex-member of Sennett's Fun Factory, was a highly gifted performer in numerous comedy silents, and starred in the lead role in *Mind Over Motor* (1923). In *Tillie's Punctured Romance*, she impersonates Tillie as a gawky runaway farm girl with pigtails and calico dress; this comic country bumpkin role was her usual persona during the 1920s. She was joined by Mack Swain, a former Keystone Kop, who played Tillie's father, General Pilsner. Swain appeared with Chaplin in numerous one-reelers and features in which his heavy-set, tall frame contrasted sharply with Charlie's smaller, waiflike tramp figure. His portrayal as Big Jim opposite Chaplin in *The Gold Rush* (1925) became the highlight of the comic duo's works together. Pairing Swain and Fazenda with Conklin was like a homecoming of Keystone graduates. Fields was now co-starring and competing with two more jokesters. The *Variety* critic felt that the comic foursome ruined the picture. "Featured comedy is strictly a single star racket," he wrote. "Four characters can't be built up for the strong hee-haw."[14] Paramount failed to realize that among the four, Fields should have been the star comic. The studio instead let him share the spotlight with three other comics.

Fields role in *Tillie's Punctured Romance* led to a second rendezvous with Eddie Sutherland, who directed the film. Sutherland helped create the story during an ocean voyage to Paris and back with Al Christie and the writers Monte Brice and Harry Edwards. After spending most of the trip carousing, the writers developed a story overnight, and read it to Christie, who was delighted. Sutherland and Brice continued to work on the story during their train trip to the West Coast.

Except for keeping several characters' names from the original *Tillie*, they created a new circus movie, knowing Fields thrived in such a setting. To serve as the big top, a huge 500-foot-long tent was set up next to the Christie studio on the old Paramount lot. To produce inside lighting, numerous sun arcs were connected to a dozen ten-ton portable generators. Cameras were placed at various vantage points in the "biggest tent ever used for a cinematic production." To recreate a circus environment, "bands, acrobats, charioteers, wild animals, clowns, calliopes, and crowds" were used.[15]

Before shooting began, Sutherland and Fields discussed the film's problematic script over drinks in the Sutherland home. Louise Brooks, Sutherland's wife, recalled the afternoon: "I remember Bill sitting quietly, listening and drinking martinis from Eddie's two-quart cocktail shaker: I remember him teasing me by dropping my fragile Venetian wine glasses and catching them just before they hit the floor; but I can't remember one word he said about the idiotic plot contrived for the remake of the film." The afternoon foreshadowed an ominous outcome. "This story that Brooks and I knew wasn't very good.... And it wasn't. It was just a bad picture," recalled Sutherland.[16]

Fields plays the ringmaster, who plans to murder the circus owner Horatio Q. Frisbee (Conklin) so he can steal the circus. The part of the violent assassin was far removed from his usual roles as a con man or henpecked husband. The plots centers on the ringmaster's plan to feed Frisbee to the lions. His plan backfires, and instead he is almost eaten by the lions. When World War I begins, the ringmaster and Frisbee decide to help the Allies by bringing their circus to entertain the troops in Europe. However, after the circus lions escape, running into German lines, the two men chase after them. The ensuing confusion causes the Germans to retreat, thereby helping the Allies win the war.

Surviving stills capture some of the movie's flavor. One photograph shows Fields, Conklin, and Fazenda cutting up as privates in uniform. The studio's press book reported that during the war sequence, Fields lost his clip-on mustache and juggled hand grenades. Another still from a circus scene depicts the smiling strong woman (Babe London) with her arms around Fields's girth as the

*Figure 16.3 Battle scene from* Tillie's Punctured Romance. *Bison Archives/HollywoodHistoricPhotos.com.*

latter cringes, afraid he either will be strangled to death or unable to escape her romantic advances. In the picture she hurls hundred-pound weights at the defenseless ringmaster. A photograph of a vengeful Fields attacking a fearful Conklin using an open-mouthed stuffed lion captures the enmity between the two arch rivals.[17]

Many critics believed that the acting, directing, producing, and story line in the seventy-minute movie was second-rate. The film lost money due to its distribution as a split week feature mainly in second-run houses. Indeed, the film opened in Manhattan in a second-run venue. The *Variety* reviewer felt the movie was too long. "In a two-reel version it would have been a scream, but it spreads out over too much time. Fields has some comedy moments" but the overly long film has "frequent let downs. It hasn't quite robust enough knockabout or gags, lacks sufficient speed, and a smashing climax of roughhouse, which seems to be essential to the big money laughs." Louise Brooks wrote the film's epitaph. It was "the worst mess of filmmaking that I have ever observed.... It was filmed with groans, previewed with moans, shown in a few theaters, and then buried in the vaults. Poor old Tillie had not a single mourner."[18]

*Figure 16.4 The pool game between Gabby Gilfoil (Fields) and Sheriff Holden (Chester Conklin) in* Two Flaming Youths.

*Fools for Luck*, the last film in the Fields-Conklin trilogy, suffered the same fate. After two circus movie flops, Paramount placed Fields in a small town locale, playing the slick con man Richard Whitehead. The character's last name is possibly a reference to Fields being called Whitey due to his white hair while a youth in Philadelphia. Whitehead is described "as the most successful villain that the screen has exploited for many a day." He purchases an option on a worthless sand lot and sells fake oil well stocks in collusion with Ray Caldwell (Jack Luden), son of affluent parents. At a large gala dinner and dance held in Caldwell's honor, Whitehead pitches his fake stocks to the crowd. "Friends, I have had my eye on Huntersville for some time. I started life as a newsboy, and since then honesty has been my motto. In conclusion, I will quote you a quotation from Shakespeare, 'He that sees me—knows me—but says nothing!'"[19]

The movie's highlight is the pool game between Fields and Conklin. When Fields went to Hollywood he insisted that his pool table accompany him. "I felt sort of lonesome without it," he confessed. "It's such an old friend that I like to have it around."[20] He had performed his pool routine in *Tillie's Punctured Romance* (1928), but it was cut from the final version.

Although a visual record of Fields's skill is unfortunately lost, the scene is described in a review. The contest is between Whitehead, a pool hustler, and Hunter (Conklin), the town's champion. Whitehead pretends he is an inept "mark" by handling the cue as a baseball bat and golf club. "The players get down to the last ball, with an easy shot for Mr. Hunter," wrote the *New York Times* reviewer. "Just like taking candy from a baby," a confident Hunter says. He pockets his ball, but it strangely bounces back. Whitehead has rigged the pool table, allowing him to sink his own ball. "I'm just one of those fools for luck!" Whitehead exclaims. The *Times* reviewer explains: "As Mr. Whitehead has nothing that could be termed a conscience or sporting instinct, he discovers a way to trick Mr. Hunter and win the game." The *Variety* critic called the pool table sequence "the comedy standout."[21]

Besides the pool table sequence, reviewers praised the scene in which Hunter climbs into bed with his "wife." "A city slicker cheated me at pool tonight," he grumbles. "If I ever see him again, I'll fill him full of lead. I'll be with you in one minute, Snooky-ookums!" Hunter takes his gun and puts it under his pillow. "How about Papa's good-night kiss? By golly, you will kiss me!" He uncovers the sheets to discover not his wife but Whitehead, whereupon he angrily grabs his gun and aims at his pool opponent. After they hear a gunshot, Hunter's wife and daughter rush into the bedroom and see Whitehead with his hands raised. Mrs. Hunter takes the gun and chastises, "What do you mean by threatening my house guest, Mr. Whitehead, the oil king?" "An oil king to you, perhaps," Hunter responds, "but an oil can to me!"

Like their first two films, the third Fields-Conklin movie was given mixed reviews, with the bad comments outweighing the good ones. The pair "succeed in giving a second or so of fun," but after that, "originality is successfully avoided," wrote the *Times* reviewer. "They are either very funny in their films or very silly. In this one the silly ideas predominate." Other New York papers agreed. The *Morning Telegraph* called it "a feeble comedy," the *Graphic* "a mediocre flicker," and the *Herald Tribune* "a patchwork more or less entertaining." By contrast, *The Telegram* labeled it "a good comedy for any program," the *Sun* called it "fairly successful," the *American* critic believed it "will have a wide public," and the *Post* reporter found it "entertaining [only] at those moments Mr. Fields chooses to be funny." The *Morning Telegraph* journalist wrote the film's epitaph: "To allow the talents of the screen's finest comedy teams to be squandered on such mediocre piffle is to us inexcusable and justifiably censorable."[22]

While Paramount developed its film sound equipment and wired its theaters, the studio sunk Fields's pictures with poor scripts, stilted plots, and mediocre direction. (In 1928, the studio released its first all-dialogue sound film, *Interference*.) The fault stemmed from the shoddy material the studio gave him. On April 18, 1928, he wrote his estranged wife Hattie that he needed to reduce her allowance. "I am at a stage where I cannot get an offer at all. I have been badly handled and am now out of the movies. I have worked sixteen weeks in the last thirteen months. Have had two big law suits, lost both, and am entering upon a third. After income tax, lawyer's fees, agent's [commissions] and damages have been deducted from my income, there is little if anything left."[23]

Conklin made a successful transition to sound films, but was mostly relegated to playing secondary roles and bit parts. Conklin appeared with Chaplin in *Modern Times* (1936) as a factory mechanic, and in *The Great Dictator* (1940) as a customer who is shaved by the barber (Chaplin) to the tune of the *Hungarian Rhapsody*. In 1931, he joined Fields for the final time playing a bit part as Emil in *Her Majesty Love*. As a member of Preston Sturges's stock company, he performed in six of the director's films during the 1940s. A man of incredible stamina, he performed cameo and secondary roles in countless films until the 1950s. By 1954 his reputation had plummeted to such an extent that he took a job as a department store Santa Claus. Once commercialism dominated the film industry, his style of physical comedy became outmoded. "Work got awfully scarce," he remembered. During the 1960s he lived at the Motion Picture Country Home and Hospital, where, at age 79, he met his fourth wife, June Gunther. They moved to Van Nuys in 1965, and a year later he made his last film, *A Big Hand for the Little Lady*. He died at age 85 on October 11, 1971, from heart failure. Among people viewing his star on the Hollywood Walk of Fame at 1560 Vine Street, few realize how much this tireless, walrus-mustached trouper, who made nearly 100 films within a span of fifty-three years, contributed to the advent and evolution of silent and sound films.

As Whitehead, Fields added an epitaph to his last silent film, the third Fields-Conklin picture lost to posterity. Using the title he said, "I'm just one of those fools for luck! I just wanted to make people laugh."[24]

**Notes**

1. *LAT*, July 9, 1927, A6.
2. *LAT*, October 23, 1927, 28.
3. *Fools for Luck*, Paramount Press Sheet, 2, MPD-LOC.
4. *Fools for Luck*, Paramount Press Book, May 7, 1928, MPD-LOC.
5. Mary Brian interview by Anthony Slide, MMIOHP; Mary Brian remarks, "W. C. Fields: Centennial Tribute," January 29, 1980, AMPAS; Anthony Slide, *Silent Players*, 46.
6. All quotes are taken from the *Two Flaming Youths* script, Paramount Script Collection, AMPAS.
7. *WCFALOF*, 63.
8. Frank Scully, ed., *Beside Manna: The Third Fun in Bed Book* (New York: Simon and Schuster, 1936), 156.
9. *LAT*, October 5, 1927, A1; *NYT*, October 4, 1927.
10. *LAT*, October 5, 1927, A1.
11. *NYA*, January 2, 1928; *CHE*, January 13, 1928; Deschner, *The Films of W. C. Fields*, 58; MOMA, Film Department Collection.
12. Deschner, 58; Pare Lorentz, *Judge*, scrapbook #14, WCFP; *WCFALOF*, 63.
13. "W. C. Fields Settles Down," *New York Sun*, October 8, 1927; see also undated clipping, ca. 1927-28, HTC.
14. *Variety*, June 20, 1926, clipping, AMPAS production file.
15. *LAT*, October 30, 1927, 27.
16. Brooks, *Lulu in Hollywood*, 82; Sutherland interview, CUOHP, 112.
17. *WCFALOF*, 66-67; Nicholas Yanni, *W. C. Fields* (New York: Pyramid Communications, 1974), 34; Everson, *The Art of W. C. Fields*, 56.
18. *Variety*, June 20, 1928, AMPAS; Brooks, *Lulu in Hollywood*, 82.
19. *NYT*, June 12, 1928, 33; dialogue quotes are taken from the titles found in the script outline, Paramount Script Collection, AMPAS.
20. *Six of a Kind*, Paramount Press Book, MPD-LOC.
21. *NYT*, June 12, 1928, 33; June 13, 1928, box 9, clippings 1920-29, WCFP.
22. *NYT*, June 12, 1928, 33; *Fools for Luck*, box 9, clippings 1920-29, WCFP; *NYMT*, June 10, 1928, scrapbook OS-49, WCFP.
23. *WCFBH*, 76.
24. *Fools for Luck*, Paramount Press Book, May 7, 1928, MPD-LOC; *LAT*, October 11, 1971.

# Afterword

## Fields's Silent Movies: The Basis for His Fame in Sound Films

After Fields finished *Fools for Luck* in early 1928, Paramount refused to renew his contract. He sought other acting roles in Hollywood, but was unable to find a studio willing to hire him. The year 1928 was a terrible time to be unemployed in Hollywood. Not only did his films get mediocre reviews, but the studios were racing to develop sound systems. Few, if any, then recognized his unique voice as a precious gem for Talkies. Fields's three lost movies in Hollywood might have also yielded significant information about his evolution as a screen comedian.

Later in 1934, Fields bitterly recalled his debacle in Hollywood. Bill was shocked when he discovered the bureaucratic system Paramount had created to produce their pictures. "The first time I came to Hollywood I was taken gently but firmly to one side, and spoken to in a fatherly tone," he said. "I was told that my days of worry and toil were over. Hollywood, it seemed, was a community of specialists working in a mass-produced film factory. There were specialists who did nothing but sit down and think of plots for stories, others who embellished these into screen plays, still others to write dialogue, and more to think up funny situations. All I had to do, I was told, was to go out and play golf. When they were ready for me, they would let me know. I would come to the studio, make a few faces and [read] a few previously written remarks, and I would be paid regularly. I tried it, and in six months I was out of a job. Not only was my option not renewed, but nobody else would hire me."[1]

Fields had been pushed aside by a studio atop the film industry. No other mega-film facility among the Big Five matched Paramount's power. Its slogan was "If It's a Paramount Picture, It's the Best Show in Town." Under Zukor's leadership, Paramount reported earnings of $8 million in 1927, and by decade's end, $15.5 million. The studio was so profitable that the dividend on its stock increased by 25 percent at the end of 1929. Its Publix theater chain numbered 1,210 venues in 1930. With so many stars and theaters, the studio created "block booking," forcing exhibitors to purchase a whole year's worth of Paramount pictures. Once the Great Depression worsened and theater attendance plummeted, its profits fell to $6 million in 1931, and the following year, it lost $21 million, causing the studio to fall into bankruptcy and receivership in 1933.

The studio promoted other performers in 1927, a cast list that included Clara Bow, Charles "Buddy" Rogers, who starred in *Wings* (winner of the first Academy Award for Best Picture in 1929), and actors such as William Powell, Adolphe Menjou, and Gary Cooper, among others. In the area of comedy, Fields faced competition from the likes of Harold Lloyd, who remained an audience favorite in *The Kid Brother* (1927) and *Speedy* (1928). New comedians with fresh faces were contracted by Paramount, such as the Marx Brothers, who turned their Broadway smash *The Cocoanuts* into a film in 1929. The studio was also producing sophisticated comedy feature films directed by Berlin-born Ernst Lubitsch whose feather-light touch in *The Love Parade* (1929) proved extremely popular.

Lost among the luminaries, Bill became a sacrificial lamb thrust aside by a system that worshipped screen idols who assured box-office profits. Fields was not among them. He had learned an important lesson during his inaugural Hollywood experience. When Paramount offered him a contract in 1933, he demanded complete control over his films. "I do have a hand in everything that goes on—from the writing to the casting," he said in 1934. "If I flop now, it'll be my own fault, and I'll have no kick coming."[2]

As mentioned earlier, six of Fields's twelve silent pictures, which represent one half of his oeuvre in the medium, have perished. His silent film negatives contained flammable material, which required expensive fire insurance to store properly. Because of its silver content, the negatives had some value as scrap. Opting to make money rather than pay high storage bills, studios consequently sold many silent pictures to scrap companies.

The loss of his work was costly to his reputation as a silent picture comedian. The films' disappearance makes it difficult to assess his entire career in the medium. Without more of his work available, several questions remain unanswered. What stage characteristics did he transfer to these lost silent pictures? How did the acting techniques he learned in the silent comedies influence his Talkies? If available, how would these lost Paramount silent features play today?

With only one half of his canon available for viewing, judgment of Fields's work as a silent comedian is challenging. He had a late start as a silent screen comedian. Putting aside his two movies in 1915, he completed most of his pictures between 1925 and 1928—the tail end of the silent era and the advent of the Talkies revolution. These factors prevented Fields from ever joining the top pantheon of silent screen comedians: Chaplin, Keaton, and Lloyd. Digital technology, however, has given viewers a second chance to evaluate Fields's pre-sound movies and to observe a great pantomime at work. With his existing silent films now available on DVD, a new generation of Fields aficionados can now see signs of the great sound comedian to come.

Although often forgotten among his entire oeuvre, Fields's silent movies were exceedingly significant stepping stones to his success in the initial era of sound films. During the 1920s, he took his two main characters that he created in his sketches in the *Ziegfeld Follies*, the henpecked husband and the benevolent con man, and enhanced them in his silent movies.

Equally important was Fields's ability to rework his silent pictures into the new medium of sound. The remaking illustrates his reliance on recycling his earlier work. For his sound films, Fields often borrowed from his silent screen pictures. These remakes, however, were not exact carbon copies from the original work, but more like bits and pieces and elaborations. Whether complete or part conversions, these adaptations greatly added to his success as a film star during the 1930s. According his grandson and film scholar Ronald Fields, *The Potters* "is a precursor of such top titles in the Fields canon as *It's a Gift* and *The Bank Dick*. While a strict blueprint for neither, *The Potters* does foreshadow many of the same peccadilloes of life dealt with so admirably by Harold Bissonette and Egbert Sousé."[3]

Whether similar in plot and/or characterizations, other silent pictures reappeared in Fields's sound films:

*Sally of the Sawdust* (1925)→*Poppy* (1936)
*It's the Old Army Game* (1926)→*It's a Gift* (1934)
*So's Your Old Man* (1926)→*You're Telling Me* (1934)
*Running Wild* (1927)→*Man on the Flying Trapeze* (1935)
*It's the Old Army Game* (1926)→*Fools for Luck* (1928)
*That Royle Girl* (1925)→*Man on the Flying Trapeze* (1935)

Without a renewed Paramount contract or any offers from other studios, Fields had no idea what to do next. Returning to the Broadway stage was an option, but after dedicating himself to a film career, it seemed a backward step. New York had its excitements, but half the year the weather was cold, compared to perpetually pleasant Southern California. Bill had fallen in love with the Sunshine State, its warmth, its slow life style, and its pristine beauty, from the low desert and the Sierras to the blue Pacific Ocean. "If the West didn't want me, I wanted it. I wanted sunshine and warm weather. I wanted a house and a bed to sleep in and a closet to hang my clothes in. . . . I wanted to be out in the open and play golf and tennis. . . . But for that, I had to have work."[4]

Fields again found himself stranded, an experience he had endured on many occasions during his years on the stage. He lost count of how many times he rode a precarious roller coaster from the depths to the summit and from the apex spiraling back to the bottom. With his ambition for a film career buried in Hollywood's quicksand, Fields remarked, "Hollywood is the gold cap on a tooth that should have been pulled out years ago."[5]

Despair set in once the stock market crashed, ushering in the Great Depression, which added economic uncertainty to Fields's hellish season in Hollywood. Fortunately, it did not last long. His reputation on the stage saved him. He starred in the 1928 *Earl Carroll Vanities*, where he wrote new sketches that would reappear in his sound films. He was also the leading light in the Broadway musical comedy, *Ballyhoo* (1930-31).

While treading the boards again, Fields kept wondering when a producer would sign him for a sound movie. He got a start doing pieces from his *Follies* golf sketch in the March 1929 *Fox Movietone* newsreel, in which he tells gags, quips, and plays with props while giving a woman golf lessons and bragging about his game. A more

*Figure Afterword.1  Illustration by Al Hirschfeld showing the cast in* Ballyhoo *(1930). In the center is Fields in a Baby Austin.*

important breakthrough occurred when his mentor William LeBaron (now vice president at RKO) recommended Fields to do his entire *Golf Specialist* sketch for the RKO series, *Broadway Headliners*, a twenty-one-minute comedy short in sound (released July 24, 1930). Added were extra scenes depicting the arrest of his character, a wanted thief. Moviegoers could now hear Fields's remarkable intonations on the screen. "W. C. Fields clicks a lot of laughs in this amplification of the golf act he used for many years on the stage," wrote the reporter for *Motion Picture News*. "Fields' voice is ideal for [talkies] and his camera presence excellent. All types of audiences will enjoy it."[6]

With the Broadway theater business collapsing due to the Depression in 1931, Fields packed up his belongings and left New York, heading again to Hollywood. Without a contract, he had no idea what his future might be like. For a moment, it hurt. He felt as if all he had done in show business had evaporated. Needing confirmation that his fleeting thought was not true, he looked back at the New York high rises remembering how the city had shaped his successful show business career on the stage and in silent pictures. "I twisted around for a last look at the skyline. I had an idea somehow that I wouldn't see it again." His premonition was right— Fields never saw New York again. "But I felt young, and I know it was good, and it was a wonderfully sunny day. So I drove on towards a very uncertain future, about the same as I had in the past."[7]

As he continued to Hollywood, Fields was unaware that ahead lay the pinnacle of his career during the golden age of sound comedy during the 1930s. "Critics today should rate this comedian as the king of the Thirties because of his uniqueness, innovation, and many-faceted character," wrote Donald W. McCaffrey, distinguished scholar of film comedy. "We have begun to associate the man with the character, and when that happens, the artist's works become creations for all seasons—for the ages."[8]

**Notes**

1. *NYT*, June 12, 1928, 33; June 13, 1928, box 9, clippings 1920-29, WCFP.
2. *Fools for Luck*, box 9, clippings 1920-29, WCFP; *NYMT*, June 10, 1928, scrapbook OS-49, 3, WCFP.
3. *WCFALOF*, 52-53.
4. *WCFBH*, 76.
5. *Fools for Luck*, Paramount Press Book, May 7, 1928, MPD-LOC; *LAT*, October 11, 1971.
6. *Motion Picture News*, July 5, 1930.
7. Taylor, *W. C. Fields*, 211.
8. Donald W. McCaffrey, *The Golden Age of Sound Comedy: Comic Films and Comedians of the Thirties* (New York: A. S. Barnes, 1973), 172. For Fields's career during the 1930s see Arthur Frank Wertheim, *W. C. Fields from Sound Film and Radio Comedy to Stardom: Becoming a Cultural Icon* (New York: Palgrave Macmillan, 2019).

# Index

*Abraham Lincoln* (1931) (film), 118
Academy Awards, 204, 209, 233
Academy of Motion Picture Arts and Sciences, xiii
ad-libbing. *See* improvisation
*Adorable Lion, The* (Broadway play), 187–188
*Adventures of Dollie* (1908) (film), 80
African Americans: *Birth of a Nation* and, 23, 82–83; *A Fool and His Money,* 17–18
Agee, James, 5, 38
agents, 143
Aitkin, Harry E., 20
Albert, Katherine, 94
alcohol, use of: during *It's the Old Army Game* filming, 148; La Cava, 194; WCF, 148, 202
Alden, Mary, 179
Allen, Fred, 208
Allen, Judith, 142
"All-Star Comedies" (Gaumont one-reel), 20–21
"Amazing Peregrinations and Pettifoggery of One William Claude Dukenfield..., The" (museum exhibit), xiii
*America* (1924) (film), 53, 55
American Mutoscope and Biograph Company, 80
*American Venus, The* (1926) (film), 91
Anderson, Sherwood, 141
animation, 168, 187
*Annie Dear* (1924-25) (musical), 124
Arbuckle, Roscoe "Fatty," 7
arguments about content inclusion, 25, 147; golf routine, 172–173; with La Cava, 168, 172–173, 190–191; pool routine, 33, 34; *Poppy* (play), 62–63; *Running Wild,* 190–191;

*So's Your Old Man,* 168, 172–173; tendency diminishes in later years, 222
army shell game, 69, 73, 155–156, 218. *See also* con man character; *It's the Old Army Game* (1926) (film)
"Art of Breaking a Neck, The" (Scully), 220
*Art of the Moving Picture, The* (Lindsay), 113
*Art of W. C. Fields, The* (Everson)
Arvidson, Linda, 5
Astoria studio (Famous Players-Lasky/Paramount), 84–89, 167; closes, 194–196, 210; reopens, 207

Baby LeRoy, 129, 186–187
*Ballyhoo* (1930) (Broadway musical), 235
Balmer, Edwin, 106
*Bandits Waterloo, The* (1908) (film), 115
*Bank Dick, The* (1940) (film), 99, 139, 175, 190
Bara, Theda (née Theodosia Goodman), 7
*Barbershop, The* (1933) (film), 153
Barré, Raoul, 168
Barrymore, Ethel, 18
Barrymore, Lionel, 5, 7, 18, 28, 81
*Beau Geste* (1926) (film), 195
*Bedside Manna: The Third Fun in Bed Book* (Scully), 220
*Behind the Front* (1926) (film), 209
*Be Natural* (documentary), 18
Berlin, Irving, 50
Bernhardt, Sarah, 23
Berry, Wallace, 209, 214
*Big Broadcast of 1938, The* (1938) (WCF film), 36–37

*Big Con, The* (Maurer), 67–68
*Big Hand for the Little Lady, A* (1965) (film), 229
Bijou Dream Theater (New York City), 22
Bijou Theatre (Philadelphia), 22
Biograph Company (silent film studio), 23; Griffith at, 5, 80–82, 92, 115, 203; image, 83; *In Old California*, 203; *Ramona*, 203; Sennett at, 6, 92
*Birth of a Nation, The* (1915) (film), 8, 23, 82–83, 108, 118
Bitzer, "Billy," 94
Blackburn, Linelle, 141–146, 157, 200
Black Maria studio (Edison's studio), 4
Blanche, William "Shorty" (WCF's stooge on stage, films and personal assistant), 63, 116, 119, 153, 173
Bolton, Whitney, 87
Bosch, Hieronymus, 155
Bow, Clara Gordon, 208–209, 233
Bradford, F. G., 20–21, 40
Brennan, Jay, 214
Brenon, Herbert, 110, 195
Brian, Mary: in *Man on the Flying Trapeze*, 217; in *Running Wild*, 186, 188, 191, 216; in *Two Flaming Youths*, 216–217
Briant, Roy, 187–188
Brice, Monte, 223
*Bringing Up Father* (comic strip), 175
*Broadway Headliners* (sound shorts), 236
*Broken Blossoms* (1919) (film), 83–84
Brooks, Louise, 148–152; in *The American Venus*, 91; on Astoria studio, 85, 86; on Blackburn, 143; dancing of, 91, 150–151; *Dixie Dugan* character modeled on, 125, 178; on Griffith, 92, 96, 118–119; on Griffith and Dempster, 96; in *It's the Old Army Game*, 148, 149, 150, 152, 153, 159, 160; on LeBaron, 48;

*Lulu in Hollywood*, 150, 152; marriage to Sutherland, 143, 152, 224; "The Nagger" sketch described by, 135; "Other Face of W. C. Fields," 151–152; in *Pandora's Box*, 152, 206; on Paramount's factory-like operations, 206; studies WCF's performances, 150; on *Tillie's Punctured Romance*, 225; on WCF screen acting, 91–92; in *Ziegfeld Follies*, 91, 135, 149–150, 151
Broun, Heywood (critic), 48, 183–184
Brown, Karl, 94
Buck, Gene, 51, 124, 126
Burke, Billie, 44, 124

*Camille* (French production), 23
Cantor, Eddie (né Israel Itzkowitz), 124, 210
Capone, Al, 114
Capra, Frank, 120
cartoons, 125, 168, 175, 178, 187
Cavanna, Elise, 130, 153–154
"Celebrated Jumping Frog of Calaveras County, The" (Twain), 66–67
Champion Film Company, 6
Chaplin, Charlie, 14, 146–147, 234; *Circus, The*, 79; Conklin and, 215, 228; *Gold Rush, The*, 101, 147, 223; *Great Dictator*, 228; with Keystone, 24, 29, 45, 215; *Making a Living*, 29; *Modern Times*, 228; Sennett and, 24; Sutherland and, 147, 152; Swain and, 223; *Tillie's Punctured Romance* (1914), 146, 215, 222; tramp character, 24, 98; WCF comparisons, 24, 45, 98, 101, 175, 190; *Woman of Paris*, 147
*Chicago* (1927) (film), 115
Chicago, Illinois: Jazz-Age era crime in, 114–115; *That Royle Girl* filmed in, 108, 111, 114
*Chicago Daily News*, 111
*Chicago Evening Post*, 135
*Chicago Herald Examiner*, 221

children characters, mischievous: Baby LeRoy, 129, 186–187; in *Comic Supplement*, 128, 129; in *It's the Old Army Game*, 156, 158–159; in *Pool Sharks*, 30; in *Running Wild*, 186; in *So's Your Old Man*, 186
Christie, Al and Charlie, 222–223
Christie Film Company, 223
cigar box tricks, 28, 69, 74, 95, 202
*Circus, The* (1928) (film), 79
circuses, 70, 79. *See also Sally of the Sawdust* (1925) (film); *Tillie's Punctured Romance* (1928) (silent film)
Cité Elgé (Gaumont studio), 14
*Citizen Kane* (1941) (film), 51
"City Alley" (sketch), 128–130
cliff hanger, term origins, 7
*Cocoanuts, The* (1929) (film), 209, 233
Coconut Grove nightclub, 204
Cohl, Émile, 15
*Collier's Weekly*, 49
Collins, Charles, 135
comedy duos, 214, 223
comic strips, 125, 168, 175, 178, 187
*Comic Supplement, The* (1925) (revue), 125–136, 140, 189; cartoon influences, 125; "City Alley" (and "Sleeping Porch") sketch, 128–130, 156; closes early, 134–135; cuts to, 133, 134; "Drug Store" sketch, 128, 130–131; henpecked husband character, 125, 126, 128, 129, 135, 136; "House by the Side of the Road" ("Picnic Scene") sketch, 128, 135; "Joyride" sketch, 128, 131–132; McEvoy writes, 125–128, 132–134, 178; plot synopsis, 129–132, 133; realism and satirical themes in, 125–126, 134, 178, 183; reviews, 133–134; WCF revises script, 127–128, 132; Ziegfeld unhappy with, 132–133, 134. *See also It's a Gift* (1934) (film); *It's the Old Army Game* (1926) (film)

"Commotion Picture" (*Follies* sketch), 8
*Confidence Game, The* (Konnikova), 65
*Confidence-Man, His Masquerade, The* (Melville), 65, 66
*Confidence Man, The* (play), 65
"Conjurer, The" (Bosch), 155
Conklin, Chester, 10, 200; career overview, 214–215, 228–229; Chaplin and, 215, 228; death, 229; *Fools for Luck*, 34, 226–228; *Her Majesty Love*, 228; mustache, 34, 214, 215, 216; *Tillie's Punctured Romance*, 223, 224–225; *Two Flaming Youths*, 214, 215, 216, 217–218, 221; on WCF Hollywood house, 201. *See also* Fields-Conklin duo
con man character, 71, 128, 180; in *Fools for Luck*, 34, 226; origins of, 64–68; in *Poppy* (play), 48, 60, 62, 64, 68–76; in *That Royle Girl*, 116; in *Two Flaming Youths*, 210, 216; WCF life as inspiration for, 68–69; in *Ziegfeld Follies*, xiv, 139, 234. *See also* henpecked husband character
*Consequences of Feminism* (film), 17
contracts: Conklin, with various studios, 215; Griffith, with Famous Players-Lasky/Paramount, 84, 106, 110–111, 115; Paramount's terms with its actors, 208, 209; WCF, negotiates his own, 143; WCF, with Famous Players-Lasky/Paramount, 139–140, 195–196, 200, 208, 221–222, 232–233; WCF, with Gaumont, 21, 27, 40; WCF, with Goodman, 102; WCF, with Ziegfeld, 21, 102, 127. *See also* Paramount Pictures; salary, WCF
Cosmopolitan Productions studio, 49, 52, 56
crime and fraud: con artists, 64–68; gangster films, 114–115; in show business, 70–71. *See also* con man character

critics. *See* film reviews; stage reviews
Cukor, George, 85
*Curtain Pole, The* (1908) (silent film), 5–6

Dailey, Bill, 69
Dale, Alan, 75
Darnton, Charles, 75
*David Copperfield* (1935) (film), 139
Davies, Marion: Hearst and, 50–52, 53; *Janice Meredith,* 52, 53–57
Davies, Reine, 50
*Day I Drank a Glass of Water, The* (1945) (radio performance and recording), 103
DeMille, Cecil B., 103, 114, 120, 195, 207
Dempster, Carol, 93–94, 116–117; Gish, Lillian, rivalry between, 93, 95; *Sally of the Sawdust,* 93, 95, 96, 113; *That Royle Girl,* 108, 116
Denishawn (Ruth St. Denis-Ted Shawn) Dancers, 150
*Dentist, The* (1932) (film), 42, 153
*Dial,* 48
Dickens, Charles, 80, 117–118, 139
Dickson, William K. L., 3
Dietz, Howard, 61
Directors Guild of America, 120
Dix, Richard, 168
*Dixie Dugan* (comic strip), 125, 178
Donnelly, Dorothy, 61–63, 75
Dooley, Ray, 128, 129
Dressler, Marie, 146
"Drug Store" (sketch), 128, 130–131, 140, 148, 152–156, 167
*Drums of Love* (1928) (film), 117
*Drunken Mattress* (film), 17
Dukenfield, John (WCF paternal grandfather), 41
Dukinfied, George (WCF great grandfather), 41
Durand, Jean, 15
Dwan, Allan, 50

dysfunctional family trope. *See* henpecked husband character; satire, of domestic harmony

Eagels, Jeanne, 207
*Earl Carroll Vanities* (1928), 235
Eaton, Walter Prichard, 44
Éclair (French film company), 6
Edison, Thomas A., 3–4, 12, 23; MPPC/Edison Trust, 4–5, 6, 20, 80, 203
*Educational Screen,* 55–56
Edwards, Harry, 223
Egan, Jack, 180
Eisner, Lotte, 151
Epoch Production Corporation, 82
Errol, Leon, 8
Essanay Company, 14, 24
Everson, William K., 115, 212

Fall, Albert B., 71
"Family Ford, The" (*Follies* sketch), 187
Famous Players-Lasky (later Paramount), 23, 101, 195, 203, 207, 208; Astoria studio, 84–89. *See also* Paramount Pictures
Famous Players Motion Picture Company, 23, 203, 207. *See also* Zukor, Adolph
*Fantomas* (1913) (film), 14
*Fatal Glass of Beer, The* (1933) (film), 139
Fazenda, Louise, 223, 224
Fears, Peggy, 151
Feature Play Company, 23. *See also* Famous Players-Lasky; Lasky, Jesse; Paramount Pictures
female directors: Guy, 15, 16–18, 19; Weber, 18
Fendick, Maud, 142
Feuillade, Louis, 14, 15
Fields, Claude (son), 51, 126, 187

Fields, Harriet Veronica "Hattie" (née Hughes) (wife), 51, 126, 142, 187, 202, 228
Fields, Lew, 214
Fields, Ronald J. (grandson), 234
Fields, Walter (brother), 41–42
Fields, W. C.: affairs: Allen, Judith, 142; Blackburn, Linelle, 141–146, 157, 200; Fendick, Maud, 142; George, Grace, 142; Monti, Carlotta, 142; Poole, Bessie, 52, 141–142; alcohol use, 148, 202; career (*See also* contracts; salary, WCF); after Paramount contract ends, 232, 235; duration on stage *vs.* in films, 140; fame, 161; financial problems, 228, 232, 235; leaves *Follies* in 1925, 56, 139; multiple genres represented, xiii–xiv, 103; overview, xiii–xv, 196; radio performances, xiv, 103; characteristics of (*See also* arguments about content inclusion); accident-prone, 219–221; contradictions in, 179; dislike of early rising, 128, 181; fond remembrances by friends and loved ones, 62, 75, 120, 173, 186–187, 193, 216–217; house in Hollywood, 200–201; house in New York, 87–88; insecurity, 196, 222; interest in literature, 117; physical appearance, 2, 142, 215–216, 226; tall tales by, 35, 67, 103; voice, 10, 55, 74, 176, 210, 232, 236; wanderlust, 142; comedic style; Brooks studies, 150; improvisation, 40, 63, 64; mustache humor, 29, 92–93, 116, 181, 188, 215–216, 224; pantomime, 35, 91, 99, 161, 172, 175; physical comedy, 172, 175; prop use, 29, 32, 35, 174; reflections on his own, 22, 29, 63, 91; slapstick, pressures to employ, 24–25; stage training to film studio setting, difficulties of adapting, 22, 43–46, 91–92, 180–181; timing in, 54–55, 91, 92, 180; comic characterizations (*See also* con man character; henpecked husband character); card shark, 74; developed in *Ziegfeld Follies*, xiv, 46, 128, 139, 166, 234; frustrated Everyman, 29, 32, 102, 131, 149; inspiration from life events, 68–69, 129, 148; pun names, 140; tramp juggler, 2, 24, 69; contracts (*See* contracts); costars (*See also* Brooks, Louise; Fields-Conklin duo); Alden, Mary, 179; Blanche, William "Shorty," 63, 116, 119, 153, 173; Brian, Mary, 186, 188, 191, 216–217; Cavanna, Elise, 130, 153–154; Davies, Marion, 51, 54, 56, 57; Dempster, Carol, 93, 95–96, 108, 113, 116; Dooley, Ray, 128, 129; Egan, Jack, 180; Fazenda, Louise, 223, 224; Fitzgerald, Cissy, 218; Gallagher, Richard "Skeets," 180; Harris, Ivy, 180; Harris, Marcia, 169; Joyce, Alice, 170, 171; Kennedy, Madge, 61, 62, 63, 75; Leedom, Edna, 135; LeRoy, Baby, 129, 186–187; Luden, Jack, 226; Page, Lionel, 36; Reichart, Catherine, 169; Rogers, Charles "Buddy," 171, 173, 209; Shotwell, Marie, 188; Sinclair, Johnny (stuntman), 153, 220; Swain, Mack, 223; Wynn, Ed, 8–9; Young, Tammany, 34–35, 153; death, 201, 202; directors (*See also* Griffith, David Wark; La Cava, Gregory; Sutherland, Eddie); Haddock, "Silent Bill," 40; McCarey, Leo, 34; Middleton, Edwin, 28; Waters, John, 221; family relationships: brother Walter, 41–42; grandson Ronald, 234; paternal lineage, 41; son Claude (with Hattie), 51, 126, 187; son William (with Bessie Poole), 52; wife Hattie, 51, 126, 142, 187, 202, 228; film performances (*See*

film performances, WCF; films, WCF's attitude toward); friendships: Cavanna, Elise, 154; Conklin, Chester, 216; Geraghty, Thomas J., 166; Grady, Bill, 143; La Cava, Gregory, 192–194; LeBaron, William, 48; McEvoy, J. P., 127; Rogers, Will, 7; Sutherland, Eddie, 147–148; health, 33, 142, 148, 154, 202; accidents, 219–221; life events: birth and youth, 67, 129; death, 201, 202; as inspiration for comic characterizations, 68–69, 129, 148; lives in Hollywood, 196, 200–201, 236; lives in New York, 87–88; similarities to Griffith, 79–80; travels of, 80; radio performances, xiv, 103; salary (*See* salary, WCF); scripts, revisions to and influence on (*See also* arguments about content inclusion); *Comic Supplement*, 127–128, 132; stage performances (*See* stage performances)

Fields, William Claude, III (grandson)

Fields, William Claude, Jr. (son), 51, 126, 187

Fields-Conklin duo, 10, 200, 210, 211, 214–229; *Fools for Luck*, 34, 226–228; *Her Majesty Love*, 228; mustache humor, 215–216; reviews, 221, 227–228; *Tillie's Punctured Romance*, 223, 224–225; *Two Flaming Youths*, 214, 215, 216, 217–218, 221. See also *Fools for Luck* (1928) (silent film); *Tillie's Punctured Romance* (1928) (silent film); *Two Flaming Youths* (1927) (film)

Fields Papers, xiii

Film Booking Offices of America, 208

*Film Daily*, 100

*Film d'Arte* productions, 23

film distribution, 56, 225; Edison Trust, 4; Mutual Film Corporation, 20, 21, 24–25, 43, 82; Paramount, 50, 106, 139, 194, 207, 222, 223; shorts screened in vaudeville venues, 22–23

film industry: financial motivations in, 106, 109–111, 206, 207–208, 211–212, 222, 232; transition from silent films to Talkies, 205–206, 210. *See also* film studios (companies); Hollywood, California; New York City, filmmaking in

filmmaking process: benefits of Hollywood locale for, 203; Griffith's directorial style, 81, 92, 94, 97, 108, 117; Griffith's editing techniques, 23, 81, 93; Griffith's influence in, 120; La Cava's editing techniques, 168; special effects, 108–109; WCF unfamiliar with, 92–93

film performances, WCF, 140; "All-Star Comedies," 21; *Big Broadcast of 1938*, 36–37; *Follow the Boys*, 37; Fort Lee *Follies* short, 3, 8–9; *Golf Specialist*, 10, 42, 172, 210, 236; *Her Majesty Love*, 228; *His Lordship's Dilemma*, 27, 40–46, 172; *It's a Gift*, 128, 136, 175, 182, 183, 189–190, 235; *Janice Meredith*, 52, 53–57; *Man on the Flying Trapeze*, 186, 217, 235, 287; *Old Fashioned Way*, 70, 221; *Pool Sharks*, 27–33, 37, 43, 44; *Poppy*, 103, 235; *Potters, The*, 87, 178–184, 196, 234; *Running Wild*, 50, 87, 186–191, 196, 200, 216, 235; *Six of a Kind*, 34–36; *Tillie's Punctured Romance*, 34, 70, 222–225; *You Can't Cheat an Honest Man*, 71; *You're Telling Me*, 176, 189, 235. See also *It's the Old Army Game* (1926) (film); *Sally of the Sawdust* (1925) (film); *So's Your Old Man* (1926) (film); *That Royle Girl* (1925) (film); *Two Flaming Youths* (1927) (film)

film reviews, 22, 23; *Big Broadcast of 1938*, 36; *Broadway Headliners*,

236; *Follow the Boys*, 38; *Fools for Luck*, 227–228; Fort Lee *Follies* short, 9; *His Lordship's Dilemma*, 43; *It's the Old Army Game*, 160; *Janice Meredith*, 53, 55–57; *Pool Sharks*, 32; *The Potters*, 183–184, 196; *Running Wild*, 190, 196; *Sally of the Sawdust*, 99–102, 113; *Six of a Kind*, 35–36; *So's Your Old Man*, 174, 175; *That Royle Girl*, 111–113, 115–116; *Tillie's Punctured Romance*, 223, 225; *Two Flaming Youths*, 221. See also *New York Times, The* (reviews); stage reviews

film reviews, Griffith's films, 84, 118; *America*, 53, 55; *Birth of a Nation*, 82; *New York Hat*, 5; *Sally of the Sawdust*, 99–102, 113; *That Royle Girl*, 111–113, 115–116. See also Griffith, David Wark, films directed by

films, lost, 111, 216–217, 233–234; *Fools for Luck*, 34, 226–228, 229, 232, 235; *His Lordship's Dilemma*, 27, 40–46, 172; *The Potters*, 87, 178–184, 196, 234; *Tillie's Punctured Romance*, 34, 70, 220–221, 222–225. See also *That Royle Girl* (1925) (film); *Two Flaming Youths* (1927) (film)

films, popularity growth of, 22–23, 102

films, silent. See silent films

films, sound. See Talkies

films, WCF's attitude toward, 102, 120, 160, 161, 195–196, 221; stage training, adapting to film setting, 22, 43–46, 91–92, 180–181

film studios (companies): Big Five, 106, 207–208, 232; Goldwyn, 7; Nestor Studios (and mergers), 222–223; Preferred Pictures, 208–209; RKO, 106, 207, 236; United Artists, 101, 208; Universal, 5, 18, 20, 223; Vitagraph, 12, 20; Warner Bros., 56, 206, 207. See also Biograph Company (silent film studio); film industry; Gaumont Film Company; Keystone Pictures Studio; Paramount Pictures (was Famous Players-Lasky)

film studios (production facilities): Astoria (Famous Players-Lasky/ Paramount), 84–89, 167, 194–196, 207, 210; Cosmopolitan Productions, 49, 52, 56; fires, 9, 10, 56; Flushing, 12–13, 20; Fort Lee, 3, 4, 5–10, 17; Fox, 7; Ideal Studios, 10; Nestor Studios, 222–223; Reliance-Majestic (Mutual), 82; Solax, 7, 17; storage issues, 233; Universal, 7, 19; Vitagraph, 12. See also filmmaking process

*Film Weekly*, 36

Fits and Convulsions Club, 193

Fitzgerald, Cissy, 218

*Follies. See Ziegfeld Follies*

*Follow the Boys* (1944) (film), 37–38

Fontaine, Lynn, 97

*Fool and His Money, A* (1912) (film), 17–18

*Fools for Luck* (1928) (silent film), 226–228, 229, 232; *It's the Old Army Game* remade as, 235; plot synopsis, 226–227; reviews, 34, 227–228

*Fool There Was, A* (1914) (silent film), 7

Ford, Harrison, 108

Fort Lee, 5–10; film studios proliferate in, 4, 6; *Follies* short, 3, 8–9; Griffith's films in, 5–6; image, 7; Solax moves to, 17. See also New York City, filmmaking in

Fox, William, 7

Fox studio, 206, 215

France, filmmaking in, 13, 15

"French Comedy, Gaumont Style" (Museum of Modern Art exhibit), 14–15

*Freshman, The* (1925) (film)

frustrated Everyman character, 29, 32, 102, 131, 149
Fulton, James, 71

Gallagher, Richard "Skeets," 180
gangster films, 114–115
Gaumont, Léon, 13
Gaumont Film Company, 12–25; Feuillade at, 14, 15; Guy at, 15, 16–18; Haddock at, 40; *His Lordship's Dilemma*, 27, 40–46, 172; moves to New York, 13, 20; Mutual as distributor, 20, 21, 24–25, 43; *Pool Sharks*, 27–33, 37, 43, 44; slapstick and, 15, 24–25; WCF, contract with, 21, 27, 40; WCF shorts produced by, 83; Weber at, 18
Gaumont-Palace movie theater (Paris), 14
Geddes, Norman Bel, 133–134, 135
George, Grace, 142
*George White's Scandals* (play), 196
Geraghty, Thomas J., 166–167
*Gilded Age, The* (Twain), 66
*Girl Who Stayed at Home, The* (1919) (film), 93
Gish, Dorothy, 5, 7, 81, 84
Gish, Lillian, 5, 7, 113; Dempster, rivalry between, 93, 95; Griffith and, 81, 84, 93, 95, 109; *Musketeers of Pig Alley*, 115; *Orphans of the Storm*, 84
*Glorifying the American Girl* (1928) (film), 210
Glyn, Elinor, 209
Goldfish (Goldwyn), Samuel, 61, 207
"Goldie" (Ziegfeld's secretary), 124
*Gold Rush, The* (1925) (film), 101, 147, 223
Goldwyn Pictures, 7
golf, WCF plays, 172, 192–193
golf routines: *Dentist, The*, 42; *Golf Specialist*, 10, 42, 172, 210, 236; *Hip Action*, 172; *His Lordship's Dilemma*, 42, 172; *So's Your Old Man*, 42, 171, 172–173
*Golf Specialist, The* (1930) (film), 10, 42, 172, 210, 236
Goodman, Phillip, 60–62, 74, 102, 167
Grady, Bill, 142–146
Graham, Martha, 150
*Graphic*, 228
Grauman, Sid, 204
Graves, Richard, 95
Great Depression, 233, 235
*Great Dictator, The* (1940) (film), 228
*Greatest Question, The* (1919) (film), 94
*Greatest Thing in Life, The* (1918) (film), 93
Great White Way, The, 2
Griffith, David Wark (D. W.).: at Biograph, 5, 80–82, 92, 115, 203; Dempster and, 93–94, 95, 96, 116–117; directorial style, 81, 92, 94, 97, 108, 117; editing techniques, 23, 81, 93; end of life, and death of, 118–120; at Famous Players-Lasky/Paramount, 84, 106, 110–111, 115; Fort Lee as filming location, 5–6; gangster films by, 115; Gish, Lillian and, 81, 84, 93, 95, 109; Hollywood move, 203; image, 110; influence of, 120; life events, as inspiration for films, 98; life events, WCF similarities, 79–80; prolific output, 81–82, 118; scripts, dislike of, 94, 97, 108; special effects used by, 108–109; voice of, 94; Watson and, 88–89. *See also* film reviews, Griffith's films; *Sally of the Sawdust* (1925) (film); *That Royle Girl* (1925) (film)
Griffith, David Wark, films directed by: *Abraham Lincoln*, 118; *America*, 53, 55; *The Bandits Waterloo*, 115; *Birth of a Nation*, 8, 23, 82–83, 108, 118; *Broken Blossoms*, 83–84; *The Curtain Pole*, 5–6; *Intolerance*, 83,

93; *Isn't Life Wonderful?*, 117; *The Musketeers of Pig Alley*, 115; *In Old California*, 203; *One Exciting Night*, 109; *Orphans of the Storm*, 84; *The Politician's Love Story*, 6; *Ramona*, 203; *Sally of the Sawdust*, 79, 89, 92–93, 94–101, 113; *The Sorrows of Satan*, 117; *The Struggle*, 118; *That Royle Girl*, 106–115, 117. See also film reviews, Griffith's films; *Sally of the Sawdust* (1925) (film); *That Royle Girl* (1925) (film)
Griffith, David Wark, WCF works with: amiable relationship, 117, 120; directorial style conflicts with WCF comedic talents, 92; *Pickwick Papers* interest, 117–118; on *Sally of the Sawdust*, 79–80, 89, 92, 95–96, 97, 99–101, 107; similar life events, 79–80; on *That Royle Girl*, 107, 109; WCF admires directorial style, 117; WCF eager for opportunity, 79, 89, 107
Griffith, Linda, 6
*Guardsman, The* (1931) (film), 97
Gunther, June, 229
Guy Blaché, Alice, 15, 16–18, 19

Haddock, William F. "Silent Bill," 40
Hall, Mordaunt, 175, 183, 190, 221
Hal Roach Studio, 211
*Ham Tree, The* (1905) (play), 61
Harding, Warren G., 71
Hardy, Oliver, 211
Hardy, Sam, 153
Harris, Ivy, 180
Harris, Marcia, 169
Hatton, Raymond, 214
Hearst, Phoebe, 49
Hearst, William Randolph, 49, 168; Davies and, 50–52, 53; *Janice Meredith*, 52, 53–57; media synergy strategies of, 52–53
Heath, Thomas, 61
Held, John, Jr., 133

Henderson, Alice Corbin, 111
henpecked husband character: in *Comic Supplement*, 125, 126, 128, 129, 135, 136; in *It's the Old Army Game*, 140–141; in "Mr. Bisbee's Princess," 166; origins of, 125–126; in *The Potters*, 178, 180, 182, 183; in *Running Wild*, 186; in *So's Your Old Man*, 161, 170, 175, 183, 189; in *You're Telling Me*, 183, 189; in *Ziegfeld Follies*, xiv, 139, 234. See also con man character; rich-in-the-end scenario; satire
*Her Majesty Love* (1931) (film), 228
*Hiawatha* (1909), 5
*Hip Action* (1933) (film), 172
*His Lordship's Dilemma* (1915) (film), 27, 40–46, 172; image, 45; plot synopsis, 41–42; reviews, 43
Holland, Andrew, 4
Hollywood, California, 200–205, 235; commercial growth in, 204; image, 201, 205; incorporation and marketing, 202–203; naming of, 200–201; Paramount concentrates filmmaking in, 194–196; population increase and demographics, 203–204; WCF in, 196, 200–201, 236. See also New York City, filmmaking in
*Hollywood on the Hudson* (Kozarski), 12
"House by the Side of the Road" ("Picnic Scene") (sketch), 128, 135, 140, 157–159
*Huckleberry Finn* (Twain), 66
*Humoresque* (1920) (film), 49
*Hypocrites!* (1914) (film), 18

Ideal Studios, 10
*Immortal Alamo, The* (1911) (film), 40
improvisation, 40, 63, 64
Ince, Thomas Hart, 161
*In Old California* (1910) (short film), 203

International Movie Data Base (IMDB), 43
*Intolerance* (1916) (film), 83, 93
*Isn't Life Wonderful* (1924) (film), 84, 117
*It* (1927) (film), 209
*It Can't Happen Here* (Lewis), 167
*It's a Gift* (1934) (film), 128, 136, 182, 235; rich-in-the-end scenario, 99, 175, 183, 189, 190. *See also It's the Old Army Game* (1926) (film)
*It's the Old Army Game* (1926) (film), 87, 140–161, 180; army shell game in, 155–156; cast and crew's drinking on set, 148; *Comic Supplement* sketches recycled in, 128, 136, 140, 156, 160; "Drug Store" scene, 140, 152–156; Geraghty coauthors screenplay, 166; henpecked husband character, 140–141; image, 149, 151; "Joyride" scene, 140, 156–157; Ocala location shots, 146, 148, 157; "Picnic" scene, 140, 157–160; plot synopsis, 148–149, 152–153, 154–155, 156–160; remade as *Fools for Luck,* 235; reviews, 160; rich-in-the-end scenario, 99, 183, 189–190; "Sleeping Porch" scene, 140, 156; Sutherland directs, 146, 147, 148, 152, 157; WCF, Blackburn, and Grady road trip to Florida for filming, 141–146. *See also It's a Gift* (1934) (film)

Jacobs, Lewis, 114, 115
Jaffe, Adeline, 210
*Janice Meredith* (1924) (film), 52, 53–57; budget, 53, 55; image, 57; plot synopsis, 54; reviews, 53, 55–57
Javier, Emma, 61–62
Jazz Age Chicago, 114–115. *See also That Royle Girl* (1925) (film)
*Jazz Singer, The* (1927) (film), 222
Joyce, Alice, 170, 171

"Joyride, The" (sketch), 128, 131–132, 140, 156–157
juggling routines, xiv, 29; cigar boxes, 28, 69, 74, 95, 202; cut from *Sally of the Sawdust,* 95; *His Lordship's Dilemma,* 42; *Pool Sharks,* 30; *Poppy,* 74; *Tillie's Punctured Romance,* 224; tramp juggler character, 2, 24, 69; tricks of, 28, 69; *Two Flaming Youths,* 217, 218
J. Walter Thompson advertising agency, 103

Karno, Fred, 45
Keaton, Buster, 45, 234
Keith and Orpheum circuits, 23
Kennedy, Joseph P., 208
Kennedy, Madge, 61, 62, 63, 75
Kern, Jerome, 74, 102
Kerr, Walter, iv
Keystone Pictures Studio, 6; Chaplin with, 24, 29, 45, 215; Conklin with, 215; Mutual as distributor, 20; Sutherland with, 146–147. *See also* Sennett, Mack
*Kid Boots* (1923-25) (musical), 124
*Kid Brother, The* (1927) (film), 209, 233
"Kid Strips" (comics)
Killigan, Corey, 43
Kinetoscope, 3–4, 12
Kingsley, Grace, 101
Konnikova, Maria, 65
Koster and Bial's New Music Hall, 23
Kozarski, Richard, 12
Kuhn, Loeb, and Company, 20

La Cava, Gregory, 49–50; death, 194; directs *My Man Godfrey,* 193; directs *So's Your Old Man,* 50, 167–168, 175, 186; directs *Stage Door,* 193–194; editing techniques, 168; WCF conflict, 168, 172–173, 190–191, 196; WCF friendship, 192–194; writes and directs *Run-*

ning Wild, 50, 186, 187, 190–191.
See also Running Wild (1927) (film);
So's Your Old Man (1926) (film)
Laemmle, Carl, 5, 7, 19
land speculation theme, 66, 149, 155, 182–183, 189–190
Lanz, Walter, 168
Larson, Edwin S., 117
Lasky, Jesse, 23, 84–85, 86, 140; announces Astoria closing, 194; Famous Players-Lasky merger, 203, 207; leases Hollywood land in 1913, 203; on Paramount Pictures School, 173; Paramount's Hollywood move and, 194, 195; That Royle Girl and, 106; WCF-Conklin pairing and, 200. See also Paramount Pictures; Zukor, Adolph
Laughing Bill Hyde (1918) (film), 7
laughter/audience reaction, WCF on, 22, 29, 161, 168, 180, 229
Laurel, Stan, 211
LeBaron, William, 87–88; at Astoria, 167; Beau Geste credited to, 195; image, 110; It's the Old Army Game and, 148; role in WCF career advancement, 48–49, 54, 208, 236; So's Your Old Man and, 167, 168; That Royle Girl and, 106; WCF friendship, 48
Leedom, Edna, 135
LeRoy, Baby (Ronald Overacker), 186–187
Letter, The (1928) (film), 207
Lewis, Sinclair, 167
Library of Congress, National Film Registry, 176
Life on the Mississippi (Twain), 66
Lighton, Louis, 211
Lights of New York, The (1928) (film), 206
Lindbergh, Charles, 206
Linder, Max, 13–14
Lindsay, Vachel, 113
Little Old New York (1923) (film), 52

Lloyd, Harold, 45, 181, 209, 233, 234
Lorentz, Pare, 221
Los Angeles Times, xiii, 101, 190, 220
Louie the 14$^{th}$ (1925) (musical), 124
Love Parade, The (1929) (film), 233
Lubitsch, Ernst, 233
Luden, Jack, 226
Lulu in Hollywood (Brooks), 150, 152
Lumière's Cinématographe, 23
Lunt, Alfred, 97
Lux Radio Theatre, 103

MacIntyre, F. Gwynplaine, 43
Mack and Moran, 214
Madame X (1910) (play), 61
Making a Living (1914) (film), 29
Male and Female (1919) (film), 114
Man on the Flying Trapeze (1935) (film), 186, 187, 217, 235
Man That Corrupted Hadleyburg, The (Twain), 67
Marion, Frances, 50
Marion Davies Film Company, 52
Marsh, Mae, 93
Marx Brothers, 209, 233
Masters, Edgar Lee, 141
Maurer, David, 67
mauve decade, 71
Max and his Taxi (film), 14
Mayer, Louis B., 56
McCaffrey, Donald W., 126, 236
McCarey, Leo, 34
McDonald, Katherine, 208
McEvoy, Joseph P. ("J. P."), 124–128; Comic Supplement, 125–128, 132–134, 178; Dixie Dugan, 125, 178; The Potters (play), 124, 178; Slams of Life, 125, 178–179; WCF, professional relationship with, 127–128, 132, 178–179; Ziegfeld and, 124–125, 126–127, 132–134
McIntyre, James, 61
McManus, George, 175
medicine shows, 69–70
Meek, Donald, 178

Méliès, George, 22
Melville, Herman, 65
Mencken, H. L., 64, 167
*Merchant of Venice, The* (1914) (film), 18
Merman, Ethel (Ethel Agnes Zimmerman), 88
MGM, 56, 207
Middleton, Edwin, 28
Midnight Frolic supper club, 2
Miller, Marilyn, 124
milquetoast, origin of term, 187
milquetoast husband character. *See* henpecked husband character
*Mind Over Motor* (1923) (film), 223
El Mirasol estate, 157–158
*Les Miserables* (1918) (film), 7
*Mississippi* (1935) (film), 66, 74
Mix, Tom, 79
*Modern Times* (1936) (film), 228
*Monte Carlo Girls* (burlesque show), 4, 71
Monti, Carlotta, 142
*Morning Telegraph,* 228
Morris, William Rexford Fields (son of WCF and Bessie Poole), 52
*Motion Picture News,* 160, 175, 190
Motion Picture Patents Company (MPPC)/Edison Trust, 4–5, 6, 20, 80, 203
*The Movies Are* (Sandburg column), 111
movie theaters, 22, 204; Gaumont-Palace, 14; Paramount Theater, 183, 206–207; Publix theater chain, 183, 194, 207, 233; wired for sound, 206–207, 228
*Movietone News* (Fox), 206, 235
*Moving Pictures* (Schulberg, Budd), 211
*Moving Picture World* (industry trade magazine), 6, 17, 20, 43, 56, 175
"Mr. Bisbee's Princess" (Street), 166
Murray, Elizabeth, 115
Murray, Mae, 8

Museum of Modern Art, 14
*Musketeers of Pig Alley, The* (1912) (film), 115
mustache-related humor, 29, 92–93, 116, 181, 188, 215–216, 224
Mutual Film Corporation, 14; as Gaumont distributor, 20, 21, 24–25, 43; Reliance-Majestic studio, 82; slapstick and, 24–25
*My Little Chickadee* (1940) (film), 74
*My Man Godfrey* (1937) (film), 193

NAACP, 82
"The Nagger" (*Follies* sketch), 135–136
narrative feature films, 23
Nasaw, David, 50
Nathan, George Jean, 48
*National Police Gazette,* 65
Nestor Company, 203
Nestor Studios, 222–223
New Amsterdam Theatre, 2
*Newark News,* 10
Newmeyer, Fred, 181
*New York American,* 75, 221, 228
New York City, filmmaking in: Astoria studio, 84–89, 167, 194–196, 207, 210; Flushing, 12–13, 20; Gaumont moves to, 13, 20; Griffith and, 80, 84; Hearst and, 49; Paramount moves to Hollywood, 194–196. *See also* Fort Lee; Hollywood, California
*New Yorker, The,* 111, 116
*New York Hat, The* (1912) (silent short), 5, 81
*New York Herald,* 65
*New York Herald Tribune,* 35–36, 190, 228
*New York Post,* 228
*New York Sun, The,* 228
*New York Times, The,* 4, 43, 85, 173, 220
*New York Times, The* (reviews): *America,* 53; *Comic Supplement,* 134;

*Follow the Boys*, 38; *Fools for Luck*, 34, 227, 228; Fort Lee *Follies* short, 9; *It's the Old Army Game*, 160; *Janice Meredith*, 53, 56; *The Potters*, 183; *Running Wild*, 190; *Sally of the Sawdust*, 100, 101; *So's Your Old Man*, 175; *Two Flaming Youths*, 221. See also film reviews
*New York World*, 187
Nolan, William, 50
Normand, Mabel, 146

Ocala, Florida, 146, 148, 157
"Off to the Country" (1921) (*Follies* sketch), 187
*Old Fashioned Way, The* (1934) (film), 70, 221
*One Exciting Night* (1922) (film), 109
"*Onésime*" comedy series (Gaumont), 15
"Open Letter to D. W. Griffith" (Quirk), 84
orphan characters, 80
*Orphans of the Storm* (1922) (film), 84
Oscars, 204, 209, 233
"Other Face of W. C. Fields, The" (Brooks), 151–152

Pabst, G. W., 152, 206
Page, Lionel, 36
Paine, Thomas, 3
*Pandora's Box* (1929) (film), 152, 206
pantomime: in *Comic Supplement*, 132; Conklin and, 215; WCF and, 35, 91, 99, 161, 172, 175
Paramount movie theater, 183, 206–207
Paramount Pictures (was Famous Players-Lasky), 23, 206–212; actors promoted by, 208, 209, 233; Astoria studio, 84–89, 167, 194–196, 207, 210; as Big Five studio, 106, 207–208, 232; Conklin at, 215; factory-like operations at, 206, 207–208, 211–212, 222, 232–233; film distribution by, 50, 106, 139, 194, 207, 222, 223; financial difficulties, 233; financial motivations, 106, 110–111, 206, 211–212, 222; financial success, 232–233; Griffith, contract with, 84, 106, 110–111, 115; Hearst and, distribution deal, 50; Hollywood move, 194–196; LeBaron, William at, 48; logo, 207; pays for WCF pool table transport, 33–34; Publix theater chain, 183, 194, 207, 233; Schulberg, B. P. at, 208, 209; WCF, contract with, 139–140, 195–196, 200, 208, 221–222, 232–233. See also contracts; Famous Players-Lasky (later Paramount); film studios
Paramount Pictures School, 173
Paris, Barry, 152
Pathé-Frères (French film studio), 13–14, 102. See also Gaumont Film Company
Petrova, Olga, 18
*Pharmacist, The* (1933) (film), 141, 153
Philadelphia, Pennsylvania, 22, 67
Phonoscène (early talking picture system), 13, 16
Pickford, Mary, 5, 7, 81, 87, 173, 194
*Pickwick Papers, The* (Dickens), 117–118
"Picnic Scene" (sketch), 128, 135, 140, 157–159
Picture Productions, 6
*Politician's Love Story, The* (1909) (silent film), 6
Poole, Elizabeth (Bessie) Chatterton, 52, 141–142
pool routines, 27–38; "All-Star Comedies," 21; *Big Broadcast of 1938*, 36–37; *Comic Supplement*, 133; *Follow the Boys*, 37–38; *Fools for Luck*, 34, 227; origins of, 27; *Pool Sharks*, 27–33, 37, 43, 44; *Poppy* (play), 74; *Six of a Kind*, 34–36; *Tillie's Punctured Romance*, 34; *Two Flaming*

*Youths,* 226; WCF's table and props, 27–28, 33–34, 227
*Pool Sharks* (1915) (film), 27–33, 37, 43, 44; plot synopsis, 29–32; reviews, 32
*Poppy* (1923-24) (play), 60–64, 68–76, 141, 196; con man character in, 48, 60, 62, 64, 68–76; plot synopsis, 71–75; reviews, 48, 73–74, 75; *Sally of the Sawdust* deviates from, 96–97, 98–99; WCF improvises lines, 63, 64; WCF voice and, 74. *See also Sally of the Sawdust* (1925) (film)
*Poppy* (1936) (film), 103, 235
*Poppy* (radio dramatization), 103
*Poppy Comes to Town* (Donnelly), 60
*Potters, The* (1923-24) (play), 124, 178
*Potters, The* (1927) (film), 87, 99, 178–184, 234; plot synopsis, 179–180, 182–183, 184; reviews, 183–184, 196
Preferred Pictures, 208–209
Proctor's 23rd Street Theater, 22
production facilities. *See* film studios (production facilities)
Prohibition, 71, 114, 148
Publix theater chain, 183, 194, 207, 233. *See also* Paramount Pictures

*Queen Elizabeth* (French production), 23
Quirk, James R., 84

race: *Birth of a Nation* and, 23, 82–83; *A Fool and His Money* and, 17–18
radio performances, WCF, xiv, 103
rail travel, 70
*Ramona* (1910) (short film), 203
Ramsaye, Terry, 81–82
Reading, Amy, 66
Reichart, Catherine, 169
Reisner, Charles, 216
Reliance-Majestic studio (Mutual), 82
Renoir, Jean, 120
reviews. *See* film reviews; stage reviews

"revolt from the village" literary movement, 141, 167
revues. *See Comic Supplement, The* (1925) (revue); stage performances
Rex Motion Picture Company, 18
Rialto Theater, 100
rich-in-the-end scenario: *The Bank Dick,* 99, 175, 190; *It's a Gift,* 99, 175, 183, 189, 190; *It's the Old Army Game,* 99, 183, 189–190; *The Potters,* 99, 182–183; *Sally of the Sawdust,* 98–99; *So's Your Old Man,* 99, 174, 175, 183, 189; *You're Telling Me,* 99, 183, 189. *See also* satire
Ring, Blanche, 154–155
RKO, 106, 207, 236. *See also* film studios
Robinson, David, 81, 212
Rogers, Charles "Buddy," 17, 173, 209, 233
Rogers, Ginger, 194
Rogers, Will, 7, 210, 220
*Rose of Kentucky* (1911) (film), 82
Ross, Bud, 29–32, 33, 41, 45
*Runaway Roman* (1917) (film), 52
*Running Wild* (1927) (film), 87, 186–191, 200, 216; henpecked husband character, 186; image, 188; La Cava-WCF relationship during and after, 186, 191–194, 196; La Cava writes and directs, 50, 186, 187, 190–191; plot synopsis, 187–189; remade as *Man on the Flying Trapeze,* 235; reviews, 190, 196; script contention, 191
Runyon, Damon, 193
Russell, Lillian, 28

salary, WCF, 221; *Comic Supplement,* 127; with Gaumont, 21, 27; *Janice Meredith,* 54; with Paramount, 139–140; *Sally of the Sawdust,* 79, 107, 140; *That Royle Girl,* 107. *See also* contracts

*Sally of the Sawdust* (1925) (film), 87, 91–103, 107, 140, 180; cuts to, 95, 99; Dempster in, 93, 95, 96, 113; deviations from *Poppy* (play), 96–97, 98–99; Griffith directs, 79, 89, 92–93, 94–101, 113; image, 96, 99; plot synopsis, 96–99; rehearsals, 94; remade as *Poppy* (film), 103, 235; reviews, 99–102, 113; rich-in-the end scenario, 98–99; WCF nervousness about, 89; WCF screen time in, 115–116
Sandburg, Carl, 111–113
satire, 8, 13, 17–18, 135, 182–183, 184; as antithetical to escapist films, 211; of domestic harmony, 125–126, 134, 161, 178, 183, 187, 211; realism of *Comic Supplement*, 125–126, 134, 178, 183; "revolt from the village" literary movement, 141, 167; of small-town life, 141, 167, 169. *See also* henpecked husband character; rich-in-the-end scenario
Savoy, Bert, 214
Schickel, Richard, 6, 118
Schulberg, Benjamin Percival (B.P.), 195, 200, 206, 210, 211; career, 208–209
Schulberg, Budd, 210–211
*Screenland*, 100, 116
Scully, Frank, 220
Selznick, Lewis, 6
Selznick Enterprises, 7
Sennett, Mack, 5–6, 24, 153, 215, 223; at Biograph, 6, 92. *See also* Keystone Pictures Studio
Sherwood, Robert E., 100–101
Shotwell, Marie, 188
*Show Boat* (1927-29) (musical), 56, 102
*Silent Clowns, The* (Kerr), iv
silent films, 20, 52, 111, 146; early popularity, 22; remade as Talkies, 160–161, 176, 234–235; renaissance, 44–45, 234; storage and preservation, 233; transition to Talkies, 10, 205–206, 210; WCF cast in, while Talkies becoming popular, 10, 200, 222, 228. *See also* film performances, WCF; films, lost; Talkies; specific film
Silverman, Sid (Sidney), 184
Silverman, Sime, 9, 184, 190
Sinclair, Johnny, 153, 220
Sinyard, Neil, 80
*Six of a Kind* (1934) (film), 34–36
*Slams of Life: With Malice for All and Charity Towards None* (McEvoy), 125, 178–179
slapstick comedy: French origins, 15; *Pool Sharks* and, 28–32; WCF comedic style differs from, 24–25. *See also* Keystone Pictures Studio; Sennett, Mack
"Sleeping Porch, The" (sketch), 128–130, 131, 140, 146, 148, 156–157
Smalley, Phillips, 18
*Smart Set*, 48
social changes in American culture, 125, 126
Solax Studios, 7, 17
*Sorrows of Satan, The* (1926) (film), 117
*So's Your Old Man* (1926) (film), 87, 161, 166–176, 180, 209, 235; adapted from "Mr. Bisbee's Princess," 166; golf scene, 42, 171, 172–173; henpecked husband character, 161, 170, 175, 183, 189; image, 169, 171; La Cava directs, 50, 167–168, 175, 186; plot synopsis, 169–172, 174–175; remade as *You're Telling Me*, 99, 176, 183, 189, 235; reviews, 174, 175; rich-in-the-end scenario, 99, 174, 175, 183, 189
sound films, early experiments in, 4, 13, 16, 40, 206, 222. *See also under* films; silent films; Talkies
*Speedy* (1928) (film), 209, 233

*Spoon River Anthology, The* (Masters), 141
*Squaw Man, The* (1914) (film), 195
*Stage Door* (1939) (film), 193–194
stage performances, WCF, 103, 140, 235; adapting acting style to film setting, 22, 43–46, 91–92, 180–181. *See also Comic Supplement, The* (1925) (revue); *Poppy* (1923-24) (play); vaudeville, WCF and; *Ziegfeld Follies*
stage reviews: *Comic Supplement*, 133–134; *Follies*, 135; *Poppy*, 48, 73–74, 75. *See also* film reviews
star billing, WCF: double billing, with Conklin, 200, 210, 211; in *Poppy*, 75. *See also* Fields-Conklin duo
Starr, Kevin, 202
Steffens, Lincoln, 67
St. John, Adela, 95
*Stop! Look! Listen!* (1915) (musical), 50
Stotesbury, Edward T. (and wife), 157, 160
Strand Theatre, 22, 100
Street, Julian Leonard, 166
*Struggle, The* (1931) (film), 118
*Student Prince, The* (1924) (play), 61
studios. *See* film studios
Sturges, Preston, 228
Sutherland, Al, 146
Sutherland, Eddie: directs *It's the Old Army Game*, 146, 147, 148, 152, 157; directs *Tillie's Punctured Romance*, 223; with Keystone, 146–147; marriage to Brooks, 143, 152, 224; WCF, initial dislike and eventual friendship, 147–148
Sutherland, Julie, 146
Swain, Mack, 215, 223
swans, 63
Swanson, Gloria, 86
Sydney, Sylvia, 210

*Tale of Two Cities* (1917) (film), 7

Talkies: early experiments in, 4, 13, 16, 40, 206, 222; *Follies* stars in, 210; Phonoscène as predecessor, 13, 16; popularity of, while WCF cast in silent films, 10, 200, 222, 228; silent films remade as, 160–161, 176, 234–235; theaters wired for sound, 206–207, 228; transition from silent films to, 10, 205–206, 210; WCF voice and, 10, 55, 176, 210, 232, 236. *See also* silent films
tall tales, WCF tells, 35, 67, 103
Taylor, Robert Lewis, 172
Teapot Dome Scandal, 71
*Telegram, The*, 228
*Temperance Lecture, The* (1945) (radio performance and recording), 103
tent road shows, 70
*That Royle Girl* (1925) (film), 87, 106–120, 235; budget overspent, 109; Chicago locale, 108, 111, 114; cyclone effect in, 108–109, 112; Griffith directs, 106–115, 117; Griffith's hesitation about making, 106, 109–111, 113–114, 115; image, 112, 119; rehearsals, 108; reviews, 111–113, 115–116
*They Had to See Paris* (1929) (film), 210
Thompson, William, 65
Thompson, William Hale, 114
*Tillie and Gus* (1933) (film), 74
*Tillie's Nightmare* (1910) (musical), 222
*Tillie's Punctured Romance* (1914) (silent film), 146, 215, 222
*Tillie's Punctured Romance* (1928) (silent film), 34, 222–225; image, 225; plot synopsis, 70, 224; reviews, 223, 225; Sutherland directs, 223; WCF accidents during, 220–221
Times Square, 2, 22, 183
*Timid Soul, The* (Webster), 187
timing, 54–55, 91, 92, 180
Triangle Film Corporation, 20

*Trip to the Moon, A* (1902) (film), 22
Twain, Mark, 66–67
20th Century-Fox, 7, 207
*Two Flaming Youths* (1927) (film), 186, 215, 216, 217–222; image, 218, 219, 226; originally titled *The Sideshow*, 210, 214; other comedy duos in, 214; plot synopsis, 70, 217–219; reviews, 221; Waters directs, 221; WCF bicycle accident during, 219–220

United Artists, 101, 208
United Studios lot, 195
Universal City, 19
Universal Studios, 5, 7, 18, 19, 20, 223
*Unseen Enemy, An* (1912) (silent short), 81
Urban, Joseph, 50

Valentino, Rudolph, 7, 87, 93
*Variety* (reviews): *Comic Supplement*, 133; Fort Lee *Follies* short, 9; *It's the Old Army Game*, 160; *Janice Meredith*, 55; *Running Wild*, 190; *Sally of the Sawdust*, 116; *So's Your Old Man*, 174, 175; *Tillie's Punctured Romance*, 223, 225
*Variety*, Silverman founds, 184
vaudeville: Conklin on, 214–215; French origins of, 13; vaudeville theaters screen silent films, 22–23
vaudeville, WCF and, xiv, 22, 54–55, 61, 147, 202; character and story inspiration from, 80, 128; demands of, 2–3, 221; golf routine, 42; juggling routine, 2, 24, 29, 69; pool routine, 27, 36, 37; prop use, 29, 32, 216
vertical integration business model, 207–208. *See also* film industry
Victorian era, 79–80, 115
Villard, Oswald Garrison, 82
Vitagraph studio, 12, 20
Vitaphone shorts, 206

Vitascope, 23
voice of WCF, 10, 55, 74, 176, 210, 232, 236

Walsh, Frank, 94
Wanger, Walter, 200
war movies, 37
Warner Bros., 56, 206, 207
Washington, Booker T., 82
Washington, George, 3, 53
*Watch Your Step* (1914) (musical), 115
Waters, John, 221
Watson, James Sibley, Jr., 88–89
Watts, Richard, 35–36, 99–100
*W. C. Fields at the Ziegfeld Follies: Becoming a Character Comedian* (Wertheim), xiv
*W. C. Fields from Burlesque and Vaudeville to Broadway: Becoming a Comedian* (Wertheim), xiv
*W. C. Fields from Sound Film and Radio Comedy to Stardom: Becoming a Cultural Icon* (Wertheim), xiv–xv
wealth. *See* rich-in-the-end scenario
Weber, Joe, 214
Weber, Lois (née Florence Pietz), 18
Webster, H. T., 187
Welles, Orson, 51, 56
Wellman, William, 209
*What Makes Sammy Run?* (Schulberg, Budd), 210–211
*When Knighthood Was in Flower* (1922) (film), 52
White, Pearl, 7
Whitlet, H. J., 200
*Who's Who on the Screen* (1920), 85
Wilcox, Deidra, 200–201
Wilcox, Harvey, 201
Williams, Bert, 8
Wilson, Edmund, 48
*Winesburg, Ohio* (Anderson), 141
*Wings* (1927) (film), 209, 233
Wolfe, Bill, 153
*Woman of Paris, A* (1923) (film), 147

women's liberation movement, 126.
  *See also* female directors
Woollcott, Alexander, 73–74, 75
Woolsey, Robert, 62–63
*The World,* 48
Wynn, Ed, 8–9

*You Can't Cheat an Honest Man* (1934) (film), 71
Young, Tammany, 34–35, 153
*You're Telling Me* (1934) (film), 99, 176, 183, 189, 235. *See also So's Your Old Man* (1926) (film)

Ziegfeld, Florenz, Jr., 2, 44, 71; *Comic Supplement,* unhappy with, 132–133, 134; death, 56; financial problems of, 124; McEvoy and, 124–125, 126–127, 132–134; offers *Show Boat* part to WCF, 102; unhappiness with WCF's filmmaking, 21, 40; WCF, contract with, 21, 102, 127
*Ziegfeld Follies,* 2–3, 50–51, 124, 187, 196; Brooks in, 91, 135, 149–150, 151; cast members move to film careers, 20–21, 210; comic characterizations developed in, xiv, 46, 128, 139, 166, 234; Fort Lee short filmed, 3, 8–9; reviews, 135; WCF entertains from his dressing room, 151; WCF leaves, in 1925, 56, 139; WCF performs in, while filming *That Royle Girl,* 107; Ziegfeld Girls, 142, 150
Zimmerman, Ethel Agnes (Ethel Merman), 88
Zukor, Adolph, 50, 84–85, 110–111, 140, 183; Famous Players-Lasky merger, 203, 207; image, 110; imports French films, 23; life events, 207; Schulberg and, 209. *See also* Famous Players Motion Picture Company; Lasky, Jesse; Paramount Pictures

www.ingramcontent.com/pod-product-compliance
Lightning Source LLC
Chambersburg PA
CBHW051119160426
43195CB00014B/2263